The Streetsmart Guide to

Timing the
Stock Market

The Streetsmart Guide to

Timing the Stock Market

When To Buy, Sell, and Sell Short

Colin Alexander

McGraw-Hill

New York   San Francisco   Washington, D.C.   Auckland   Bogotá
Caracas   Lisbon   London   Madrid   Mexico City   Milan
Montreal   New Delhi   San Juan   Singapore
Sydney   Tokyo   Toronto

Library of Congress Cataloging-in-Publication Data

Alexander, Colin.
    The streetsmart guide to timing the stock market : when to buy,
sell, and sell short / by Colin Alexander.
      p. cm.
    ISBN 0-07-134650-3
    1. Futures.   2. Stocks.   3. Investment analysis.   I. Title.
HG6024.A3A45   1999
332.63'228—dc21   99-18009
                                                           CIP

McGraw-Hill

A Division of The **McGraw·Hill** Companies

  2 3 4 5 6 7 8 9 0   DOC/DOC   0 9 8 7 6 5 4 3 2 1 0

ISBN 0-07-134650-3

The sponsoring editor for this book was Stephen Isaacs and the production
supervisor was Tina Cameron. It was set in Utopia by North Market Street
Graphics.

Printed and bound by R. R. Donnelley & Sons Company.

This publication is designed to provide accurate and authoritative information in regard to the subject matter covered. It is sold with the understanding that the author nor the publisher is engaged in rendering legal,
accounting, futures/securities trading, or other professional service. If
legal advice or other expert assistance is required, the services of a compe-
tent professional person should be sought.

> —*From a Declaration of Principles jointly adopted by a Committee*
> *of the American Bar Association and a Committee of Publishers.*

McGraw-Hill books are available at special quantity discounts to use as
premiums and sales promotions, or for use in corporate training programs.
For more information, please write to the Director of Special Sales,
McGraw-Hill, Professional Publishing, Two Penn Plaza, New York, NY
10121-2298. Or contact your local bookstore.

 This book is printed on recycled, acid-free paper containing a
minimum of 50% recycled de-inked fiber.

Contents

Part 3: What Else You Need to Know

Part 4: Bringing It All Together

Part 5: When to Sell and When to Sell Short

Part 6: Different Perspectives

Acknowledgments

To Ruth Rodger, I owe an immense debt of gratitude. Her perceptive insights and constructive criticism were invaluable in developing a profitable system for trading futures. I have now carried these concepts forward, with substantial additions and modifications in some areas, for use in the stock market. I am also grateful to her for many valuable comments and for the contribution of her writing and editorial skills to some parts of this book.

I want to convey wholehearted thanks to Pierre Fichaud. His assistance was invaluable when it came to cross-referencing the theory in the text with the computer program based on it that we developed for trading futures markets, including stock indexes.

I am grateful to Peter Worden and the technicians at Worden Brothers, Inc., for assistance with their *TC 2000* charting package, with its excellent data management capabilities, and for allowing its use in the book.

I am also grateful to Kimball Hansen and the staff at Ensign Software for permission to use their excellent charts for futures markets and for the early history of the stock market.

Finally, a special thank you goes to Julie Gray for formatting the forms and tables and for her unflagging patience in overcoming technical challenges.

Colin Alexander

The Streetsmart Guide to

Timing the
Stock Market

The Case for Timing

CHAPTER 1

The Secret of Timing

What and When to Buy and Sell

The timing techniques in this book come from technical analysis. If the word *technical* sounds forbidding, don't be alarmed. In this context, technical does not mean complicated. This book is for all investors. It is for those already familiar with technical analysis as well as for those who know nothing about it but want to learn which stocks to buy and when, and when to sell.

Technical analysis tells you when to buy or sell a stock on the basis of what its price action says about it. It can complement fundamental analysis, which suggests which stocks to buy on the basis of financial statements and assumptions about business prospects.

From this book you will learn, step-by-step, how to use specific timing techniques to buy and sell stocks. In doing that, it discards what you do not need to know, for there are few areas of greater knowledge overload than the stock market. This book comprises, with modifications and additions, a straightforward and easy-to-learn system that works in futures markets and which is described in my book, *Five Star Futures Trades*.

A computer program developed from *Five Star* by Pierre Fichaud in Montreal delivers consistently profitable results in all financial futures markets traded in North America. He has proven with this program that this methodology works in all financial futures markets and in all market conditions over the long term. The results for stock indexes, although deriving only from data during a major long-term bull market, show profitable trades exceeding losers by more than two to one, and profits exceeding losses by almost four to one.

When technical analysis and fundamental analysis support the same conclusions, the results are likely to be spectacular. However, fundamental analysis on its own does not necessarily lead to stocks where the action is. A stock might look wonderful on the basis of its fundamentals but in the real world more people may want to sell than buy it. So the stock goes down, not up. On the other hand, when there are strong technical buy signals, it will likely be more rewarding to buy a stock about which you know little or nothing than to buy a blue chip with poor price action.

You can tell from technical analysis when an individual stock, or the market generally, is in an uptrend or a downtrend, or when the trend is sideways and ambiguous. Within that framework, the timing techniques described in this book tell when the balance of the evidence favors buying, holding a stock, selling, selling short, or doing nothing. In simple terms, that means buying a stock already showing, by going up, that it can continue to move up, and vice versa when selling or selling short in a bear market.

As long as the technical indicators remain favorable, you can let profits run for a long time, occasionally for many years. When the balance of technical evidence turns against a stock, it is time to bank a profit or prevent a loss from getting bigger. Over the years it may be appropriate to buy and sell a stock several times. Since you can never tell beforehand how far down a stock might go once it starts going down, you must also be prepared to sell as well as buy. Even the greatest stock can fade and, in extreme cases, go down to nothing. You must avoid the tragedy of losing your life savings in a major bear market.

Contrary to what many people believe, timing is not about picking exact market tops, either in the market generally or for an individual stock. That cannot be done with acceptable consistency, and there is no point in trying.

Extremely good profits should come some of the time, and you should avoid devastating losses at any time. It is certain that you will sometimes misinterpret signals. Remarkably, you might think, you have to be right less than the 50 percent of the time. When you are really right, you may succeed in buying a stock that goes up by ten times or more. That, in essence, is the secret of timing.

The Difference Between Two Stocks

Price charts and chart-based technical indicators show you what is happening. The challenge of buying the best stocks and of not buying poor ones is illustrated by comparing the monthly chart for General Motors (Figure 1-1) with the one for General Electric (Figure 1-2).

Everyone knows GM. It is a household name, so it would be natural to think of it as a solid and reliable company and of its stock as a great one to own. In the 1920s the stock was the equivalent, for its time, of Microsoft, multiplying in price by 150 times. In 1989 you could have bought GM at $50. At one point in 1998 the stock made it to $76, for a

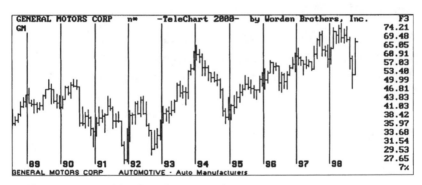

FIGURE 1-1. Monthly Chart for General Motors.

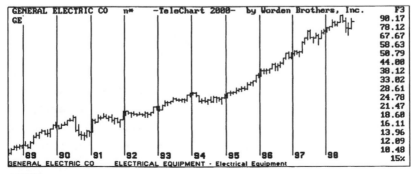

FIGURE 1-2. Monthly Chart for General Electric.

profit of about 50 percent. However, in October 1998 the stock fell to $47, to where it was almost ten years before. Meanwhile, many stocks went up by five and ten times between 1989 and 1998.

Instead of buying GM, you could have bought General Electric. At the beginning of 1989 you might have paid $12 for the stock, or you might have paid $18 at the high in 1990. Assuming that you held the stock until 1998, it would matter little how much you paid. At the 1998 top, you made between five and eight times what you invested in 1989 or 1990. When the stock fell back to $69 at the low for the decline in October 1998, you still had several times what you paid for it in 1989 or 1990.

As we shall see later, there were sometimes better times to buy GE, when the near-term prospect of gain was greater, and the near-term risk of loss lower.

What You Need

This book, a computer with charting software, and a source of end-of-day stock prices provide the tools you need to be successful. You also need to make a commitment to set aside a moderate amount of time for homework to review your current investments and potential new ones. Investing should be stimulating and rewarding in every sense, although it has to be approached responsibly and in an organized manner, as you would approach any business.

For illustration, this book uses stock charts generated by the Worden Brothers' *TC 2000* software. There are many good software programs but it is hard to beat *TC 2000* for cost and data management. Even if you have a small portfolio, you must have a package that permits unlimited access to long-term historical data. It is essential for long-term investing with the system described in this book to look at the charts for several years of market action.

The *TC 2000* software includes two excellent technical indicators not discussed in this book. They are the Cumulative MoneyStream and Balance of Power. Developed by Don Worden, one of the pioneers of volume and money-flow analysis, these indicators show buying and selling pressure. The software comes with a booklet explaining these indicators. This book uses, in new ways, the similar On Balance Volume indicator, which can also be used with other software.

Six Primary Objectives

This book shows how to:

1. Buy the stocks most likely to have above-average performance, whether in established trends or just starting a potential long-term move.

The big winners, the ones with the potential to double or better, make investing worthwhile. At any given time, no more than 10 or 20 percent of all stocks are normally worth considering. With so many stocks to choose from, there is no need to compromise on quality. It is almost always better to buy on the basis of high-quality technical signals than to rely exclusively on fundamental analysis, which says nothing about timeliness or the overall direction of the stock.

2. Run your profits and cut your losses.

This book gives objective guidelines that show how to run profits and cut losses. Although you can sometimes stay in a great stock for many years, some stocks never get going. Then you lose three times. First, there is the loss in the stock trading below what you paid for it. Second, and often worse in the long run, is the opportunity cost resulting from not reinvesting the money in a better stock. Third, you may have to pay more tax than you should. Most people need to use their losses to offset capital gains tax after they bank the profits from their winning stocks.

3. Sell when a stock, or the market generally, runs out of steam and *before* you get caught in a bear market.

Every buy-and-hold investor, by definition, makes a commitment to ride a bear market to the bottom—whether in a single stock, a mutual fund, or a portfolio that appears to be diversified but which comprises most of the same risks. This book shows how to avoid that disaster. Regardless of profit or loss, the foremost requirement is to protect your capital.

You must not make the mistake of thinking that your stocks will buck the trend in a bear market. In a general bear market 90 percent of all stocks go down. Almost no stocks go up enough to justify the risk of owning them.

In a general bear market you lose twice. You lose when your stocks go down, and you lose by not having the money available to buy bargains when the next bull market starts.

4. Look after the risks and let the rewards look after themselves.

A chapter on capital management discusses how to manage your money.

5. Sell stocks short in a bear market.

This book discusses what all investors need to know about selling short. Even if you have no personal inclination to do so, you must know how to avoid riding a stock down while short-sellers profit at your expense.

6. Take personal responsibility for your investments.

Owning stocks is like owning a business. You can employ a manager or you can do the job yourself. Few businesses do as well as they should when management is farmed out by an absentee owner.

Some people think of professionals in any field as people you can trust implicitly. Every profession includes charlatans and incompetents. The less you know, the more likely it is that your investments will be handled badly or for the benefit of the manager rather than for your benefit. Ironically, there is a rough rule of thumb that the more prestigious the organization looking after your money, the more difficult it will be to recover losses if they let you down. You can never rely on the regulators to help you—or the courts—assuming that you have money enough left to sue the financial manager that has abused you.

The Structure of This Book

The subject matter is grouped as follows:

Chapters 1 to 7 discuss the analytical techniques and how they relate to fundamental analysis, fashions in investment, and bull and bear markets. Two chapters show why you need to assume personal control over your investments.

Chapters 8 to 24 discuss how to use specific technical indicators systematically to buy and sell stocks, and how to manage your capital responsibly.

Chapters 25 to 29 show how to buy and sell stocks. They use case studies to illustrate different kinds of opportunity.

Chapters 30 to 33 describe how and when to sell short, with case studies for different kinds of situations.

Chapters 34 to 37 discuss the practical and psychological aspects involved in successful investing.

CHAPTER 2

Stock Timing and Fundamental Analysis

Why Buying Low and Selling High Doesn't Work

Many fundamental analysts do very good work, finding great stocks selling at good prices. For them it is axiomatic that a price is good because the price is below or at least not too far above their assumed value. When a fundamental analyst's work coincides with favorable market action, you can make a lot of money.

First, though, what is fundamental analysis? It comes in two different flavors, which sometimes merge. The *value analyst* looks at the potential for a stock on the basis of tangible value on the balance sheet. This approach may include such intangibles as the value of a franchise in the marketplace and perceptions of business prospects.

The *growth analyst* establishes value by projecting expected profit growth into the future and then assuming a current value by discounting the value of the expected profits. Many growth analysts have little concern for tangible value on the balance sheet. When they see a record of consistent growth, they assume that it is likely to continue. Since value in many businesses resides in people's heads rather than in bricks and mortar, there may be good reasons to move away from undue reliance on visible assets and liabilities. This approach works reasonably well in a general bull market but it suffers from two incurable weaknesses. It is almost impossible to tell whether a small interruption in the rate of profit growth is temporary or the start of a more serious reversal. It also does not account for what the market does with the stock. The stock may appear to offer good value. However, the price may be high enough to attract selling that prevents further advances for a considerable time. The market may not share the view that good times will continue, or at least not enough to justify the current share price.

Unfortunately, there are reasons why fundamental analysis without using timing techniques often achieves mediocre results. The first problem is that the information used as the basis for the analysis is certain to be out of date when it is available. A quarterly report, although it may seem recent, still looks back quite a long way by the time it is available. In any case, it may be wrong; circumstances may have changed significantly for better or for worse since the information became available. Companies always try to put the best face on their business, and you cannot rely on the auditors to keep management honest. Creative accounting practices, even when legally acceptable, sometimes create huge distortions that are impossible to analyze effectively.

The second problem is that value may already be fully reflected, or more, in the price of a great stock. So you can't buy it. The fundamental analyst may be the last to hear news on which many investors started acting long ago, when the stock was much cheaper. If you wait for value to become evident, you may be the sucker, victimized by short-term traders who buy a stock when good technical action starts and sell when the news is announced that caused the buying in the first place. Many short-term traders and market-makers operate this way.

The third problem for the fundamental analyst is that a stock logically becomes a better buy the cheaper the price. Therefore, the more a stock falls, the better the price at which you can buy it and, if you already own it, the better the price at which you can buy more. Sometimes, however, there is a good reason for the decline in price, which becomes known only long after a collapse. Then the fundamental analyst is left holding the bag. Smart money and investors using technical analysis have sold ahead of the bad news.

The fourth and most serious problem with fundamental analysis is that this discipline, used logically, requires the sale of a stock that becomes overpriced. Fundamental analysis may well dictate selling a stock that doubles in a short time on the grounds that it has become twice as expensive as it was before. Then you have to find a replacement, which may or may not do as well as the stock you started with. It often happens that the stock that doubles once goes on to double again. In due course, the price that once seemed too high is justified by what the company behind the stock achieves. When that news becomes known, the stock goes on again to a price that again seems unreasonable. These stocks constantly prove the truism that the greatest stocks always look expensive. So the investor relying on fundamental analysis can buy these great stocks only rarely, and even then, practically never stays in one that goes up by five or ten times.

Fundamental analysis should achieve the academically excellent objective of buying low and selling high. In practice, it means the exact opposite of running profits and cutting losses. When fundamental analysis and the real world are in conflict, go with stocks that show, by going up, that they can go up.

Cendant, Great Stock but Lousy Action

Sometimes the contrast between apparent value and what the market does to a stock is amazing. Consider Cendant, recommended strongly by a prominent market advisor at $40 (Figure 2-1).

One day in 1998 it turned out that there was something wrong with the company's accounting. On the announcement of this news, the price of the stock halved to $20. The advisor declared that the stock was

FIGURE 2-1. Cendant Daily Chart.

an even better buy now than before, based on his understanding after talking to the company's management. Have you ever known a company spokesman or a politician fail to put the best face on bad news? Even when the best face is correct, as it essentially was for Cendant, you should take it with a pinch of salt.

Within a few weeks the price of Cendant halved again to $10. It hit a low for the decline at $6.50, remaining all the time on this advisor's recommended list. However good the stock, the fact is that it declined in a few months from high to low by 84 percent. Hanging onto Cendant was an exercise in fighting the market. It became evident later that staying in the stock was also an exercise in fighting the largest mutual fund company in the world, Fidelity, which decided to liquidate a huge holding. Whether they were right or wrong to do so is irrelevant. Selling pressure from various sources swamped buying pressure. You could readily see by looking at the price chart that there was persistent selling and that the stock was going down.

When there is a conflict between what you think a stock ought to do and what it does, the market is always right. Either you make money or you lose it, and you can see the result on your monthly statement.

Anyone using market timing techniques and anyone living by the rule of cutting losses should have sold Cendant at $20. You should certainly not have bought more until the dust settled. This stock proves the point of the saying: First loss, best loss. Even in the strongest bull market you must run profits and get out of losers and underperformers. Otherwise, you hang onto stocks like GM and Cendant, and even buy more, while not buying and holding stocks like General Electric and Microsoft that multiply in price by many times.

There is another point to make about the Cendant story. While this stock was going down, the bulk of investment money was going into stocks in the Dow Jones Industrial Average and NASDAQ stocks with a record of reliable corporate performance or Internet sex appeal. The result was that many of the greatest stocks were extremely expensive by most valuation criteria, and they continued to become ever more expensive until the severe correction in the late summer of 1998. During this period many lesser stocks that seemed cheap went on getting cheaper, as shown by the Russell 2000 Index (Figure 2-2). Whenever there was any doubt about a company's credibility, skittish investors were heeding the one-cockroach theory, which normally stands one in

FIGURE 2-2.   Russell 2000 Daily Chart.

good stead. The theory states that there is no such thing as one cock-roach. One bit of bad news is likely to lead to more. Therefore, there is no point in taking the risk involved in buying stock in a company over which there is a question mark.

Cendant was caught in the net of suspicion at a bad time. The result was that the stock, once its uptrend was broken, established a new downtrend. According to the law of trends, the new downtrend contin-ued in force until the stock hit $6.60. Only then did value investors, those who thought the stock ridiculously cheap, finally overcome sell-ing pressure by those aggressively, if misguidedly, dumping the stock or selling short.

With Cendant, fundamental analysis, at least in the near term, failed abysmally. In all likelihood, anyone buying Cendant near the bottom of its decline bought the stock at a wonderful price. But how could you know when the stock would stop going down? At least it did stop going down. That is not always the way. If the stock of an inher-ently sound company can fall by 84 percent in a few months, think what might happen in a general bear market to the stock of a company that has real problems.

As we shall see later on, there was a technical case for assuming completion of a selling climax in Cendant when the stock reversed with an island on October 9 and closed at $9. In addition, as discussed in Chapter 19, there were signs that the general market might have completed a selling climax. There were safer stocks to buy from a strictly technical standpoint, but now there was also, at last, a techni-cal case to support the apparently good fundamentals.

You Don't Have to Get Left Behind!

The other side of the Cendant story is that there is no limit to how high a great stock can go. There have always been some stocks that go up by several times, and occasionally, by a hundred times or more. It is easy, after the event, to see a Microsoft and wish you had bought it. The challenge is not how to find them, for they are generally as obvious at the time as they are in retrospect. The challenge is knowing when to buy them when the risk is manageable.

"We don't own Microsoft (Figure 2-3), Intel, or Coca-Cola. I missed these," admitted a prominent fund manager in January 1997.

Why not? These were stocks that any manager of a major stock portfolio should have owned during the greatest bull markets of all time. A portfolio invested less than 50 percent between these three stocks, with the balance in Treasury bills, would have far outperformed the market averages and most managed money.

Logically, you should ask yourself: If I would like to own a stock, why don't I? If you like a stock that has gone up and expect it to go higher still, it is not logical to refrain from buying it. If you don't like the price and fear a big retracement, then just buy a little to start with. Then look for signals to buy more when timing techniques suggest an acceptable ratio of reward to risk. Even the strongest stock comes back, stabilizes, and then starts going again.

No doubt, this money manager was concerned that these stocks were "overvalued," which by many standard criteria they were. He may have assumed that there was too much risk in owning them. If you buy

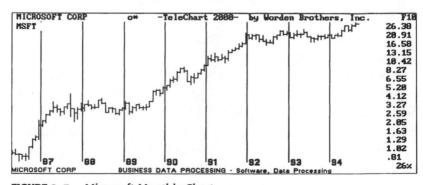

FIGURE 2-3. Microsoft Monthly Chart.

what you believe is overvalued, the more the price rises, the greater the fear of a reversal. On the other hand, the technician knows when to buy with a manageable risk. You learn to have faith in a major price trend and to expect its continuation as long as the technical indicators remain favorable.

There is a good fundamental reason why the price of many stocks goes up for a long time, and to that extent the growth analyst uses good logic. Business success or failure tends to move in very long trends. Good management, a strong franchise, and an expanding world economy can keep a business rolling forward for decades. The stock price may precede, with a long lead, new developments in the business. A company that has a long record of doing well is less likely to stumble, although all companies can stumble, and most companies do so at one time or another. Corporate success, or lack of it, and stock price action are almost invariably linked in the very long run, and that long run can last for many years. That is why the best stocks generally look expensive, and the worst ones generally look cheap.

Microsoft shows how a company can develop a franchise and grow like Jack's beanstalk. A lengthening record of success suggests that prosperity will continue. So the stock price of a great company may increase faster than corporate profits for a long time. The longer a good record, the higher the premium that investors are prepared to pay. So the price/earnings ratio (the price as measured by the stock price earnings per share) can increase even without an acceleration in the rate of increase in profits, although that divergence cannot last forever.

Buying Value Can Mean a Long Wait

There is a further problem with buying stocks on the basis of value alone and not also using technical indicators, even when the analysis leading to the decision is good.

We have noted the money manager who could not bring himself to buy some of the most dynamic stocks of the 1990s. So what do these people buy?

Another money manager, who, incidentally, outright repudiates stock timing, is on the record as saying how he sets about buying stocks. He finds a stock in which he sees great value and which he expects in due course to double. He is happy to buy the stock and sit on it. If, at last, the stock doubles in the fifth year, after he has held it through four years of sideways market action, he still achieves an average annual return of 15 percent and is very happy with the outcome.

Why not delay buying that stock until the price action begins in the fifth year? You may catch only 50 percent of the move that year, for you buy only when the stock shows that it can move higher. If you can use the money well in the meantime, a gain of 50 percent in one year is better than 100 percent spread over five years. Besides, during the four years of waiting things may change for the worse, and the stock may go down instead of up. Instead of waiting for something to happen, however good the apparent prospects, it is generally better and also safer not to be among the first to jump into a stock. Wait for confirming market action.

As we have seen with General Electric, the probabilities favor continuation of a trend in force. Therefore, the stock that doubles in the fifth year may well go on to double again in the sixth year. The long sideways consolidation increases the likelihood of that happening.

The Market Is Always Right

The case for bringing together technical analysis and fundamental analysis could hardly be stated better than it was by Peter Siris, author of *Guerrilla Investing*, when interviewed by Kathryn M. Welling for *Barron's:*

> Well, I used to completely disregard charts because I'm a fundamental investor. But over the years, as I've looked back over the stocks I've owned that have done well—as well as the mistakes I've made—I've realized that the charts very often would have shown me great opportunities to buy and sell, if I had looked at them dispassionately. What's more, when I've ignored what the charts had to tell, I've usually been wrong. As a fundamental investor, I've come to understand that what the charts are saying sometimes is that other people know more than I do about a stock. Its movement isn't just a question of momentum. If you look back at Oxford Health Plans—or almost any of the others that have cratered 50 percent in a day—in almost all cases, in the three or four weeks before they

got killed, you could see them topping out and starting down. The charts, essentially, are the early warning systems of what the professionals are doing, telling you the direction in which they're getting ready to make a major move. It's like an army getting ready to turn. Ironically, when an individual sees these patterns developing, he can often move faster than the professionals because he has much less money to move around. So one thing I say is "Never fight the tape." If a stock is getting crushed, I don't want to stand in front of it."

It is readily apparent that there can be huge swings in stock prices that relate only loosely to what you might think about a company's prospects. Apparent information about corporate prospects is often late and often wrong. As a result, many stock analysts labor mightily to produce profit forecasts that turn out to be way off the mark. By the time a change in circumstances becomes known, whether favorable or unfavorable, the stock price may have moved sharply up or down to reflect the new reality. Those close to the company, and not just its directors and financial officers, may have already voted with their money by buying or selling stock. So the price moved long before the news came out.

Since individual stocks and the overall market fluctuate enormously, it is obvious that more is required for success than trying to guess what price level is high or low. In any case, you can readily see in hindsight from looking at almost any chart that there are much better and less good times to buy, and that there are also times to sell. This book illustrates the outright necessity of doing so, and it also shows how to do it.

Without using timing techniques, you miss many of the best opportunities, and you run the risk of getting killed when conditions turn hostile. In that case, being right about the stock but wrong about the timing amounts to the same thing as being altogether wrong. When there is a conflict between market action and the price of a stock, the fundamental analyst assumes that the mind is mightier than the market. The technical analyst lets profits run and cuts losses short.

CHAPTER 3

What Does Value Really Mean?

Value Versus Price

It is tempting to be impressed when a prominent market guru declares with fanfare that the stock market values are high, low, or fair. What does that mean? What is value?

Unfortunately, it is seldom possible to establish a useful connection between value and price. For centuries many great thinkers worked on the challenge. Among them were Adam Smith, David Ricardo, and Karl Marx, as well as the stock analysts Benjamin Graham and David Dodd. These sages came up with very little that is helpful in establishing the fair price for a stock. In a perfect world, value should equal price. However, it happens frequently that the price of something sold yesterday is not the same as the price today, although nothing seems to have changed in the meantime. The price may be significantly higher or lower, as anyone familiar with art auctions knows well. Buying and selling is done by people according to a wide range of personal opinions and circumstances. Even under optimum circumstances, the willingness of a buyer or a seller to do business within a certain price range can, at best, only be estimated before the next sale takes place.

At certain times many stocks sell below apparent value. Sometimes the price responds and comes into line within a reasonable time, sometimes not—and sometimes never. It all depends on whether new buyers are prepared to pay up.

Valuation Criteria and Normality

Despite the difficulty in establishing benchmarks, there are some good rules of thumb that have stood the test of time. In the very long term, markets tend to fluctuate a very long way either side of the historic median. Here are some historic benchmarks:

1. Government bonds should yield 3 percent plus the rate of inflation.

When inflation is high and rising, bonds yield more. Rates also tend to be high after a period of inflation, when investors still fear its return. Rates tend to be lower after a period of stable prices or outright deflation, when investors do not fear inflation.

2. When prices are stable, no-growth stocks and commercial real estate should yield 25 percent more than long-term government bonds.

There were few real solid and stable no-growth stocks in the 1980s and 1990s, although some utilities came close. There have been long periods in the past when many companies simply marked time without profit growth. A yield higher than that from government bonds has been considered necessary in order to offset the perceived higher risk.

3. When prices are stable, a growth stock is assumed to represent fair value if its price/earnings ratio is equal to its expected rate of growth.

If a stock earns $1 per share and growth is expected at 15 percent annually, by this measure a stock price of $15 represents fair value. It sells at 15 times earnings, or with a price/earnings ratio of 15.

This multiple can grow as a good track record lengthens, but it cannot grow to infinity. The problem with a high multiple is what happens if growth falters. A share price based on a high expected growth rate is vulnerable. If a company with its stock selling at a price/earnings ratio of 40 or 50 starts losing money, the impact on the price can be devas-

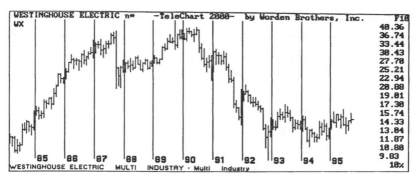

FIGURE 3-1. Westinghouse Electric Monthly Chart.

tating. Even the stock of a prestigious company like Westinghouse Electric can hit the skids when great expectations are confounded (Figure 3-1). From the end of 1989 to the end of 1992, the stock dropped from a high of $42.31 to a low of $9.38, a decline of 78 percent. This decline occurred, moreover, while stocks generally were in a strong bull market. Westinghouse was taken out of the Dow Jones Industrial Average long after the company lost its luster.

4. During the twentieth century the "normal" long-term average dividend payout for stocks in the Dow Jones Industrial Average was 50 percent, and its "normal" average price level was 23.7 times dividends.

In the 1990s dividends were paid at a rate much lower than 50 percent of earnings, and in 1997 at around 29 percent. With consensus earnings of $377 for the Dow in 1998, and a payout of half of that in dividends multiplied by 23.7, the "normalized" value of the Dow was 4467.

In mid-1980 the Dow was trading at 18.5 times dividends. In March 1998 it was trading around 65 times dividends.

Valuations in the 1970s and Early 1980s

Valuations in the 1970s and early 1980s were at an extremely low level by almost all criteria except by comparison with competing investments.

In 1975 Hilton Hotels sold down to $10, where it had a dividend yield of 10 percent and a book value of $24. In the same year, Tiffany was selling for $7.50, although its headquarters building in Manhattan was itself worth more than the company's $17 million market capitalization. In 1978 Avon paid $40 per share to take over the company. In January 1980 Gulf & Western was at $16.25, after earning $4.13 the previous year, which gave the stock a price/earnings ratio of 3.93. From 1970 to 1980 earnings had been increasing at an annual rate of 9.5 percent, and from 1975 to 1980 at a rate of 11.5 percent. Tangible book value was $16.34. In 1979 the dividend was raised to 75 cents, making it the fourteenth consecutive year of dividend increases.

In March 1980 the Dow Jones Industrial Average was at 785. Its price/earnings ratio was 6.9 percent, it had a dividend yield of 6.4 percent, and it sold at approximately 1.5 times book value. For a while the Dow Industrials responded to perceptions of value, rising to a high just over 1000 in January 1981. From there, it was hard down again into the August 1982 low of 770, a decline of 23 percent off the top.

Low valuations from the mid-1970s to the early 1980s have to be put in context of what happened earlier. The bear market that began in 1973, when combined with rising inflation, rising interest rates (and a corresponding collapse in bond prices) drove investors away from stocks. Having been burned so badly, it appeared too risky to go near the stock market.

Polaroid, for example, rose from a low of $22 in 1965 to a high of $145 in 1973. The bear market then took the stock down to $17.50 at its low the next year. Polaroid was not an isolated example of market devastation. It was a representative one. The seemingly most solid and secure growth stocks fell the most because they were the most "overvalued." For technicians they were also the most overextended on the charts. Almost none of the so-called nifty fifty, the one-decision stocks of that time, fell by less than 50 percent. From the 1972 market top to the 1974 low, declines of 75 percent or more were standard.

Valuations in the 1990s

There was an equal and opposite extremity of valuations in 1998. Internet stocks were capitalized in the billions, even when they had minuscule sales and, in many cases, no profits. At $212 Yahoo! was selling at 100 times revenues and 500 times profits. At least this stock was the market leader in one of the fastest-growing industries of all time. If profits stopped growing for some reason, you would have to live to be 500 years old for the stock to earn what you paid for it. On the other hand, if profits doubled every six months, compounding might make the stock worth its 1998 price, compared with other growth stocks, in two years or less.

Book values seemed to have lost all meaning, with the Dow trading more than six times the reported book values on the balance sheet. Somehow, Disney managed to show negative book value, which did not of course mean that the company was bankrupt. The balance sheet reflected markdowns of goodwill for tax purposes. By now Hilton Hotels was yielding less than 1 percent, compared with 10 percent in 1980, and there were still analysts recommending it as a buy for a further 50 percent gain within a year. In March 1998 the Dow Industrial Average was above 9000. It had a price/earnings ratio of 21 and a dividend yield of 1.5 percent. Remarkably, at these levels some experts were proclaiming that the overall market was still below "fair value."

Coca-Cola stock sold for 50 times earnings when its reported earnings growth rate was around 18 percent. A case could be made that the company's reported growth rate considerably overstated what was really happening. After allowing for creative accounting, the real long-term growth rate appeared to be less than 10 percent. The stock even sold at a multiple of more than five times sales, although unit sales growth was only 8 percent. Such a high multiple is generally attributable only to the stock of a dynamically growing company in the computer industry or in some other area of proprietary technological innovation. But sweet fizzy water? It hardly seems a product that someone cannot both copy and make more cheaply. In any case, it is a mathematical impossibility for profit growth to exceed unit sales growth forever. Profits cannot exceed sales.

The Japanese Experience

At the extremity of overvaluation, it is hard to beat the initial public offering (IPO) in Tokyo in February 1987 for Nippon Telegraph and Telephone. The stock was offered at the equivalent of $7770 per share. Despite an expected drop in corporate earnings in 1987, the stock rose in a few weeks to the equivalent of $17,582, where it traded at 234 times questionable earnings. The London *Financial Times* quoted Peter

Trasker of Kleinwort Benson International in Tokyo as saying: "We're talking about a social phenomenon. Everyone is buying because everyone is buying."

The difference between Yahoo! and Nippon? In both cases buying was a social phenomenon. At least the Internet was a real growth industry. Buyers had to weigh the value of market leadership versus the vulnerability to competition or new technology in such a fast-moving business.

In due course, the Nikkei Average of Japanese stocks went on from the 30,000 level in 1987 to 39,000 in 1989. Then it began a protracted decline to 14,000 in January 1998, when there were few signs of the nine-year bear market ending. It was by no means clear even then that stock values in Japan had generally become cheap, although some stocks clearly had. It is hard to say that a country's stock market is cheap when its entire banking industry is essentially bankrupt, as was the case in Japan during the 1990s, largely as a result of the fallen stock market. That is how a downward spiral, a vicious circle, can feed on itself and become the equal and opposite of an expansionary and virtuous one.

You might be tempted to think of real estate as the ultimate store of value, and in a sense it probably is in the very long term. However, like anything else, you have to buy well. Japan experienced a phenomenal real estate mania in conjunction with its stock market mania. At one point the value of real estate in Tokyo was estimated to be worth more than all of California. That imbalance was corrected between 1990 and 1998 when the market value of much previously high-priced real estate declined by 90 percent, and many properties were unsalable at any price. Japanese banks were reported to be relieved if they could recover 20 percent of the value of a real estate loan.

Investment Trusts in the 1920s

During the 1920s the persistence of the bull market seemed to make traditional tenets inapplicable, as they also seemed to be in the 1990s. In the nineteenth century, a traditional tenet of trust management was to buy stocks in a depression and to sell them in a boom. Doing this is difficult during a major bull market when the boom lasts a long time.

The challenge lies in telling how long a bull market or a bear market will last. Selling during a boom may mean selling after a stock doubles once but before it doubles again one or more times. The twentieth century has shown how far stock market booms can go. The lesson of the 1920s and also of the early 1970s is that eventually, booms invariably end.

Describing the approach taken by investment trusts during the 1920s, the equivalent of mutual funds of the 1990s, Graham and Dodd wrote in their book *Security Analysis:*

> If a public utility stock was selling at 35 times its maximum recorded earnings, which was the preboom standard, the conclusion to be drawn was not that the stock was too high but that the standard of value had been raised. Instead of judging the market price by established standards of value, the new era based its standards of value on the market price. Hence all upper limits disappeared, not only upon the price at which a stock *could* sell, but even upon the price at which it would *deserve* to sell.

What passed for wisdom in the 1920s also became generally accepted during the 1990s.

Historical Valuations

Table 3-1 shows important milestones in market value during the twentieth century up to the temporary market top at the end of June 1997. The table shows the dividend yield for the Standard & Poor 500 Index (Industrials), the ratio of price to the book value of stocks in the index, and the level of the Dow Industrials. The milestones generally mark turns in the market except for the ones from 1993 to 1997. Those stand at the respective years' ends during the seemingly perpetual bull market. At the bottom of the table are the corresponding numbers for Japanese stocks at the end of 1989, just as the market topped and began its multiyear decline.

The best of all value during the century was available in 1932, in terms of both dividends and price-to-book ratio. You might have thought that there would be a total absence of dividends at the bottom

TABLE 3-1 Milestones in Market Value

Date	Dividend Yield	Price/Book	Dow Industrials
1929	3.1	2.2	380
1932	9.0	0.35	41
1942	7.8	0.8	95
1949	7.2	1.0	168
1972	2.3	2.2	1020
1974	4.6	1.2	607
1982	5.8	1.2	770
1987	2.2	2.8	2735
1993	2.3	3.1	3754
1994	2.2	4.0	3834
1995	2.0	4.8	5117
1996	1.8	5.4	6448
1997 (June)	1.6	6.4	8222
Japan: Tokyo Stock Exchange First Section			
1989	0.5	5.6	

of the slump but that was not the case. Dividend yields were high in recognition of severe dividend cuts already made and the expectation that they would continue to be cut or eliminated. Bonds, on the other hand, yielded around 3 percent. You needed to have faith that the world was not coming to an end in order to buy such good value. It was a function of such immense general pessimism that few people were prepared to take that risk, even for three times the yield obtainable from bonds.

At the other extreme is the valuation at the top of the Japanese stock market boom in 1989. And then there is the experience with U.S. stocks during the 1990s, which required extension of the price/book baseline far beyond anything seen anywhere before. Curiously, perhaps, the extremes at the bull market tops in 1929, 1972, and 1987 came nowhere close to those in the late 1990s.

Valuation Criteria Work As Alerts

The criteria for stock valuation on the basis of fundamental analysis may suggest a stock worth looking at to see how it is acting. However, one can bluntly say that Graham and Dodd's valuation criteria require such latitude in interpretation that they serve only as alerts or as arbitrary and subjective guidelines. Even under the best of circumstances, it is very difficult to work with their benchmarks. The stock of a strong company may be very weak, and persistent selling may not seem rational. It also happens often that the stock of a company with little or nothing behind it can multiply in price by several times.

The experience of the biggest bull market of all time is that reliance on value rather than on technical analysis may lead you to do the opposite of what is required for long-term success. It tempts you to buy apparent value in stocks going nowhere. It invites you to sell, and certainly not to buy, the most dynamic stocks, because they seem overpriced. The greatest risk is that fundamental analysis could lead you to buy rather than sell when prices start to unravel during a bear market.

The great economists of earlier times were not embarrassed to admit that they were unable to define "fair value." Market analysts of our own time are not so humble. One chief investment strategist for a major New York investment house was quoted in *The Wall Street Journal* in 1998. This advisor said the S&P 500 index had a fair value between 780 and 1020. This guru was asked the question: "What if stocks overshoot, falling below fair value?"

"That," came the reply, "is too horrible to think about, because it means a fall below 780 on the S&P." This possibility was totally excluded from any "base scenario" on the grounds that it is too painful to think about.

There is no need to expose your investments to undue risk or your pain threshold to torture if you sell when the technical indicators tell you to. There is certain to be a sell signal some time for every stock you ever own.

CHAPTER 4

Bull and Bear Markets

The Long-Term History of Stocks

The overall trend in stock prices has always been upward. According to The Foundation for the Study of Cycles, stocks appear to have advanced by about ten times from 1800 to 1900. During the nineteenth century the purchasing power of money changed little, so those gains were real.

During the twentieth century stocks also appear to have advanced substantially in real terms. However, they have done so with long periods of stagnation and with huge bull markets and huge bear markets on the way. From the 1982 low to mid-1998 the advance in stock prices was also about ten times. So in those sixteen years stock prices appeared to advance by as much as they did during the entire previous century, which included the dynamic period of the Industrial Revolution. With inflation declining most of those gains were also real.

The Dow Jones Industrial Average, at the time comprising twelve stocks, was at 41 at the low in 1903. By 1998 it was over 9000 for an increase of more than 225 times. With stocks constantly coming and going from the Dow, all you can really say though is that stocks generally went up as the economy grew. You cannot say that any mindless buy-and-hold strategy applied to individual stocks held for eternity is effective. Capitalism has rightly been described as creative destruction, and entire industries as well as individual companies come and go.

There is no easy way to reconcile distortions caused by the departure of stocks from the Dow and the arrival of new ones. Of the original twelve stocks in the Dow in 1900, only General Electric remained in the index throughout the twentieth century. Compared with the constantly revised Dow, a portfolio invested in the Dow stocks of 1900 and never changed could show a much worse performance than the apparent result suggested by this index. You have to make a negative adjustment for bankruptcies and companies that fell into oblivion. You have to make a positive adjustment for reinvestment of the proceeds from Dow stocks taken over and bought out for cash.

The twenty-five years from 1972 to 1997 provide an example of the challenge of evaluating the performance of any stock index over the long term. Of the so-called nifty-fifty stocks of 1972, nine disappeared by 1997, or 18 percent of them. These included MGIC, acquired by Baldwin United, which went bankrupt, and Burroughs and Emery. A truly long-term investor has to include these stocks in the record as if they were still held, even if they became worthless.

A buy-and-hold strategy applied only to the Dow as it once was would have you still owning many lackluster stocks, and heavily weighted in steels and textiles. The list includes Bethlehem Steel, Inco, USX, Westinghouse, and Woolworth, as well as some stocks worth no more than their value as collectible certificates. All Dow stocks should have sold at one time or another. Even with GE, there was no reasonable way of knowing in advance that this single stock would come back after every bear market and continue to prosper when so many apparently great stocks did not. A one-in-twelve probability of finding and holding for a century that one great stock is not good odds. In sum, there are good reasons to override a perpetual buy-and-hold strategy that relies on finding needles in haystacks.

Logically, you could sell stocks when they are dropped from the Dow and buy the new additions when they arrive. Owning the adjusted Dow has some merit for the very long term, and this strategy would produce better results than many money managers achieve. It would be an approach sharing a conceptual relationship with the objective of this book, to buy stocks on strength and to sell them on weakness. The problem is that the call for action occurs so long after weakness in a departing stock has become apparent. There is the same problem with the strength in a new arrival, which may have its best days behind it when it arrives in the Dow. In some cases Dow stocks have been dropped only long after the price has gone down the drain, as occurred with Westinghouse Electric, illustrated in Chapter 3.

If you simply buy the Dow, there is no provision in this approach for buying stocks performing better and not those performing worse, or for avoiding major bear markets. All you can really say is that buying Dow stocks equally has the feeble merit of avoiding what many money managers do: selling winners seemingly overpriced and then buying losers.

Distortions Caused by Inflation

Inflation caused such serious distortions in the record for the stock market during the twentieth century that it is almost impossible to make adjustments for it. By some measures the U.S. Dollar in 1998 was perhaps worth $\frac{1}{50}$ of what it was in 1900. Unfortunately, attempts to measure long-term inflation are distorted by the fact that prices for almost all commodities and manufactured goods are perpetually declining in real terms as a result of constant improvements in production techniques. For example, one person can now look after 400 acres of cotton, whereas just four acres once required employment of a single worker. Looking ahead, some commodity prices might end their bear market in real terms, including fish, lumber, and petroleum. The decline in prices in the computer industry has been so remarkable that it is impossible to make a useful connection with any standard measure of inflation. There are also irreconcilable distortions because some goods and services fall into disuse completely, while new ones arrive that were not even thought of before.

By contrast with the price of commodities and manufactured goods, there has been a huge upward movement in real wages and in the purchasing-power value of prime real estate. Consequently, real estate prices may constitute the only solid long-term benchmark for inflation, although with the caveat that this asset class also experiences long periods of stagnation at certain times and immense swings in price at other times. It might seem that the advance in stock prices generally during the twentieth century has been about four times the rate of inflation as it is normally measured. However, if real estate on Manhattan Island is the benchmark, stocks as measured by the Dow Jones Industrials may not have advanced at all.

From 1972 to the end of 1997 the Standard & Poor 500 index advanced by 700 percent. However, with inflation as it is normally measured running above 5 percent, the purchasing power of the dollar declined by 73 percent. Consequently, the inflation-adjusted gain for the S&P is 112 percent, or 3.1 percent annually, compared with a nominal 12.9 percent annual rate of gain. As with the record for the Dow during the twentieth century, these numbers do not allow for changes in the composition of the S&P, which almost certainly impact the performance record adversely.

Major Bull and Bear Markets

The stock market has generally gone up about two-thirds of the time and down about one-third. About once every ten years there has been a major decline. Figure 4-1 starts with the period from the October 1919 monthly closing high at 118.92 to the 1921 low. That routine bear market took the Dow Industrials down by 44 percent. Similar bear markets have occurred at very irregular intervals, and their severity has also varied considerably. As a rule, bear markets have generally lasted longest and fallen the most when the preceding advance has been longest and greatest. Sometimes declines give back all of the previous advance.

FIGURE 4-1.   The Dow Jones Industrial Average Monthly Chart, 1920–1934.

The challenge of owning stocks in a rising market and not owning them in a bear market is really conspicuous in Figure 4-1 where it shows the Dow Jones Industrials during the bull market of the 1920s. That great bull market went from its monthly closing low in August 1921 at 67.11 to its monthly closing high in August 1929 at 380.33, for a gain of 467 percent. The crash in October followed through to a low at 198 on November 13. Then came a bear market rally, amounting to a huge 41 percent gain, to a secondary high at 279 by April 1930. When the market turned back down again, a technical analyst should have liquidated any stocks still inadvertently retained through the initial devastation. The chart shows that the bear market to the June 1932 low went to 41.22, for a total decline from the top of 89 percent. The index actually dipped slightly below the low in 1903. A full thirty years of gains disappeared.

It is clear in hindsight that you would have wanted to own stocks during most of the 1920s. It is also painfully obvious that you would not have wanted to own them for several years after 1929. The chart for the Dow Industrials shows the performance of the average for bigger stocks. As always happens, some stocks did much better during the bull market and some did much worse in the decline. There were many stocks that went to zero during the Depression. They included many banks that once seemed impregnable. They also included many investment trusts (the equivalent of closed-end funds of the 1990s) as a result of their borrowing to buy stocks on margin and then not having the means to repay their loans.

Stocks Since 1957

The bear market that began in 1929 was unusually severe, but not unique for the United States or elsewhere. For example, there was a decline of 90 percent in Hong Kong in the early 1960s.

The negative but realistic way of looking at the way capitalism works and, by extension, fluctuations in the stock market, is this: Slump follows boom as night follows day! Of equal importance, and equally difficult to embrace at the bottom of a slump, is the reverse: Boom follows slump as day follows night! The tide comes in and the tide goes back out. Within the movement of the tides there are bigger waves and smaller ones, down to the smallest ripple. Get the major direction of the market right when it is favorable to own stocks and the probabilities are overwhelmingly favorable for making money. Nevertheless, there really are times when it is important to be out of the market.

Figure 4-2 shows the Dow Industrials from 1963 to 1978, when there were immense fluctuations in the Dow but no perceptible upward progress overall. Table 4-1 shows the major highs and lows from December 1957 to March 1998, on the basis of monthly closes.

Note that the lower percentages for declines versus higher ones for advances do not balance. It takes a 100 percent gain to recover from a 50 percent loss. It took a 67 percent gain to recover from the 40 percent loss at the bottom in 1974.

If you bought the equivalent of the Dow Industrials at the top on the last day of December 1961 at 731.14, and held to the bottom July 30, 1982, at 808.60, you made a capital gain, not including dividends, of just over 10 percent. That was the total for twenty years. It amounts to less than one-half of one percent annually. Times were exceptional, but not all that exceptional, compared with the record for the previous 250 years.

Despite this sideways action of the indexes, there was big money to be made in some stocks during these twenty years. However, you had to buy stocks in specific market sectors, and you had to avoid those

TABLE 4-1 DJIA: Major Highs and Lows, 12–57 to 3–98

Date	Low	% Change High to Low	Date	High	% Change Low to High
12/31/57	435.69	—	12/29/61	731.14	68
6/29/62	561.28	23	1/31/66	983.51	75
10/31/66	807.07	18	11/29/68	985.0	22
6/30/70	683.53	31	12/29/72	1020.02	49
9/30/74	607.87	40	12/31/76	1004.65	65
2/28/78	742.12	26	3/31/81	1003.87	35
7/30/82	808.60	19	8/31/87	2662.95	229
11/30/87	1833.55	31	7/31/90	2905.20	58
10/31/90	2442.33	16	3/31/98	8799.56	260
Average		**26**			**96**

FIGURE 4–2. The Dow Jones Industrial Average Monthly Chart, 1964–1978.

performing poorly. There are almost always opportunities for making money in individual stocks far greater than the action in the Dow Industrials collectively, whether in specific Dow stocks or elsewhere. For example, fortunes were made in gold- and silver-mining stocks and in some real estate stocks during the years leading up to 1980. This was truly a period when no more than 10 to 20 percent of all stocks were worth considering. The rule almost invariably applies in good times and bad that just a few stocks offer really attractive opportunities, while the majority simply tie up money unnecessarily, or lose money.

Figure 4-3 shows the Dow Industrials during the 1980s. The bull market began from a monthly closing low at 808.60 in July 1982 and went to a monthly closing high in August 1987 at 2709.50. The intra-month low in October 1987 was at 1592.80, 41 percent down from the high.

The declines of 1963, 1973, and 1987 were nowhere near as severe as the bear market that made its low in 1932. However, the carnage was still gruesome, especially for those who bought near the top. From the 1973 top, many blue chips, including many of the greatest names of corporate America as well as almost all mutual funds, declined by 70 or 80 percent from their highs. Coca-Cola was one of the stronger stocks, declining by only 60 percent from its high.

	2790.00
	2700.00
	2610.00
	2520.00
	2430.00
	2340.00
	2250.00
	2160.00
	2070.00
	1980.00
	1890.00
	1800.00
	1710.00
	1620.00
	1530.00
	1440.00
	1350.00
	1260.00
	1170.00
	1080.00
	990.00
	900.00
	810.00
	720.00

1979   1980   1981   1982   1983   1984   1985   1986   1987   1988   1989

FIGURE 4-3.   The Dow Jones Industrial Average Monthly Chart, 1979–1989.

The Risk of Buying at a Market Top

The opportunities for making money by buying stocks in a bull market are clear. Less obvious is the risk that depends on when you buy. That risk is considerably greater than you might at first think. You cannot assume that you will buy all or most of your stocks in the early stages of a bull market. On the contrary, the probabilities are high that you buy many stocks past the halfway mark or toward its end. You could theoretically invest all your money at or near the absolute high point for a bull market. The statistical probability of doing so is small. Nevertheless, the real risk of buying at or near the top far exceeds the statistical probability. Market tops occur when there is maximum enthusiasm. Then there is no fear, and people expect the bull market to continue to infinity. It is all too easy to be drawn into the collective enthusiasm near the top of the market when all about you are making, at least on paper, their collective fortune.

Table 4-2 shows how long it would have taken to get your money back had you invested your capital at the top of some of the biggest bull markets. (Table 4-1 uses the extremities at monthly closes, whereas Table 4-2 uses intramonth highs and lows, thus showing a greater range.)

The good news for buy-and-hold investors is that stocks, overall, have always come back eventually. Also, they have always gone on to make new highs far beyond previous highs. The potentially bad news is not as good as you might think, because there is so much rotation among stocks during each revival. Some stocks make new highs twice as quickly as the averages come back, and some take twice as long or never do. There is an informal rule that the most popular stocks of the previous bull market, the ones you are most likely to own, are the *least* likely to be at the forefront of the next bull market.

After a bear market, it can take many years, and sometimes decades, for an individual stock to regain a previous high at the top of the last bull market, if it ever does. It took Avon until 1998 to recover its peak price in nominal dollars at the 1973 high, a full twenty-five years later and despite the huge bull market going on around it. Some stocks never come back, and some recovery stories are less encouraging than you might think. In 1972 IBM began its long downtrend, departing for a time from the Dow, after starting from a price/earnings ratio of 78! It was a very long road back, and even then, not to the preeminence that it once had. In inflation-adjusted terms, IBM recovered the purchasing power of what it was worth at its high in 1972 only at the end of 1998.

Why You Must Avoid Bear Markets

It should be obvious that you must buy strong stocks in a rising market and that you must hold on as long as these stocks and the market gen-

TABLE 4-2 Markets, Peak to Peak

Market Peak	% Decline	Years to Recover
1890	64	15
1906	64	10
1916	56	9
1929	89	26
1966	38	7
1973	45	10
1987	42	2
Average	**57**	**11**

erally continue rising. It is important to make that double qualification and to emphasize the significance of stock selection. About 70 percent of all stocks go up in a bull market. That means that 30 percent of all stocks go sideways or down. For example, the period from January 1 to June 13, 1997, was one of the strongest bull phases of all time for the stock market. Nevertheless, Merrill Lynch found that 26 percent of all stocks listed on the New York Stock Exchange declined during this period, and 45 percent of all NASDAQ stocks were down.

The positive side of market fluctuations is that a market technician is likely to own some stocks in a major bull market that far exceed the performance of the market indexes. Therefore, there should be room to accept substantial price fluctuations during the process of confirming a top for the overall market, and before establishing the designation of a new bear market. If you own a stock that has tripled while the indexes are up by 50 percent, it is not too painful to give back as much as a third of the value at the top when a stock shows that its bull market may have ended.

It might seem like a lot to give back a third of what you once had at the top. However, you have to allow for big fluctuations that do not violate the major uptrend. Otherwise, you never stay in a stock on its way to doubling again. Trying to anticipate market tops before the technical signals fall into place often means losing money compared with just staying with good stocks. However, all bull markets end eventually. It is essential for long-term financial survival not to get trapped in an established downtrend that gives back all or most of the gains of the preceding bull market, or worse, in stocks that go down to zero.

If it is important to own rising stocks in a rising market, it is imperative to own few stocks or none in an established bear market. In a bull market most boats rise, and even random selection of stocks is likely to make money. Many that lag eventually get moving. Even if you fail to pick big winners, it is unlikely that you will pick many serious losers. On the other hand, about 90 percent of all stocks go down in a general bear market.

The fundamental reasons for a bear market become apparent only after the event, generally in the form of higher interest rates or an economic contraction or both. Then profits decline, lowering the apparent value of all stocks as well as their price. In a severe bear market, investors don't sell just poor stocks. Some stocks become unsalable at any price. Therefore, investors also sell what they can sell, however good. Once this downward spiral becomes entrenched, you never know how far the bear market will go or how long it will last. If you park your money in Treasury bills or an equivalent safe haven during a bear market, you have that all-important cash with which to buy back stocks again at favorable prices.

It is remarkable how much more money you make and how much grief you avoid by avoiding bear markets and having money to buy stocks in the early stages of the next bull market. The difference in performance that results from avoiding even one bear market is huge. The cumulative difference resulting from missing several bear markets is staggering. Of course, avoiding bear markets is more difficult than looking at previous bear markets in hindsight might lead you to believe. It is all too easy to confuse a routine retracement, however severe, with a bear market. If you inadvertently do so, you must be prepared to buy back in. Bull markets truly die hard, and they seldom die without plenty of strong signals showing that the trend may be reversing.

You cannot, of course, both ride stocks to the bottom of a bear market and also have the money they once represented with which to buy low. The standard alternative to using timing techniques, staying fully invested all the time, cannot reconcile this conflict.

Value Fails in a Bear Market

Fundamental analysis is suicidal in a bear market. It leads you to believe that your seemingly great stocks should ride out the decline. That just does not happen in practice. Your chances of picking stocks that buck the downtrend are infinitesimal when 90 percent of all stocks are going down.

Benjamin Graham's own experience, as told in his *Memoirs*, is sobering. He recalls having a discussion with the great investor Bernard Baruch in 1929. They agreed how extraordinary it was that stocks at the time delivered a yield of only about 2 percent when a return of 8 percent was available in the money market. They both said they expected that these returns would change places in due course. This happened over the next few years.

Baruch sold out of all his stocks in good time in 1929. Graham, who came to be known as the Dean of Wall Street, did not. He went on believing in fundamental investing and stuck with it throughout the bear market that began in 1929.

Graham admits in his *Memoirs* that he should have taken his clients' money and his own out of the market and kept it out, but he did not. Emphasis on value meant that losses on his portfolio were limited to 70 percent, compared with the 89 percent decline in the Dow. During the decline he continued to make quarterly disbursements of 1.5 percent of the value of the investments. As a result, by the end of 1932 only 22 percent remained of what he was managing in 1929. His loss in 1930 was 50.5 percent, for 1931 a further 16 percent, and for 1932 only 3 percent. During the following years Graham recovered all his losses by sticking with his value approach to investing. He made the approach work for him again when the market was going up again.

In the final analysis, all that Graham and Dodd really proved was that fundamental analysis works spectacularly in a rising market when you start from a very low level.

CHAPTER 5

Fashions in Investment Change

Industries Come and Go

Anyone telling you to hold stocks for the long term still has to tell you which stocks to hold steadfastly even in good times—never mind during a bear market.

Hard as it may be to believe, almost every line of business has had its time in the sun. For much of the nineteenth century and into the early years of the twentieth, there were no more rewarding places to invest than in railroads, steel, and shipping. The wreck of the *Titanic* was caused by the quest for prestige and power in a profitable line of business. By contrast, for long periods during the twentieth century, rails, steel, and shipping were totally out of favor, and rightly so. Owning gold stocks was a bonanza during the 1970s. After 1980 they were generally lackluster investments, and at worst, a bust. Even the most seemingly stable companies in the most seemingly stable industries can go through bad times as well as good, and they may or may not come back into the sun.

There is an informal law that the favorites of the previous secular boom are extremely unlikely to be the favorites of the next. The probabilities favor the discovery of some completely new attraction or the return to favor of one that was once utterly discredited.

General Motors in High Gear and Low

Owning General Motors was wonderful during the 1920s, the equivalent of owning Microsoft during the 1990s. $10,000 invested in General Motors in 1919 grew to $1.5 million by the top in 1929, for an increase of 150 times. Just 10 percent of a portfolio invested in GM in the early 1920s would have resulted in a wonderful performance overall, even if all the rest was in cash equivalents and showed no gain. If you rode the stock down for an 80 percent decline into the 1932 low, you still had 20 times what you put into the stock in 1919. You would also have had three times the total value of the portfolio that you started with, having risked only 10 percent of its starting value. GM was a stock for those times. It is worth noting that GM never had a losing quarter during the Depression. Its inventory controls and profit margins were all so good that its worst results were break-even.

Graham and Dodd, writing in 1934 about stock market conditions in the previous decade, said: "The history of industrial companies was a hodgepodge of violent changes in which the benefits of prosperity were so unequally and so impermanently distributed as to bring about the most unexpected failures alongside the most dazzling successes." They could have been writing about any time of industrial boom before or since.

After the 1930s, GM went out of the sun. The experience of GM in the 1920s and of Microsoft in the 1990s shows that you do not have to pick many big winners or invest heavily in them to work wonders for the long-term performance record of an investment portfolio. The necessary condition for success is that you know how to buy a winner and how to stay with it as long as you should. Then you have to get out. If, on the way, you get out inadvertently when the technical evidence merely falters, you must also know how to buy the stock back again.

Coca-Cola in Low Gear and High

Coca-Cola is a remarkable stock for its time in sun and shade. In 1939 the stock was perceived as having one of the world's great business franchises and unlimited growth potential, as it was during the 1990s.

Yet in 1959 the stock price was no higher than it was twenty years earlier. During those twenty years the Dow went up by three times, and some stocks went up by five or ten times. Coca-Cola came out of the Depression with a reputation too high for investors' expectations. The stocks that did well over the next two decades were often those that had sold down to bargain-basement price levels. So investors no longer found it necessary to pay champagne prices for Coke.

By contrast, during the 1980s and 1990s there was hardly a more popular favorite than Coca-Cola (Figure 5-1). Depending on when you bought it, the stock was up ten, twenty, or fifty times. It just went on doubling and doubling again. In 1998 it was selling at a multiple of five times sales, had a price/earnings ratio of 50, and had a dividend yield of 0.8 percent.

Instead of buying Coca-Cola in 1939, you could have bought Intertype Corporation, the leading maker of typesetting equipment. Coming out of the Depression of the 1930s, Intertype was selling in 1939 for just $8, although its underlying asset value was $20. Finally, Intertype started moving up. It was an extremely good buy once it went back up through $12. Then it was on its way to $98 in 1959 for an increase of more than ten times its price in 1939. It was enough to get on this escalator at $12 or $20, or at $30 or $40, in order to make a huge profit. However, it was not a stock to buy on the way down just because its price reached its book value.

The lesson of General Motors and Coca-Cola shows that there is no standard of quality so favorable that you can expect to hold any stock forever. The lesson of Intertype is that you can make a huge profit by

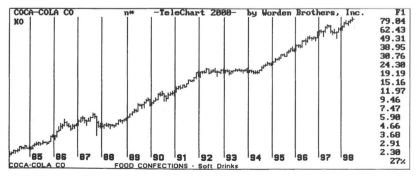

FIGURE 5-1. Coca-Cola Monthly Chart.

buying a depressed stock with a solid balance sheet and a strong franchise, once it starts moving—and only once it starts moving. Intertype also shows that there is no point in buying until other investors are prepared to join the party. However good a stock, do you really want to ride it from $22 down to $8 when it is in a clearly established downtrend? In the 1980s and 1990s buyers of many apparently low-priced stocks knew the painful answer.

Digital Equipment Goes Out of the Sun

Figure 5-2 shows a great stock going from sun into shade. Once regarded as an investor's dream come true as it reached for its high at $199.50, the stock of Digital Equipment Corporation was to decline to a low of just $18.50.

No doubt, as the stock continued to grind lower, it was tempting for many investors to try their hand at picking a bottom on the basis of apparent value and of price relative to where it once was.

There have been many successes and many failures, even in the computer industry—especially in the computer industry. Exasperatingly, DEC was in many ways a success. Unfortunately, while Microsoft, Intel, Compaq, Dell and many others never seemed to end their major uptrends, things never quite came back together for DEC. This company, along with Apple and IBM, was one of those in the industry that ran into difficulties, with dire consequences for the price of the stock.

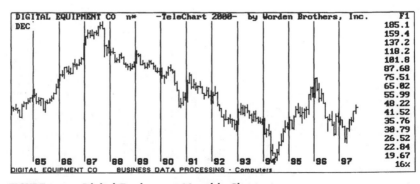

FIGURE 5-2. Digital Equipment Monthly Chart.

Success and Failure Come and Go

The lesson of DEC is that you have to be vigilant to watch market action even in the best of all stocks. Realistically, it almost never happens that you find a one-decision stock, although some stocks may be worth holding for many years. If there is one constant, it is that success and failure come and go. Prosperous companies fade. New ones take center stage. Apparently moribund war-horses of an earlier age regain their former glory. Fashions change. Technology changes. Competition changes. Corporate tycoons become senile. Eventually they leave and new blood arrives, which may or may not be better.

There was hardly a better company than Fruehauf Trailer in the early 1980s, when it was the market leader in transport trailers, selling one in three of all units sold in the United States. Yet financial mismanagement of this great company led to bankruptcy, despite the prosperity of the times. There are always winners, and there are always casualties. Market action may not necessarily show you what is happening in a company's business, but it will show whether buyers or sellers are the more aggressive. If a stock is going down relentlessly, knowledgeable sellers may be selling in order to salvage what they can while they can.

Many of the best stocks represent participation in companies profiting from the technology of their time. However, technological innovation creates a business environment where things move fast. There are spectacular successes, and there are surprising failures if a successful company takes a wrong turn. Eventually, the new technology loses its significance or becomes obsolete, and few companies profiting from the technology of one age successfully make the transition to that of the next. Fortunes were once made in typewriters. Only Olivetti made a successful transition to computer technology. No shipbuilder made a successful transition to building airplanes.

Owning a stock is not like a marriage. Above all, there are bear markets as well as bull markets, and stocks decline by far more than ever seemed remotely possible when conditions looked so good that nothing could go wrong. Airlines, especially airlines, are a classic example of technological progress and an apparent market opportunity to make money in a growing industry. Despite that, there is hardly an industry that has delivered more opportunity for losing money as well as making it. The conclusion is inescapable: You must buy stocks when the technical indicators are favorable and you must sell stocks when they are no longer favorable.

The good news about obsolescence and market rotation is that letting profits run while cutting losses short should result in gains that far outweigh losses. When a stock or the market generally goes to a level that appears conspicuously high, it may not necessarily mean that the next major move is down. You have to heed the futures trader's saying: There is no price so high that it cannot go higher still. That is the experience of hundreds of great stocks in many, many bull markets. In a bear market, however, you have to heed its counterpart: There is no price so low that it cannot decline further. In the stock market that can mean going down to nothing.

In the 1980s and 1990s, failure to stay with a Coca-Cola or to act on new signals to buy the stock was an exercise in arguing with the market. When there is more buying pressure than selling pressure, the stock price remains high and can continue higher. All you can say at apparently nosebleed price levels is that you cannot afford to relax. To that extent and only to that extent does value analysis serve as an alert to keep an eye on the exit, on the technical indicators that may suggest a trend reversal. You cannot afford to wait until there is a stampede and everyone wants to get out at the same time, as occurred in October 1987.

Fashions in Asset Classes Change

In the big picture for the twentieth century, you should have owned stocks from 1903 to 1929. Then you should have owned bonds until 1945. From then until 1966, you should have gone back into stocks and real estate. Then you should have owned gold, silver, real estate, and collectibles. Finally, from 1980 you should have owned stocks and depending where, real estate. Bonds also came out of the doghouse and began to do well after 1981, as inflation wound down.

However, if you were a truly committed long-term investor, you could have both taken a long-term view and also gone against the century's long-term trends.

Unless you think it improbable that anyone could ever do so, here is a true story about the trustee department of a prominent insurance company in London. From 1928 to 1945 they owned stocks and real estate. Thereafter, until the trusteeship ended in 1996, they owned mostly bonds and mortgages. In the process, the trustees took 68 years, starting in mid-1928, to turn US$100,000 into US$25,000. (To put the value of $100,000 in 1928 into perspective, in 1934 Standard Oil of California paid $275,000 for the entire oil rights in Saudi Arabia. Walt Disney's original budget for making *Snow White* was $250,000. It took $2000, representing a 10 percent interest in the show, to save the musical *Oklahoma!* from going under before it reached Broadway.)

The trustees incurred only a minor loss of capital between 1928 and 1945. Unfortunately, there was almost no income paid out between 1930 and 1945; the capital was invested in stocks that stopped paying dividends and which could not at that time be sold at any price. Having delivered almost no income for fifteen years, the trustees were paranoid about the risk of making that mistake twice. Throughout the great inflation beginning in the 1950s, they maintained that their responsibility was to achieve a balance between income for the current beneficiaries and capital appreciation for the eventual recipients. They could not arbitrarily reduce the income by buying lower-yielding investments. In fact, they did not do what they said they intended to do when they had the chance. Stocks yielded more than bonds from 1945 until about 1960. However, the trustees were long married to 30-year bonds with 3-percent coupon and bought at par in 1945. In the end, the trustees lost over 99 percent of the purchasing power of both capital and income.

This is an extreme example of how badly things can turn out when investing for the long term. But it did happen.

Where Mutual Funds Fail

Trading Versus Investment

The mutual fund industry says that you should invest "for the long term." Unfortunately, many fund managers do not live by what they say.

The industrywide turnover for the U.S. mutual fund industry during 1997 was running at almost 100 percent, up from 30 percent in 1977. That means that on the average, every fund turned over almost its entire portfolio every year. Looking at it another way, mutual funds themselves seldom hold any stock for longer than a year, while many stocks are bought and sold within a much shorter time. Since some funds hold stocks for years, it follows that there are others that rotate their holdings constantly. Their managers are traders, not investors, and trading is, for all practical purposes, a completely different kind of business. It is one with similarities to playing at a casino. That might be construed as a legitimate business if it were marketed as such, with disclosure of the trading approaches used. However, the main difference is that the probabilities do not vary at a casino, but they may change enormously for a stock trader when market conditions change.

The television advertising for one mutual fund group showed a group of young investment managers making investment decisions in the boardroom. Trying to impress prospective fund buyers with his sagacity, one of them says, "We must focus on next week's important economic numbers . . ." Perhaps they do focus on every straw in the wind, since this fund group has a mediocre record. In any case, such a focus must be myopic. Economic news announced in any one week practically never changes a long-term trend, and it seldom helps toward knowing what to buy or sell or when to do it.

There are many problems with investing in a mutual fund that constantly rotates its investments. For many investors every realized profit is subject to capital gains tax, and the rate may be higher on short-term gains. If you buy late in the year, you may have to pay capital gains taxes on someone else's profits, not your own.

In addition, there is a transaction cost for every purchase and another one for every sale. There is also a spread on both sides of the trade between the market-maker's bid and ask. You might pay $85.50 when you are buying, but you receive only $85.25 when you sell. The spreads are normally small for actively traded stocks. However, they widen when you want to buy at the same time as a lot of other people or when you want to sell at a time of general selling. Also, spreads often widen substantially when buying a big block in a strongly rising market or if you are selling when the price is collapsing. Mutual funds, because of their size, are at a disadvantage compared with the small investor when trading big blocks of shares. Sometimes the spread for a large block can be several points when going with the flow of a big surge, as in two or three dollars on Microsoft at $100. So transaction costs can start to amount to real money when there is a high frequency of trading.

The mutual fund industry constantly trumpets from the rooftops the merits of holding for the long term. They also trumpet the benefits of compound interest, and the corresponding exponential growth for those who start investing regularly at a young age. However, the benefits of compound interest diminish significantly when capital is constantly eroded by transaction costs and withdrawals to pay capital gains tax.

Frequent trading is great for brokers, and it is no coincidence that many mutual funds are run by brokers or by institutions that own brokerage houses. There is not supposed to be a conflict of interest. However, there is no question that mutual fund commissions make brokers salivate. Even when there is no direct connection, those who place the business and those who broker it are likely to know each other socially and to send business to each other. Bernard Shaw perceptively observed that all professions are a conspiracy against the laity. Charles Dickens observed in *Bleak House* that the business of lawyers is making business for lawyers. Things do not change. The investment business is not immune to mutual back-scratching at the expense of the public.

Unlike retailing, frequent turnover of the stock in trade is not the way to go in the stock market. There is no doubt that rapid turnover of stocks is one reason why so few funds come close even to equaling the performance of the stock indexes.

Within any broad stock market average there are always winners, losers, and stocks going nowhere. Why is it so difficult to find winners and to stay with them? You can readily see that there are stocks that keep on going. Why is it so difficult to stay away from losers and stocks going nowhere? A relatively small shift from the mediocre and the bad to the obviously good would result in a much better performance than the mediocrity of averages. It is not as if mutual funds retain big cash balances that bring down their performance record, because they do not. On the contrary, they mostly invest almost all they have all the time.

Warren Buffett's Berkshire Hathaway has shown that the stated policy of the mutual fund industry does in fact work, at least in a bull market. That company is, in effect, a closed-end fund, which means that it mostly owns stocks and it trades like a stock. Buffett finds stocks in first-class companies and stays with them. It is ironic that investors have been prepared to pay a huge premium over asset value to buy Berkshire Hathaway, with its passive investment strategy, when they could buy into mutual funds without paying any premium. On the face of it, the alternative choice of buying mutual funds at their exact asset value should have paid far better. Unfortunately, there was no contest, at least during the Great Bull Market, when it came to evaluating which managements did better. It paid hand over fist to be a patient long-term investor in great stocks, whether owned directly or through a company like Berkshire Hathaway.

What Do the Funds Hold?

In 1997 equity funds in the United States owned $2 trillion in stocks, up from $34 billion in 1977. As a result of the parabolic growth in funds, they grew to a point of controlling 22 percent of the entire $9.5 trillion capitalization of all U.S. publicly traded stocks. However, their ownership of the ten largest companies, the ones that generally enjoyed the greatest capital appreciation, was far below the 22 percent level that would correspond to their overall position in the market. The following table shows the percentage of shares in the ten largest companies owned by the funds in mid-1997.

Company	Percentage Held by Active Mutual Funds
General Electric	8.1
Coca-Cola	3.6
Exxon	5.9
Microsoft	7.3
Merck	8.8
Intel	14.3
Philip Morris	19.6
Procter & Gamble	7.4
IBM	13.7
Johnson & Johnson	9.8

Warren Buffett's Berkshire Hathaway owned more Coca-Cola than the entire mutual fund industry put together.

Expert Funds

Consider a fund family, which we call Expert Funds. Expert's promotional literature sounds great: "We are committed to excellence in investment management . . . Our approach to equity investing is based on:

- Focused, fundamental research and analysis
- Careful selection of a limited number of securities
- A long-term perspective

". . . We don't try to time the market or base our decisions on short-term expectations. We invest for the long term because achieving results takes time. Although typically we hold equities for three to five years, we do not have a definite time horizon. We may sell an existing investment to make room for an investment with greater potential, *or when an investment is no longer undervalued in the market.* [Our emphasis.]"

What does this mean?

Expert says they hold for the longer term, which ought to be good. However, it appears that any time they hit the jackpot with a big winner like Intel, Microsoft, or Coca-Cola, they sell it because it is "no longer undervalued in the marketplace." Expert appeared to hold no stock in those companies in any of their funds in 1997. On the other hand, they held large positions in several stocks doing very poorly during 1997 and, from a technical perspective, with little or no justification for owning them at all.

Expert had great difficulty in finding and staying with first-rate performers. Unfortunately, the group had no such difficulty staying with its second-rate performers. Most serious of all is that the group was in bad trouble when faced with a real bear market in Asian and Pacific stocks, one of its areas of special interest. By all normal valuation criteria, these stocks were extremely expensive during 1997. For a long time they no longer fitted Expert's criteria of being "no longer undervalued in the marketplace." Expert's fund specializing in Asian and Pacific stocks went down with the ship in the 1997 market meltdown in that sector.

Superfund

There is another billion-dollar group of funds, which we call Superfund. In 1997, this group also appeared to own no stock in Intel or Microsoft and only a small position in Coca-Cola. On the other hand, they held big positions in Boeing and Texas Instruments. Think about it! They did not have big positions in the major airline stocks which were flying high, but Boeing, which was quite clearly going nowhere, was one of their largest holdings! The same thing happened with their large holding of Texas Instruments, which was going nowhere, while Microsoft continued to levitate.

More serious still is how Superfund handled a general bear market in one of its specialized funds. What they call "excellent expertise in investment management" should be able to identify a major bear market in a niche for which they have a sector fund. They should know how to handle the decline by selling stocks when it is timely to do so. Then they would have cash available to buy stocks again at bargain prices. That would fulfill the objective of making money over the long term that investors are supposed to live for.

During 1997 it was obvious for all to see that gold was going down. Figure 6-1 shows the price of gold to the end of June 1997. How much would you want to own gold or gold mining stocks compared with owning Coca-Cola or General Electric? Or cash? Is there a contest? In any event, gold was on its way down to $275, from $335 at the end of June, and gold mining shares still had to go down a very long way after June 1997.

Superfund's performance with its gold fund during 1997 is interesting for another reason. It appears to contradict this fund group's stated policy with respect to undervalued shares. Their prospectus states: "The objective of this fund is to achieve long-term growth through investment primarily in securities of companies dependent on the value of gold, silver, platinum, and palladium . . ." For many years, this

FIGURE 6–1. Gold Monthly Chart.

objective was largely a contradiction in terms insofar as it related to growth in gold stocks.

It is patently absurd on the basis of value analysis, common sense, or any other standard investment criteria to own gold stocks priced at 20, 30, or 40 times earnings when the metal is in a full-fledged bear market.

There are times to own gold stocks, even though they always seem expensive. Naturally, you should own them only when it is timely to do so, when they are going up or showing that they may be starting to move up. There is no point in owning them in a full-fledged bear market.

On June 30, 1997, Superfund's precious metals fund had the following allocations in its Precious and Strategic Metal Fund:

Common shares	93.6%
Cash, short-term notes, and other assets	6.4
	100.0

You could hardly have a higher percentage than 93.6 percent of a fund invested in this relatively speculative and illiquid market or a lower percentage than 6.4 percent in cash. A few fundholder redemptions would soon deplete the entire cash balance. It could easily become necessary to sell stocks just to meet redemptions. Then there would be no cash at all available to buy stocks at low prices near the bottom of the market.

In June 1997 most of Superfund's portfolio of gold stocks was severely under water, with the market value of some stocks 75 percent or more below cost. So selling stocks would have meant selling at a severe loss. Fund managers may know in theory about running profits and cutting losses, but living by it is not necessarily what they do. On the contrary, many of them cut profits off at the knees and let losses run.

There is even worse to tell about Superfund than its commitment to gold in its precious metals fund during the bear market in the metal. In 1997 the group also invested heavily in gold mining stocks in some of its other funds not designated as precious metals or natural resource funds. There was a significant weighting in gold mining stocks during the third quarter of 1997 in one fund where the stated objectives are "to provide investors with superior investment returns over the long term, having regard to safety of capital . . ."

How to Tell Long-Term from Short

One test of whether a fund manager stays with winners and cuts off losers is to compare the book value of a stock in the portfolio with its market value. There should be a huge spread between the two numbers if the fund bought a stock at a good price and has held it for a long time when it was going up. If the differential is small, it probably means that the fund manager has only recently bought the stock.

Superfund owned the following stocks in mid-1997 in its Larger US Company Fund: Johnson & Johnson, Merck, Coca-Cola, Eli Lilly, Reebok, Centocor, and Gillette. Unfortunately, the market value of these combined holdings was less than 5 percent above their average cost, despite the fact that the stocks had been soaring for years! By contrast, Warren Buffett held Coca-Cola and Gillette for years, and his average cost was a tiny percentage of their 1998 market value.

Index Funds

Given the indifferent results achieved by many advisors and professional money managers during the 1980s and 1990s, it became fashionable to buy so-called index funds. The idea was that a basket of stocks comprising an equal weighting in stocks in the index would produce, on the average, a superior long-term result.

That approach is like putting your head in the oven and your feet in the freezer and expecting, on the average, to be comfortable. Almost any index generally comprises some stocks clearly going up, some going hard down, and others going interminably sideways. Therefore, it is not logical to replicate an index. Just buy the stocks going up and avoid like the plague the ones that are not. As we saw in Chapter 1, that means buying General Electric but not General Motors; the one is going up and the other one is not.

Mutual Fund Management Fees

Most mutual fund investors have a serious problem with onerous management fees. High management fees often negate the apparent attractions of low entry or exit fees, otherwise known as sales commissions or loads. A steady increase of 15 or 20 percent annually in fund values looks very good, even if the fund underperforms relative to the market indexes. It is easy enough to accept having between 1.5 and 3 percent taken out of your fund when there are double-digit gains. But what if stocks revert to the norm of advancing by 8 or 10 percent annually? What if the gains are no more than the fees? Worse, what if fund performance turns negative? How would you feel about living through a decline in the value of your fund of, say, 30, 40, or 50 percent and, in addition, paying someone so heavily to lose your money?

Management fees are particularly onerous for some fixed-income funds. How can you justify paying 1.5 to 2 percent in management fees when the total income yield on the capital is 6 percent? A management fee of 1.5 percent of the capital takes 25 percent of the income. Unlike selecting stocks, finding bonds to buy is not a two-pipe problem for Sherlock Holmes. In any case, how often do you have to make changes in a bond fund? You can own a 30-year bond for 30 years, as and when it is right to own it at all. Were it not for the fact that bonds have been in a bull market since 1981, there would certainly have been loud protests about fees from investors in bond funds.

The burden of management fees is illustrated well by the largest fund that invests intentionally in the ten highest-yielding stocks in the Dow Jones Industrial Average. Evidence over the very long term shows that it has been more profitable to buy and hold these ten stocks at the beginning of the year than it has to buy the entire index. This strategy normally calls for an annual adjustment, generally in January, so that the portfolio drops any lower-yielding stocks and brings in ones that now yield more. The reason this approach has worked over the very long term appears to be that it avoids buying the highest flyers and carrying them from top to the bottom, when their popularity wanes. It is not that this approach is particularly good at picking winners. High yields tend to provide protection from substantial declines. But if downside risk is low, so may be upside potential when market conditions are leading to a double in a stock like Wal-Mart or IBM. This approach requires no management capability as such. Yet the biggest fund using this strategy charges a 1 percent up-front sales charge and thereafter, an annual management fee of 1.75 percent.

Warren Buffett's Berkshire Hathaway has never needed to charge management fees on the scale charged by mutual fund managers. A more passive, long-term investment strategy does not require an army of analysts and traders. Like any successful investor, Buffett makes his mistakes. But making mistakes is part of life. They just have to be put in perspective.

Mutual funds' annual charges can be as much as 3 percent on the value of a fund for a specialist fund investing, say, in Russia or China. Relatively few funds charge much less than 1.5 percent, but they do exist. An example is the low-turnover T. Rowe Price International Stock Fund, which has an expense ratio of 0.88 percent and does most of what you should reasonably expect from a mutual fund.

It is reasonable to compare mutual fund charges with the actual cost of running a major pension fund. That is normally between 0.1 and 0.2 percent of the assets in a very large investment portfolio similar in size to that of a major mutual fund. Some managers of private portfolios are well satisfied with annual fees of between 0.5 percent and 1 percent of assets under management, although most individual portfolios tend to be much smaller than that of any mutual fund. There is a relationship between the size of an investment holding and administration costs. Even so, mutual fund fees for any size of investment are exorbitant when they are many times the reasonable cost of doing business.

When stocks generally were rising strongly, Expert and Superfund reported rates of return for their funds roughly in line with the average for the industry, although well below the performance of the stock indexes. Good performance in some areas obviously concealed the disasters that should have been avoided altogether.

The record for most mutual funds is that if their mandate is larger stocks, they fail to surpass the Standard & Poor 500 or the Dow Industrials. If their mandate is small stocks, they do not surpass the Value Line or the Russell stock indexes. It is not difficult to see that they and most other fund managers could and should do much better, even during the good times and especially during bear markets.

CHAPTER 7

The Risk in Mutual Funds

A Mutual Fund Is Just Another Stock

A mutual fund is really no more than another stock, a conglomerate comprising a basket of other stocks. You merely buy and sell it differently. Whereas banks invest predominantly in a loan portfolio and insurance companies in a policy portfolio, mutual funds invest in a portfolio that may include stocks, bonds, or cash. In practice, a mutual fund involves almost as much risk as investing in any huge financial institution.

Mutual funds have the strengths and weaknesses of any corporate management. They suffer from the corporate tendency toward group acceptance of politically correct ideas. The view of the future tends to focus on short-term results as it does for many corporations—*See how much money we just made in the last quarter!* Most decision making is based on recent experience rather than on a longer-term historical perspective. Youth, energy, enthusiasm, and, especially, consensus-thinking are the prerequisites for career success in the industry. Since few of the people running mutual funds in the 1990s were in the industry in 1973, experience does not generally include living through the last hamburger-grinding bear market. During the 1980s and the 1990s you could buy almost anything and expect to make money on balance. So it was never necessary to do better or to read the history books.

A bear market is the polar opposite of youth, enthusiasm, and positive energy. Unwillingness to face the negative side of life no doubt partly explains why, collectively, mutual funds have an almost infallible record of being fully invested at market tops. It is probably no coincidence that in April 1998 institutional cash holdings were at a 25-year low of less than 4 percent of assets. This was the average. Since some institutions must obviously have had more than 4 percent cash, some must also have had less. That month, the broad-based Russell 2000 index of smaller stocks made a significant and potentially long-lasting high.

For investors in mutual funds, it should be extremely alarming how most managers interpret their job description. When pressed, they say it is not their job to avoid bear markets, and few of them have the desire or the knowledge with which to try to do so. One guest on the television program *Wall Street Week* said that there was no need to avoid bear markets because they seldom last more than eight months! In fact, the long-term record for U.S. stocks shows that bear markets last, on the average, between 25 and 30 percent of the duration of the preceding bull market. Some bear markets have lasted very much longer, sometimes for many years like the one in Japan that began in 1990. Forecasting the duration of a bear market on the basis of the preceding bull market requires determination of when the preceding bull market really began. Did the major bull market of the 1990s begin in 1982, 1987, or 1990? The two-month decline in 1987 before the market low and the three-month decline in 1990 are not representative of bear-market normality. They might be described as interruptions in a long-term bull market.

If money in a mutual fund is not invested, it may suggest that the manager is not doing what the fund is paid to do. It does not show that keeping money out of the market may be an exercise in prudence. In any case, money not invested in the market is vulnerable to being taken away and placed with a more aggressive manager. Except for money market funds, it is not part of a fund's mission to hold large cash balances.

The fundholder is told to take personal responsibility for the bad as well as the good that markets bring—by "diversifying." Often as not, that means buying several different funds that are variations on the same theme. It does not mean diversification into different asset classes, such as Treasury bills and money market funds, or even bonds.

Risk assessment for the individual is not part of the mutual fund sales pitch, and the word *sell* is not part of the vocabulary of sales or of diversification. You are supposed to invest "for the long term"—*Everyone knows that!*—even if that means having most of your eggs in the same kind of basket and carrying your investments through a full-fledged bear market.

Do You Want to Hold for That Long Term?

What is the risk of your fund going down with the ship in a major bear market? What happens in a repetition of the market crash of 1987? What happens in a replay of the major bear markets that began in 1907, 1919, 1929, 1937, 1972, 1981, or the many lesser bear markets occurring from time to time? Will the loudly proclaimed expertise of mutual fund managers preserve capital in a bear market?

The answer, based on previous experience, is *No!* Like banks, mutual funds are accident-prone. Managers' enthusiasm almost invariably goes to extremes in embracing the current investment fashion. The almost universal experience of the money management industry is that they have never sold out anywhere near market highs. On the contrary, their buying extends market highs beyond where they otherwise might stop. Instead of selling at market tops and buying at market bottoms, fund managers almost invariably do the opposite. The standard pattern is that funds, fully invested at the top of the market, then ride stocks to the bottom of a bear market. As a result, they never have money to buy when stocks are really down.

Funds' selling at or near market bottoms forces prices to lower levels than would otherwise occur. It may prove a typical contrary indicator that many precious metals funds went into liquidation in 1998, when this asset class fell into utter disrepute. (A *contrary indicator* is a measure of sentiment so extreme that the market is soon likely to do the opposite of what most people expect. The masses have pigged out on buying at a top or, as the case may be, have thrown in the towel in despair at a market bottom.)

Fluctuations in sentiment from one extreme to the other are a constant in all areas of investment, and many people are reluctant to sell a loser until there is no choice but to do so. Managers of funds devoted to specific market areas that experienced bear markets in the 1990s always took a fully invested position down in a bear market in that sector. It happened in Japan funds. It happened in Mexican funds. It happened in precious metals funds. It happened in Asia funds. It happened in stocks generally in the crash of 1987. The same can be expected in a general bear market. It has always happened in the past, in every major bear market in the twentieth century.

The manager of one of the world's biggest funds wrote a book about his life as a fund manager. Between August and October 1987 the fund's value fell by more than a third. "I had to sell a lot of stock to pay off shareholders who got scared out of their assets," he wrote. "We had $689 million in sales in October and $1.3 billion in redemptions. The sellers outnumbered the buyers by two to one, but the vast majority . . . stayed put and did nothing."

Unlike the humility of Benjamin Graham and Warren Buffett in acknowledging their mistakes, there is a curious lack of remorse or humility in this observation. With the wisdom of hindsight, the money manager can claim to have been more prescient than the market. The investor who got scared was wrong, not the money manager who was oblivious to the risks of high valuations on a collision course with rising interest rates. The result was that this fund did not have cash enough on hand to meet redemptions at the bottom. That is like the individual investor having to sell stocks to pay the rent or a retail store running out of working capital to buy stock. Every business needs working capital as well as the capital investment, which, for a mutual fund, means owning stocks. The more risk of a market decline, and therefore of redemptions, the more a fund manager should raise cash.

Few funds had cash with which to buy stocks at a good price after October 1987. At the market top they were overexposed in stocks when the general market was higher by most valuation criteria than at any time since the summer of 1929. It is sad to think that many of those who sold out at the bottom were almost certainly among those least able to handle losing money, even if the loss should turn out to be recoverable in time. One of the first rules of investment is to "sell down to your sleeping level." There is no point in putting all your life savings at a risk beyond your control with a manager who may disturb your sleep. That is like buying a dog and having to bark yourself.

It would be a wonderful sales pitch to stop investors cashing in if one could say: "Why exchange your fund for cash now? The fund has cash. Now we can buy stocks low, and you can buy low too if you invest more now!"

Fortunately, investors were most likely making money within a few years, even if they bought mutual funds at the high in August 1987. Of course, the results since 1987 are enormously better for those who bought in October and November, compared with those who bought in August. Here is an example of how timing, when you get it right, can make a huge difference in long-term performance. No thanks are due to fund managers that there is such a big difference according to the month when one might have bought. Nor are thanks due to fund managers for the fact that the recovery from the 1987 low back to its high came so soon. They were lucky compared with investors who had to wait from 1929 to 1954 to get their money back.

Berkshire Hathaway is not immune to a bear market. Warren Buffett showed in 1987 that he does not sell ahead of a major market decline. At least he missed selling before that one, and he may miss the next major decline. It is well known that Buffett hates paying taxes with a passion. That includes paying the capital gains taxes incurred by selling stocks bought at much lower prices. Of course, if you hold stocks that have gone up by ten or more times, you have considerable flexibility in deciding what to do. Except in a major and long-lasting bear market, it might cost less to hang on than to pay capital gains taxes. There might not be enough of a difference between the selling price and the price where you buy the stock back. Nevertheless, risk management still dictates avoiding a major bear market in case it becomes cataclysmic.

How the Funds Say It

Funds don't blatantly admit their commitment to incompetence. The pill comes sugared like this line from the literature for one multibillion-dollar mutual fund group:

EVERYONE Has Different RISK TOLERANCES
That's why everyone has different investment needs.

Individual mutual funds typically hold a variety of invest-ments. This diversification spreads around the risk so that the performance of a fund is not tied to the performance of a sin-gle investment.

You can't eliminate risk entirely, but you can manage it by:

- Diversifying your investments
- Thinking long term
- Keeping a level head
- Seeking professional management.

Logically, if everyone has a different risk tolerance, everyone should have a personal investment portfolio, even if it is very small. Any mutual fund, by definition, involves a merging of individual toler-ance for risk into that of the collective.

Calculating Investment Returns

You have to beware of the way the investment industry measures its results. The standard method for calculating investment returns is to measure performance on the basis of total returns. Gains include both income and increases in the market price of investments. Money man-agers then assume reinvestment of the income in that pot.

That basis for calculating gains is indulgent at best, and for many people it does not meet the demands of the real world. It assumes that the investor has other income to live on, which may not be the case. It is certain to be a false assumption for many pensioners.

One test of a successful company, as Graham and Dodd correctly observed, is whether there is a real disposable income available to pay out each year as dividends. If there is, then you know that the invest-ment is truly earning its keep. Corporate growth without payment of dividends might mean that the company does not in fact have the abil-ity to pay dividends, even if it wanted to. All the cash generated by the business might be required just to keep the business going.

Given all the challenges of trusting a mutual fund with your money, there will still be many people who decide to do so. When considering this course of action, prudence dictates finding out what may be involved in terms of risk, reward, and costs. Here is a list of questions to ask.

You Ask the Questions: Fund Quiz

1. How Much Does It Cost to Get into the Fund?

Some funds charge no entry fee or "load," but they charge heavily for management fees and exit fees. The no-load feature may be offset by milking the fund with high annual management fees once they have your money.

2. How Much Does It Cost to Get Out of the Fund?

Some funds charge a hefty exit fee unless you keep the money in for many years. You should be entitled to change your mind at any time without having to pay exorbitantly to do so. You should plan for the possibility that you may need the money for something else that cannot be foreseen when you invest.

3. What Are the Management Fees as a Percentage of (a) the Total Value of My Investment and (b) the Income Received in the Fund?

As we saw in the previous chapter, some money managers operate profitably with a management fee of the order of 0.5 percent of the funds under management, that is to say, one-half of one percent. In many cases, that level of fees applies to a more passive approach to investment. There are, of course, advantages to passivity, or taking the long-term view, and disadvantages to active management. Warren Buffett exemplifies the long-term approach *par excellence.* It is hard to envision circumstances where annual management fees should much exceed 1.0 percent of assets under management, except possibly in out-of-the-way niche funds.

4. How Much Does the Fund Manager Pay Out in Sales Commissions?

Sales commissions often amount to several percentage points right off the top of your investment as soon as you make it. It might not seem that way, but the effect is the same as driving a new car off the dealer's lot. The commission to the sales representative comes out of your hide one way or another. Even if there is no visible sales commission and the fund managers have to find the money up front to pay their salespeople, you had better believe that they soon get their money back one way or another. What you pay in commissions and management fees will pay for a lot of advice and commissions elsewhere. It is just that you are told not to notice what it costs you or how you pay for it.

5. *How Does the Market Value of Investments in the Fund Compare with the Book Value of Those Investments?*

A big difference is good; a small one, or a negative one, bad. When there is a big difference, it suggests that the fund does, in fact, invest for the long term, staying with its winners, and weeding out its losers.

6. *How Has the Fund Done in the Very Long Term?*

The standard question the industry answers for you is how much money they have made in each fund over different lengths of time. The industry has expanded considerably in recent years with so many new funds. So you often have no idea how the fund you choose might perform in the really long term, or in a bear market. Many funds advertise their performance over one, five, and ten years.

For statistical significance, you really need a hundred samples, although thirty samples generally constitute an acceptable shortcut for a statistical assumption. In the investment business, there are not many thirty-year records, and none of a hundred years, that indicate with any degree of reliability what you might expect in the future. In practical terms, you really need to see a performance record that includes a bear market or two, which requires going back to about 1970. Such a long time covers almost an entire working career for many an investment manager, so even very long-term performance records are highly suspect. Still, performance during the 1987 market crash is very much worth looking at, where it is available. There was an opportunity to make a huge return during the first nine months of the year and then a huge opportunity either to keep those gains or else to lose them in September and October. If a historical record is not available, then it is worth prying to see whether the fund managers show any signs of knowing any history.

7. What Has the Fund Group Done in a Bear Market in Any of Its Sector Funds That Have Recently Experienced Bear Markets?

One shortcut for determining statistical probability and managerial competence is to see how your fund managers handled sector bear markets in Japan, Mexico, Asia, precious metals, and in Russia. Of course, this shortcut is applicable only where there were sector funds in these areas within the fund family.

8. What Can the Fund Do for Me That I Can't Do for Myself?

The answer may truly be that you do not have the time, interest, or energy to look after your own investments and that you should buy mutual funds or go to a professional portfolio manager. For many people, however, there is no reason why you should not be able to do the job yourself and probably do it better than anyone else. If you know that you want to invest in some niche market such as growth stocks in India, then a mutual fund specializing in that area makes a lot of sense. Even then, you are probably better off in a publicly traded closed-end fund which you buy or sell as you would any other stock.

You Should Do the Job Yourself

As we have seen, times change both for individual stocks and for the market generally. There are bull markets and there are bear markets. There are times when the only place to invest is in common stocks. There are also times to own no stocks. During those times, it is almost certainly no help to look to a mutual fund for diversifying your investments, thinking long term, keeping a level head, or seeking professional management. A level head also needs to be one that is responsive to a changing environment for stocks of all kinds, including mutual funds.

As a worst case, ask how long you are really prepared to wait before you make any money. Would you stay the course in common stocks if you had to live through a replay of what happened after the general market turned down in 1929? In other words, are you prepared, as a worst case, to wait for twenty-six years just to get your money back?

The bottom line is what the mutual fund industry says about protecting you from bear markets: *"It's not our job!"* One thing we learn from history is that people do not learn from history.

Since investing for the long term is not extraordinarily difficult or time-consuming, why pay a high cost for someone else to do the job? If you need help to do the job yourself, supplement your own homework with a subscription to an advisory service. Alternatively, you can look for the services of a broker who understands the importance of timing and preservation of capital. A single really good idea can pay many times over for the subscription to an advisory service or for the additional commissions paid to a personal broker compared with what you pay at a discount house.

PART

TWO

How and When to Buy Stocks

CHAPTER 8

Defining a Bull Market

Upward Zigzags

A bull market or an uptrend in a stock occurs when its price action shows a succession of higher highs and higher lows on its monthly price chart. This pattern produces an upward zigzag (Figure 8-1).

The monthly bar chart for General Electric shows that interpretation of this definition can sometimes be difficult, particularly when a market is going sideways as this stock was in 1988 and 1989 (Figure 8-2). The remedy is to use a monthly line chart, which joins closes on the last trading day of each month (Figure 8-3). Most charting software automatically produces a line chart that connects closing prices. A moving average set at 1 produces the same result.

Sometimes market action is so strongly bullish that you can identify an uptrend at a glance. There was no questioning the strength of General Electric during 1995 and 1996. Retracements stopped well above previous lows, and the stock was constantly reaching for new highs. In the strongest bull markets, which are generally also the safest

FIGURE 8-1. Bull Market Zigzag.

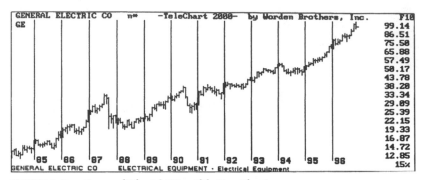

FIGURE 8-2.   General Electric Monthly Bar Chart.

ones to trade, upward market action shows persistence, without either major surges or major plunges.

In practice, even a strong bull market has aberrations, particularly when a bullish trend has been in force for some time. It can be all too tempting to sell a stock when it appears to be faltering, but it may be doing no more than digesting its earlier gains before continuing the uptrend. This means that some investors want to take profits in the stock, so the price sags a little. When the stock goes down further, additional investors want to lock in their profits. Moreover, recent buyers want to make sure that their small profit does not turn into a loss and they sell too. After a time selling decreases and buying pressure again predominates as investors wanting to buy low on the retracement become more aggressive than the fearful investors baling out. Then the stock begins to move higher again.

It is essential to distinguish between a normal retracement and one

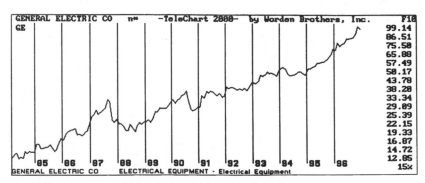

FIGURE 8-3.   General Electric Monthly Line Chart.

that may signify the start of a more substantial decline. It is a matter of common sense, as well as prudent capital management, to retain confidence in a stock that violates an upward zigzag by an amount that is insignificant and probably aberrational. Accordingly, it is generally valid to continue a bull market designation when the price decline does not exceed the previous low by more than about 5 percent on the basis of the monthly closing price. A little more than 5 percent is acceptable where there is an identifiable round number just below the 5-percent calculation.

Look at General Electric in October 1985. A strict 5 percent calculation of 75 cents from a low at $15 allows for an acceptable retracement to $14.25, but there is a high probability that there will be open orders to buy the stock at or just above $14. Therefore, in this case a monthly close in GE below $14 would constitute a violation of a bull market designation.

(An open order is one entered to buy at a fixed price below the market as and when there is a decline to that level. Many investors use this technique to buy on dips, taking advantage of routine fluctuations rather than simply doing business at the current market price. There are always routine fluctuations, but you cannot tell in advance when they may occur. Excess traders make their living by ironing out the aberrations by buying low and selling high within the underlying trend or when they think there may be a climax of buying or selling. Market-makers will buy or sell to all comers, like a dealer in any other commodity. They post a higher price where they are prepared to sell and a lower one where they are prepared to buy, making money on the spread the same way as any other retailer.)

Using the definition of an upward zigzag with acceptable retracements, General Electric was in a bull market from $12 in 1984 until the 1987 stock market crash. The bull market designation ended with its close at the end of October 1987 at $22.80. At that level its close was significantly more than 5 percent below the April 1987 low close of $25.63. (Other indicators, discussed later, signaled an earlier exit than waiting for the low monthly close after the 1987 stock market crash.)

The next bull market designation began with the monthly close at the end of August 1991 at $37.25. This designation failed, as occurs quite frequently, for all market signals are an exercise in probability

theory. The adverse market action causing the failure showed that
General Electric was not yet ready to move higher and might never be.
As it turned out, the stock continued moving sideways for a full year,
although with an upward bias, before resolving its ambiguous market
action. The upturn in November 1992 with the monthly close at $40
confirmed the new bull market designation. From there it was ever on
upward. Significantly, the low in mid-1994 did not violate the prior low
by more than 5 percent, although it came close to doing so.

The following is a summary of the profits and losses during the bull
phases in General Electric stock from 1984 to publication cutoff and
before adjustment for a stock split:

Starting Date	Price	Ending Date	Price	Profit/Loss
March 1984	$12.00	October 1987	$22.75	$10.75
April 1989	$24.50	August 1990	$31.75	$7.25
August 1991	$37.25	November 1991	$33.25	$(4.00)
November 1992	$40.00	November 1998	$180.75	$140.75
Total Net Profit				$154.75

The total profit per share over the period of the chart from a buy-
and-hold strategy was $168.75, based on a last price of $180.75 minus
the starting price of $12. This was $14 more than was available by holding General Electric only during designated bull markets and selling it
when market action negated a bullish phase. However, you would have
been out of the stock at the following times:

Time	Months
October 1987 to April 1989	17
August 1990 to August 1991	12
November 1991 to November 1992	12
Total	41

There was no bull market designation for 24 percent of this
fourteen-year period. At those times you could have parked your

money in Treasury bills or the money market, or you could have used it to buy stocks with stronger charts. Given the quality of General Electric and the wisdom of hindsight, you might have simply stayed in the stock. Nevertheless, you could not tell in advance that it would continue doing so well and that it would overcome adverse price action and weakening technical indicators.

If it turns out that you were right to tough out a rough patch in the market, you come out of it a hero, but if you were wrong to do so, you lose money, sometimes a lot. Once negative technical indicators become entrenched, it is psychologically difficult to take a large loss because you always expect that the decline has gone far enough. On the other hand, it is relatively easy to take a small loss and then to buy a stock back if the indicators again turn positive. You are not burdened with the memory of old and hurtful psychological and financial wounds.

Timing indicators to buy or sell a stock are not infallible; however, they are right often enough that probabilities do not favor overriding them.

Many stocks in companies as fundamentally attractive as General Electric failed to maintain upward momentum during some of the best years of the big bull market. The chart for Wal-Mart Stores shows a stock that required a long rest (Figure 8-4). Between 1991 and 1996 the company's sales doubled, and so did earnings per share. But what did the stock do? It went down! The price of the stock got too far ahead of market expectations.

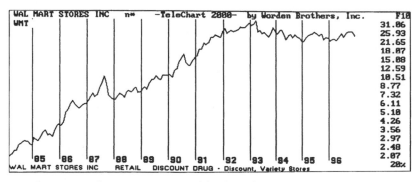

FIGURE 8-4. Wal-Mart Stores Monthly Line Chart.

W Formations: The Start of a Bull Market

A bull market starts with a zigzag in the form of a W on the monthly line chart. Of course, there are many more W formations than there are valid new bull markets. You have to consider these formations in conjunction with other technical indicators described in later chapters. Also, the reliability of an emerging bull market is often proportional to the length of time needed to develop it. The longer a stock prepares for an upward move, the greater the probability of a valid W formation and the farther the bull market is likely to go in due course. (Chapter 18 discusses breakouts after long periods of sideways price action.)

Everyone loves to buy at the lowest possible price and to sell as high as possible. But the reward is often greater and the risk is usually much lower when buying into a strong bull market, like General Electric. Trying to get in on the ground floor of a possibly emerging bull market can be exciting when you get it right, but the odds against success are considerable. For most products and services, it is generally preferable in the long run to buy quality. For investors, that means buying stocks with the highest quality charts. Remember the futures trader's adage: Buy the strongest market and sell the weakest!

The W formation that starts a bull market has two variants, depending on whether an initial higher high or higher low occurs first (Figures 8-5 and 8-6).

W Formation: Initial Higher High

To identify a W formation with an initial higher high on a line chart:

1. Assume that the low at (2) is the bottom of the market after the closing high (3) has exceeded the previous high (1).

2. After the higher high at (3) is in place, expect a retracement. Then look for a bottom and a new upturn to occur.

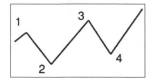

FIGURE 8-5.   W-Formation: Initial Higher High.

3. The retracement from (3) to (4) may take longer than you expect and may give up 50 to 100 percent of the gain between (2) and (3).

4. The closing price low at (4) should go no lower than the low at (2). However, it is remarkable how often lows occur at almost exactly the same level, forming what is called a *double bottom*.

A lower closing price at (4) invalidates the emerging W formation and also increases the probability that the stock will go lower. The safest buys generally occur when the low at (4) is significantly higher than the previous low. That shows that buyers are eager to buy rather than to wait patiently to buy at the previous low. It sometimes seems hard to buy something that looks expensive compared with an earlier lower price. Remember, though, that the probability of making money favors buying strength, not weakness or lackluster performance.

W Formation: Initial Higher Low

To identify a W formation with an initial higher low on a line chart:

1. Look for a low at (4) that goes no lower than (2) and which, ideally, is well above (2).

2. When there is a monthly close above the close at (3), a W is confirmed.

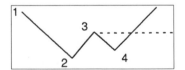

FIGURE 8-6.   W Formation: Initial Higher Low.

After a stock has broken above (3) in either variant of the W formation, it may retrace to the breakout level. This is normal price action. Some technicians suggest buying only on this expected retracement. However, the strongest stocks never retrace, and you can never tell in advance which these will be.

The monthly chart for Halliburton, the oil services company, shows both variations of W formation (Figure 8-7). In February 1992 the stock made a routine bounce in a designated bear market, with a closing monthly high at $27.62. In June the stock turned down from its May

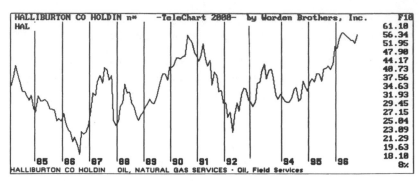

FIGURE 8-7. Halliburton Monthly Line Chart.

closing high at $29.88, after exceeding slightly the February high. There was a mere single month's retracement to a closing low at $26.88. The July monthly close at $30.37 completed a W and signaled the start of a new bull market designation.

The trend change after the October 1987 stock market crash was more dramatic. The stock went sideways for a year and a half between the 1987 high and the 1987 low. Finally, in February 1989 there was a higher low than the previous one, and it held on the next retracement. The March 1989 new high close completed a W formation and signaled Halliburton as a stock to buy at the March monthly closing price of $30.25.

Zigzags Apply to All Indicators

The counterpart of a W at the start of a bull market is an M at the start of a bear market, discussed in the next chapter. The general principle of directional zigzags and of W and M formations applies to charts of all durations: monthly, weekly, daily, and even intraday. There is a general principle that the reliability of Ms and Ws increases in proportion to the length of time they take to form. In practice, there are very big M and W formations within which there are little bumps that signify nothing. The difference between a significant wrinkle and one that is not can generally be quantified on the monthly price-line chart by the 5-percent rule.

In addition to using Ms and Ws with price charts, the concept of Ms and Ws and of directional zigzags applies to all indicators amenable to lineal plotting. These indicators include On Balance Volume, Moving Average Convergence/Divergence (MACD) and Stochastics, which are discussed in later chapters.

CHAPTER 9

Defining a Bear Market

Downward Zigzags

A bear market has the opposite characteristics of a bull market. The monthly price chart for a stock shows a succession of lower highs and lower lows in a downward zigzag (Figure 9-1).

The monthly chart for Digital Equipment shows a general uptrend from 1984 to 1987, roughly in line with the overall stock market (Figure 9-2). Digital sold off severely during the October 1987 market crash and rallied only very little when the general market stabilized. The downturn in January 1988 completed an M, in effect, an upside down W, that started the stock's relentless downward zigzag. The crest of the December 1987 rally in the stock, to $137.50, was far below the record monthly closing high at $189.75. Not only was this not a stock to buy at an apparently low price, but for a stock timer it turned out to be one that might have been sold short. Once Digital turned down in January 1988, the stock established a bear market designation that took the stock a long, long way down. The company

FIGURE 9-1. Bear Market Zigzag.

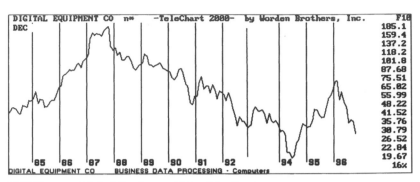

FIGURE 9-2. Digital Equipment Monthly Chart.

was having serious problems and its stock still had much farther to fall.

Digital's bear market designation was briefly negated in April 1993 when the monthly closing price was substantially higher than the preceding one. That did not, of course, mean that the stock was a buy in the absence of other confirming indicators. On the contrary, it turned out that when the rally crested, there was a great opportunity to sell, which was confirmed by other indicators. From that crest the stock was to fall by almost 60 percent before the final bottom. There was no new bull market designation until January 1995. Even then, Digital was still not an attractive stock to buy. The overall chart pattern was not encouraging. It suggested, at best, the prospect of an extended period of going sideways.

M Formations:
The Start of a Bear Market

Although you may not be interested in selling stocks short, you must know what a bear market looks like. Otherwise, you will not know when a stock that you own may be starting to go down the drain.

Stocks that have been rising strongly for a long time seldom turn down sharply unless they have been driven to absurd heights in a speculative frenzy or there is some unforeseen cataclysmic occurrence affecting the company or the economy. You can generally live by the futures trader's saying: A bull market dies hard!

Almost all bear markets start with a downward zigzag in the form of an M on the monthly line chart (Figures 9-3 and 9-4). There may be several successively lower highs and lower lows over time. The rallies are caused by the buy-the-dips crowd and short-sellers taking profits.

M Formation: Initial Lower Low

To identify an M formation with an initial lower low on the line chart:

1. Assume that the high at (2) may be the top of the market, after the low at (3) has exceeded the previous low at (1).

2. After the lower low at (3) is in place, expect a retracement. Then look for a top and a subsequent downturn at (4) that is below the one at (2).

3. When there is a close below the close at (3), an M formation is confirmed. When the amplitude of the swings forming the M is small, an initial M formation may not be meaningful. However, after completion of any M on the chart for a stock that you own, review the other technical indicators discussed in this book. If you do not have a cushion of profit, it generally pays to err on the side of selling rather than to take your chances on how future market action will unfold. The best stocks to own should not develop an outright bear market chart pattern.

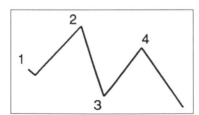

FIGURE 9-3.   M Formation: Initial Lower Low.

M Formation: Initial Lower High

When the lower high comes first, modify the approach as follows:

1. Look for a downturn at (4) that goes below the one at (2).

2. When there is a close below the one at (3), an M formation is confirmed.

As with an emerging bull market, there may be a retracement back to the breakdown level before a more sustained decline gets under way. Be careful not to be fooled into thinking that a retracement is putting the stock back on track for further gains.

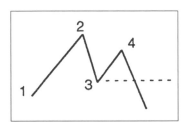

FIGURE 9–4.   M Formation: Initial Lower High.

The monthly chart for IBM shows both variations of an M formation in 1991–1992, when the stock was setting up for its big plunge (Figure 9-5). This chart had a clear downward bias. You could have sold the stock short at the end of August 1991 when there was a downturn after a lower low than the previous one. Then you would have had no difficulty accepting adverse fluctuations of 5 percent. Once the price broke down in September 1992 through the March low at $85, the stock was in free fall for a collapse of $40.

In 1991 the monthly chart for IBM formed a must-sell kind of pattern; you must sell any stock you own with such a pattern in case the ensuing decline becomes unmanageable. You do not need to sell short. Nevertheless, continuing to own the stock through IBM's debacle was clearly avoidable. Did you or your mutual fund own IBM during its decline?

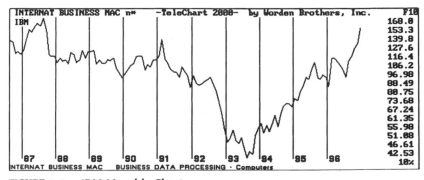

FIGURE 9–5.   IBM Monthly Chart.

It is worth mentioning that the extent of the washout in IBM was so climactic that you could have been looking for a place to buy the stock when the dust settled—but not before! When IBM turned, its price traced out a classic double bottom with a higher second low. So you might at last have bought a small position in stock. Although there was much risk of failure when buying after the first W at the bottom, because of a relative lack of other confirming indicators, here was a time when the disciplines of the technical analyst and of the bottom-fishing value analyst would have produced an excellent result. Then in March 1994 there was a second W formation—with a much higher high than the previous one—when the stock turned up at $58.25. At last, there was a technical case for assuming a recovery in IBM that could be powerful. You did not have to be the first early bird to do very well once the stock finally turned up again.

CHAPTER 10

Sideways Markets

Endless Chop

You are in the stock market for one reason: to make money. Therefore, it is as important to know about sideways, or trading-range, markets as about bull and bear markets. It is very hard to make money in a stock that is stuck in a trading range. Moreover, you are almost certainly tying up money that could otherwise be invested in real winners.

Figure 10-1 shows a sideways, or trading-range, pattern.

There are intermittent uptrends and downtrends, but they never seem to last. Often the stock stops going up somewhere around the level of the previous highs and stops going down somewhere around the level of a previous low. In other words, it seems to chop around endlessly without going anywhere.

You must understand and internalize the fact that most of the time, most stocks are not worth trading. Sideways action, ambiguity, and perversity represent normality in the stock market. Even in the strongest bull market, as few as 10 or 20 percent of all stocks show really good

FIGURE 10-1. A Sideways, or Trading Range, Pattern.

technical action. In a bear market, the percentage of stocks in a confirmed downtrend may be higher than 80 or 90 percent because a general decline is almost always more comprehensive than a general bull market.

A major problem for many investors is that a stock going sideways may appear to have substantial underlying value that the investor hopes the market will recognize eventually. However, a stock is almost certainly going sideways because of a lack of interest in either buying it or selling it, for whatever reason.

Trading-Range Examples

The monthly chart for General Motors shows how the stock provided short-lived opportunities to make money during 1988–1989 and 1993 (Figure 10-2). Overall, however, the stock was a dog. It would have been a demanding challenge to buy the stock and to sell it at a profit at any time during the twelve-year period shown. You should have been able to see at the time what this chart was saying: This is not a good place to invest your money.

One of the problems with owning a stock going sideways is that it can be very difficult to avoid banking a loss when you sell it. False rallies (bull traps) encourage you to hang on. False declines (bear traps) encourage you to sell in case the stock goes lower still. A sideways market is full of sucker traps and invitations to buy high and sell low, the exact opposite of what is required to make money.

The only justification for owning a stock like General Motors is if it

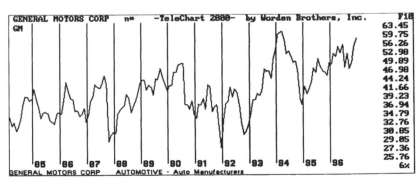

FIGURE 10–2. General Motors Monthly Line Chart.

pays a large dividend and, in addition, you need to invest for income. Even then, the financial statement should be sound, as far as you can tell, and the chart pattern not outright bearish. (Analysis of financial soundness is far more difficult than you might think. Corporate financial statements often do not show the true picture, let alone trends, and the information is always out-of-date.)

Figure 10-3 shows market action in Homestake, another big stock that was a total dog for many years. (It may seem as if the fluctuations in Homestake were big enough to make money, but this appearance is deceptive. It is partly a function of the way the amplitude of the price range fills the entire chart, regardless of whether the range is big or small.) Some people always want to own gold. However, in this stock shareholders received a mere 1 percent or so on their money in dividends. At least GM paid shareholders something most of the time and sometimes quite a lot.

Even if you need income, the chances are that you will make more in the long run—say, a span of ten years or so—by not buying stocks like General Motors. Put half your money into stocks like General Electric and half into bonds or term deposits of some kind—almost any kind. In the long term, if not initially, the dividends from a true bull market stock should outperform those of a GM. In addition, you will have the capital gain from owning stock in a better company.

Owning stocks like General Motors and Homestake generally involves, at best, an opportunity cost. At worst, you lose money, sometimes a big part of your investment. The potential reward seldom justifies the risk of holding stocks in a sideways pattern. From 1984 to 1996

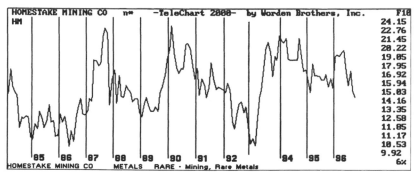

FIGURE 10–3. Homestake Monthly Line Chart.

and for many years before, General Motors stock never acted well because the company was floundering. Worse, it was not even a safe stock to own. Its technical market action confirmed its financial reports.

Stock market history has many examples of once-great companies that went out of business, leaving their shareholders with nothing. A stock going sideways can just as easily make an eventual downside break as an upside one, if it ever moves decisively at all. As a rule, strong companies have stocks that act strongly, at least compared with the overall market. Weak and ambiguously strong companies seldom have stocks that perform well.

Chapters 11 to 14 discuss specific technical indicators and other aspects of technical analysis that show whether to consider a stock and when to buy or sell it.

CHAPTER 11

On Balance Volume (OBV): Some Innovative Uses

Volume Can Forecast Price

All things being equal, increasing demand for any goods or services in short supply drives up the price. On the other hand, you sometimes hear of a product being dumped at amazingly low prices because it is in oversupply. This chapter harnesses together the quest for making money with the forces of supply and demand for stocks.

The next best thing to having tomorrow's newspaper with its stock quotations in your hands today is to look at buying and selling pressure. When there is a pattern of strong and increasing buying pressure, a stock is almost certain to continue going up. More people want to buy than sell the stock at current prices. Buyers are prepared to pay steadily higher prices, and sellers keep raising their asking price. When demand exceeds readily available supply, the same thing happens in stocks as happens with the price of other goods and services. When there is a correspondingly clear pattern of selling pressure in a stock, it is almost certain to go down.

Trading volume provides the raw data with which to analyze buying and selling pressure. The standard approach to interpreting trading volume is to assume that in bull markets, there should be higher volume on days when the market goes up and lower volume on days when it declines. A bear market should have the reverse, higher volume on down days and lower volume on up days.

To create the On Balance Volume indicator (OBV), each day's total trading volume is added to the cumulative sum when the closing price is higher than the close of the previous day. When the closing price is lower, the day's volume is subtracted. When the cumulative sum is plotted on a chart, it should normally rise steadily when price is rising and decline steadily when price is going down. In a rising market there are normally more days when the price goes up rather than down. Also, total volume tends to be higher on those days when the price goes up. On days when the price goes down in a rising market, buyers take a rest but sellers are not aggressive. In a declining market, selling pressure predominates and rallies are generally weak.

Joe Granville and Don Worden, working independently, noticed that when there is divergence between OBV and price, volume generally precedes price. This means that volume tends to give advance warning of the direction in which the price is likely to go eventually. Consequently, it may forecast a trend reversal, sometimes quite a long time before the reversal occurs. The idea is that smart money starts to build a position, or to liquidate one, before the price of the stock responds.

Early warnings from OBV are particularly useful when a stock has been going sideways for some time. Price action alone may not tell you anything about which way the stock is going to break out or when. But OBV may show that a move outside the range is shaping up, especially when there is a pronounced increase in overall volume.

New Applications for OBV

Granville originally used OBV on daily charts. But OBV is even more useful when used with monthly and weekly data. There is no more powerful indicator of the potential for a major long-term trend to continue. Since most fluctuations in price occur within a major trend (whether up, down, or sideways), it is invaluable to confirm the direction and soundness of that trend. As we saw in Chapter 8, the best stocks to own are ones in a long-term uptrend on the basis of zigzags on the monthly chart. OBV often confirms this price action for a very long time in a strongly trending market. When OBV remains positive during retracements, it can help you maintain the confidence required to stay with a stock.

We have also extended Granville's use of OBV in a second way, by plotting the OBV line (OBV 1) together with a ten-bar *moving average* of OBV (OBV 10). If possible, therefore, use software that can perform these functions. (With the *TC 2000* software, you must superimpose a ten-month moving average of OBV 1, using the moving average command.)

Let's proceed now to a list of the principles for using OBV that are applicable to charts of all durations: monthly, weekly, and daily.

Interpreting OBV

This section describes how to interpret and apply OBV. These points apply to monthly, weekly, and daily charts.

1. The most bullish pattern occurs when OBV 1 has established an upward zigzag above a steadily rising OBV 10 on the monthly chart.

   There can be minor aberrations, particularly when the two lines remain close together and the deviation from the trend is barely perceptible. As when using the monthly price line to interpret the major trend, it is important to try and see the big picture and avoid being distracted by little bumps on the chart.

2. The most bearish pattern occurs when OBV 1 has established a downward zigzag below a steadily declining OBV 10.

3. OBV gives a buy signal when OBV 1 crosses the rising OBV 10. A downside crossover constitutes a sell signal when OBV 10 is pointing down.

4. OBV also gives a buy signal when OBV 1 has been above a rising OBV 10 and it makes a new upturn. We assume that both OBV and price should be starting the next leg of an upward zigzag. A corresponding downturn below a declining OBV 10 constitutes a sell signal.

5. The strongest and most reliable bull moves generally begin after the two OBV lines have started rounding upward for many months on the monthly chart. Rounding on a chart of any duration shows gathering momentum.

6. A bulge in OBV 1 far beyond OBV 10 may indicate a buying climax when occurring to the upside, or it may indicate a selling

climax when occurring to the downside. A climax means that there has been a scramble to buy or sell. Such panic buying or selling often occurs prior to a significant retracement, which may turn into a trend reversal.

7. Many of the most extended market declines start with a pronounced weakening in the OBV line for many months. This pattern is a reflection of smart money liquidating stocks that have probably been bought at much lower prices a long time ago, and possibly also of smart money entering new short positions.

8. When a stock makes a higher high in price that is *not* accompanied by a higher high in OBV 1, it is likely that buying pressure is fading.

    The next move in the stock may be down, not up. Smart money may be selling or even going short. Similarly, when OBV 1 fails to accompany price to a new low, it is probable that knowledgeable investors are starting to accumulate the stock.

9. When buying a stock, the *weekly* and *daily* OBV charts should normally confirm an OBV buy signal on the monthly chart. When selling short, they should confirm the OBV monthly sell signal. Sometimes, however, only the monthly and the daily chart confirm, with confirmation from the weekly chart lagging after a major retracement in price.

OBV and General Electric

The monthly chart for General Electric shows OBV 1 trending above OBV 10 in 1986–1987 (Figure 11-1). Note the bulge in OBV 1 beyond OBV 10 before the 1987 market crash. After the crash OBV 1 established an M formation and the stock continued drifting lower. The intra-month low in price occurred in April 1988 and the closing price low in October. In December 1988 OBV 1 completed a small W. From that point, price and OBV both continued gathering strength until July 1990. After an initial surge from the October 1990 low, both OBV and the stock did little until the end of 1992. Once the consolidation lasting through 1994 had run its course, the OBV lines gave a buy signal with an upward crossover in January 1995 as the stock was starting its next big move up.

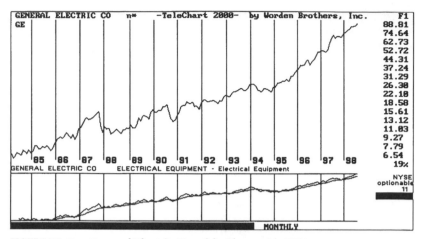

FIGURE 11-1. General Electric Monthly Chart with OBV.

The weekly chart for General Electric shows OBV basing in the second half of 1994, even as the price of the stock went to a new weekly closing low for the year (Figure 11-2). Price, however, did not go lower than the intraday low at $45, which occurred in June (not shown on the line chart). When OBV 1 crossed above OBV 10 and made a new six-month high, the stage was set for price to begin a major move up. Underlying strength in OBV preceded the move in price.

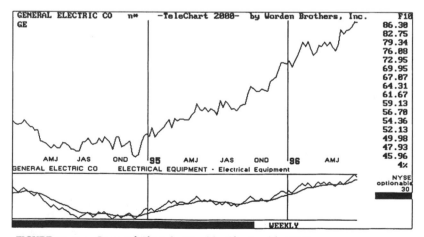

FIGURE 11-2. General Electric Weekly Chart with OBV.

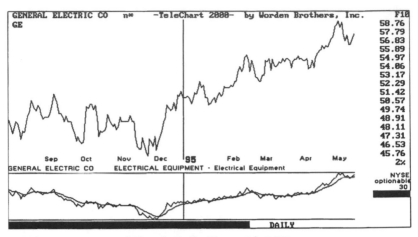

FIGURE 11-3. General Electric Daily Chart with OBV.

The daily chart for General Electric shows a downside bulge in OBV 1 and then a double bottom and an upside crossover in December 1994 (Figure 11-3). If you missed buying the stock near the late 1994 low, there were several more upturns in OBV 1 and upside crossovers in January and February 1995. The upward rounding during April provided a particularly strong indication that the stock might be setting up to accelerate higher, given the positive action on the monthly and weekly charts for price and OBV.

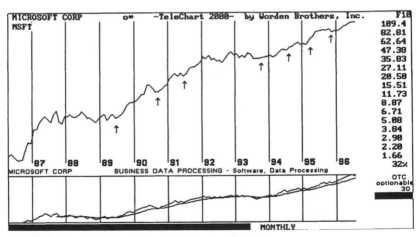

FIGURE 11-4. Microsoft Monthly Chart with OBV.

OBV and Microsoft

The monthly chart for Microsoft shows that even a stock that seems to go endlessly upward can be bought with a low risk at clearly defined points on the technical charts (Figure 11-4). Never mind that you failed even to hear about the stock when it was selling for pennies compared with its current price. What goes up in the stock market does not necessarily come back down. The table below shows when OBV and the monthly price line gave concurrent buy signals between 1989 and 1995.

Date	Price
August 1989	$ 6.60
October 1990	$14.40
July 1991	$23.70
December 1993	$41.25
August 1994	$54.65
March 1995	$71.00
December 1995	$91.00

Microsoft also provides a prime example of how to own such a stock by buying at specific times when the necessary technical buy signals occur. This stock and many others with similar technical characteristics show the importance of buying a stock that other people are also buying consistently, *on balance.* Microsoft is not such an unusual stock that you could never expect to find others like it. There have been many such stocks in the past, and it is certain that there will be many more in future. Nor do you have to go beyond the mainstream to find them.

The way to handle the risk when buying such an apparently expensive stock is to buy a little at a time and to diversify among several potential Microsofts. Don't think you are playing it safe by buying a cheaper stock but one which has a chart pattern like the one for General Motors shown in Chapter 1.

OBV and Cognos

The chart for Cognos shows that you can be early without having to be up at the crack of dawn (Figure 11-5). You might have been a very early bird in 1990 at around $2.20. The outcome should have been an exit by stop at $4.70 after the stock topped out in 1991. (Stops are discussed in Chapters 21 and 22.) The stock then took the better part of three years building a rounding base before it moved from a low of $1.90 to a high of $34.75 in five years.

You did not have to buy the stock at the low. Price and OBV action started confirming that this stock was in motion only in December 1993. By that time the stock had almost doubled from its low (when, no doubt, many value investors would want to take their profits). By doubling, Cognos was starting to show what it could do. Thereafter, it was enough to let price action and OBV speak for themselves.

OBV and IBM

IBM's monthly chart provides an excellent example of how to use OBV to identify a stock going up, down, or sideways (Figure 11-6). Although OBV gave a false buy signal in January 1991, OBV 1 quickly reversed and plunged below OBV 10. Note that the February 1991 high in OBV 1 barely exceeded the high of the previous May, although the price of the stock surged to a higher high. Once OBV 1 fell below its previous lows

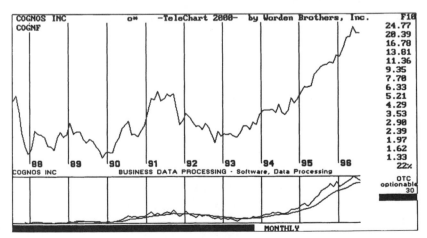

FIGURE 11-5. Cognos Monthly Chart with OBV.

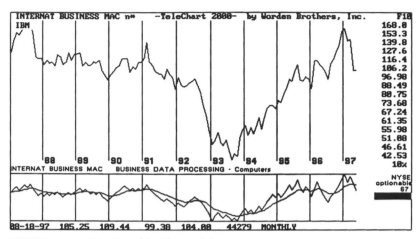

FIGURE 11–6.   IBM Monthly Chart with OBV.

and started trending down below the declining OBV 10, it was clear that this was no stock to own. This action, together with powerful signals from other indicators, called for an exit that preserved capital from the ensuing devastation.

In March 1994 a strong correlation between price action and OBV finally suggested that IBM was a stock to buy. The monthly price line completed a W after OBV 1 had been basing for almost a year and had started its own upward zigzag.

On Balance Volume is not an infallible indicator. There is no such thing. Nevertheless, OBV comes as close to a magic bullet as you are likely to get when it is used in conjunction with our other indicators on the monthly, weekly, and daily charts.

CHAPTER 12

Moving Average Convergence/ Divergence (MACD)

Direction and Momentum

Moving Average Convergence/Divergence (MACD) is an important technical indicator for showing shifts in momentum and confirming the likelihood of a trend remaining in force. A shift in momentum often provides an early warning of a trend change.

Although it is not necessary to know how MACD functions in order to use it, it may be helpful to have a general idea. It is a combination of three exponentially smoothed moving averages that are expressed as two lines. The MACD fast line (fast MACD) is an oscillator constructed by subtracting a shorter moving average from a longer one. The shorter moving average is constantly converging toward and diverging away from the longer one. Hence its name. The slow line (slow MACD) is generated from an exponential moving average of the oscillator.

As with OBV, turns in fast MACD are a signal for action, while slow MACD indicates the probable major price trend.

MACD is a standard indicator available on all good charting software packages. The recommended setting (often the default setting) is: 12, 26, 9. A decimal setting of 0.15, 0.075, 0.20, used on some software, produces an almost identical result.

Using MACD

The MACD fast and slow lines, as well as crossovers and zigzags, act much the same way as OBV 1 and OBV 10. MACD and OBV often produce remarkably similar results, despite the fact that their data sources are totally different. That difference means that these two indicators are particularly powerful when in clear agreement. Conversely, they deliver a valuable warning when they diverge.

MACD is a broad-brush indicator and may therefore be a lagging indicator at market turns, particularly when they occur quickly. So it is essential to use MACD in conjunction with other indicators, especially with price action. When other indicators are leading, you can often tell whether MACD's lagging performance is likely to lead to its confirmation coming through in the next bar or two.

MACD has the following uses, which are applicable to the monthly, weekly, and daily charts.

1. MACD delivers a buy signal when fast MACD crosses slow MACD and both lines are rising. Generally, the signal occurs with the crossover. When there is a fast turn in a stock, it may take a little longer for the direction of fast MACD to bring all three components of the signal together. The most reliable signals occur after fast MACD has had time to form its own W. The reverse applies for a sell signal.

   MACD is our slowest indicator to turn, making it the last to respond to changing circumstances, particularly on the monthly chart. Other indicators are therefore likely to confirm a new trend on the monthly and weekly charts before MACD confirms the change in direction.

2. MACD also gives a buy signal when fast MACD has been above a rising slow MACD and it makes a new upturn after turning down. You can assume that both MACD and price are starting the next leg of an upward zigzag. A corresponding downturn below a declining slow MACD constitutes a sell signal.

3. MACD can serve as a leading indicator for price by showing a shift in momentum that is not evident on the price chart. However, MACD suggests far more trend changes than actually

occur. The loss of momentum reflected by MACD may just mean that the stock needs time to consolidate its gains or losses.

When price makes a higher high but MACD makes a lower high, the stock is losing upward momentum, and vice versa when there is divergence in a declining market. Sometimes there can be a very big difference between price action and MACD that continues for a long time. The greater and longer-lasting the divergence, the greater is the likelihood of an eventual trend change in price.

4. An established uptrend is likely to remain in force when fast MACD is above slow MACD and both lines are rising. Similarly, MACD confirms an established downtrend when fast MACD is below slow MACD and both lines are falling.

   When MACD is strongly rising on the monthly and weekly charts, it is highly likely that the trend will continue. You can buy into corresponding long-term uptrends, or sell short into corresponding long-term downtrends, with relatively low risk by using signals generated by MACD and other indicators.

5. The zero baseline provides for a distinction between confirmed bull and confirmed bear markets. However, crossing over the zero baseline seldom provides a useful trading signal because it generally occurs too late. Sometimes the zero baseline helps to interpret the momentum of MACD. A steep MACD suggests a powerful move, while a shallow one indicates a lack of power.

6. Fast MACD normally draws away from slow MACD when price momentum in the stock is accelerating. The most reliable price trends generally occur when the two lines establish and maintain a constant distance between each other. When there is an upward bulge in fast MACD after a stock has made an extended move up, this bulge may show completion of a buying climax. Although there may not be an impending trend change, it is likely that the stock will at least have to go sideways or down slightly for a while. The reverse occurs in a stock that has been going down for some time, but with a higher probability that the decline may have ended. Relatively few stocks go down to zero, although many stocks maintain a very long-term uptrend.

7. In a strongly trending stock, MACD can go flat or change direction without necessarily signaling a trend reversal. It may simply be showing that the momentum has gone out of the stock for the time being. The stock may just need to consolidate its previous gains in a bull market or its losses in a bear market. After a period of consolidation, the trend may resume.

   Much more than OBV, MACD often seems to deliver a false signal by turning in the opposite direction after a stock has been trending strongly. The stock is doing no more than losing speed in its rate of climb or descent. Since MACD shows changes in momentum, not necessarily in price, it must be used in conjunction with other indicators, especially with price action. Ignoring other indicators in conflict with MACD can easily lead to selling a good stock too soon.

8. The likelihood of an impending change in direction for a stock increases when MACD makes a double top or a double bottom or multiple declining tops or rising bottoms. It often traces out its own M or W zigzags a considerable time before price changes direction.

9. It seldom pays to stay in a stock, let alone to buy it, when MACD is clearly trending down on the monthly and weekly charts and, in addition, when price on the monthly chart has violated its 5-percent allowance.

MACD and General Electric

The monthly chart for General Electric shows the MACD fast line rounding out in the second half of 1988, as price and OBV were also doing, as we saw in the previous chapter (Figure 12-1). A buy-signal crossover occurred in April 1989, one month after the monthly price line, as well as OBV, confirmed this as a stock to buy.

Note the negative divergence in MACD at the July 1991 high compared with its high in July of the previous year, when price was at approximately the same level. Rounding was feeble compared with what it did in 1988 and 1989. MACD was delivering a clear and correct message. The probabilities, on the basis of momentum, were not particularly favorable for buying. The stock might go up, but it was un-

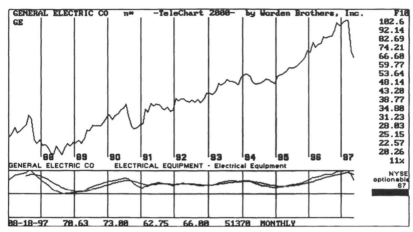

FIGURE 12-1. General Electric Monthly Chart with MACD.

likely to make a strong move until there was more strength in both price and MACD.

There was something of a false start in February 1993. However, there was a valuable reward for buying GE during the latter stages of the upward rounding, and when there was an MACD crossover in the first half of 1995.

The chart for General Electric shows why MACD should not be used on its own. When momentum goes relatively flat after a very strong move in price, the MACD lines lose their sense of direction. During 1991 and 1992 MACD for General Electric was flat to down, even as price was working erratically higher. It also turned hard down in 1994, when momentum relative to recent price action turned sharply negative.

A long-term investor should not have been perturbed by the downturn and crossover in April 1994 as long as the stock did not violate the uptrend in the monthly single-price line. An investor taking a shorter view might have used weakness in MACD as justification to sell. Although indicators for the stock had not turned outright negative, the underlying positive strength had gone out of it for the time being. MACD's action in 1994 indicated that GE was not a stock to buy at that time. In April 1995 MACD gave a new buy signal. Note how the two MACD lines subsequently maintained a strong upward and evenly spaced trend while price moved strongly upward.

On its own MACD is generally a better indicator to use when buying stocks than it is for selling one that has previously been acting well. It seldom pays to put new money into a stock until MACD turns positive or is showing signs that it may do so.

MACD and Coca-Cola

The monthly chart for Coca-Cola shows even more clearly than the one for GE how MACD confirms strength but does not necessarily forecast a substantial decline when it turns in the opposite direction (Figure 12-2).

From 1989 to 1992 MACD trended higher in conjunction with an immensely strong move up in the price of the stock. In August 1992 MACD crossed and trended down until mid-1994, while the price of the stock merely went sideways. MACD turned down so strongly because the previous upward momentum had been so strong. It did not mean that Coca-Cola was necessarily going to start trending down. A long-term investor would not likely want to sell stock, but it would have been a waste of time to buy more until the new upturn in MACD in October 1994. Then the combination of a buy signal in MACD and price action following an extended period of consolidation showed that the stock was preparing for a new leg up.

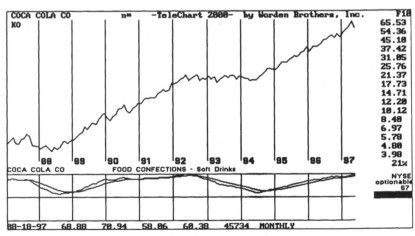

FIGURE 12-2. Coca-Cola Monthly Chart with MACD.

MACD and Cognos

The monthly chart for Cognos shows how MACD can steer you toward a junior stock as it is starting a big move (Figure 12-3). It also shows how MACD can keep you in a stock during fluctuations on its way to a much higher price. In a strongly advancing stock like Cognos, there may be price fluctuations that seem big at the time, but which do not damage the major uptrend.

During 1992–1993 the fast MACD was beginning to round out, and the stock price made a significantly higher high in June 1993. When fast MACD crossed its slow line in August 1993, you could be reasonably confident that the stock should at least be on its way toward the 1991 high. Although price action in the first half of 1994 might have seemed worrisome at the time, MACD barely faltered. There was a prime buying opportunity when the monthly price line turned up at $5 in December 1994 and soon broke out to a new high. Then all you had to do was to let your profit run while MACD showed the same even and strongly trending pattern as in Coke.

Figure 12-4 shows the weekly action in Cognos during its basing period in 1992–1993. MACD shows a good example of divergence. Although price went lower in the fall of 1992 than in late 1991, MACD was higher. MACD on the weekly chart gave a buy signal in May 1992 and a new buy signal in June 1993, well before the monthly buy signal

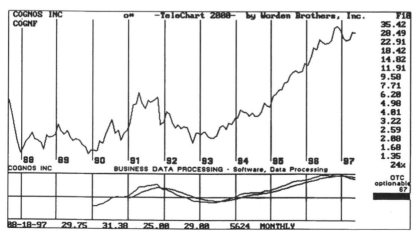

FIGURE 12-3. Cognos Monthly Chart with MACD.

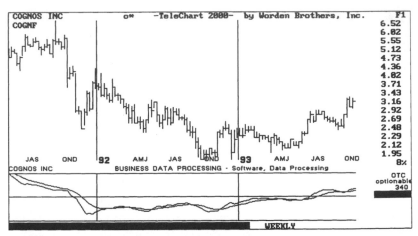

FIGURE 12–4.   Cognos Weekly Chart with MACD.

in August. The pieces fell into place to qualify Cognos as a stock to buy on the basis of the monthly chart when the monthly price line started turning up in October, putting in place a new upward zigzag on the monthly chart.

The daily chart showed fast MACD crossing over the slow on October 7, also in conjunction with powerful price action (Figure 12-5). Given the strong confirming action on the monthly chart, the key one for finding stocks with major long-term potential, it was opportune to buy Cognos on October 7 at a price of $2.79 or the next day at $2.83. It made little difference exactly which day you bought. The daily MACD crossover coincided with a 10 percent surge that showed that the stock might be on its way, which, indeed, it was. The eventual high for the major bull market in the stock was $39.50.

Many advisors and money managers recommend selling a stock when it doubles in price or at least selling half your holding. This is one of the prime reasons why so many stock traders fail to make the money they should. It cannot be said too forcefully: *Let your profits run—as long as price action and the technical indicators confirm the bull market!* When a stock is acting as well as Cognos, there is a strong case to buy more when there are new buy signals. Although it is true that some stocks fail after doubling, on balance you do far better to stay with winners. The stock that doubles can double again. If you sell it arbitrarily and prematurely, you never stay with a Microsoft, and you are unlikely

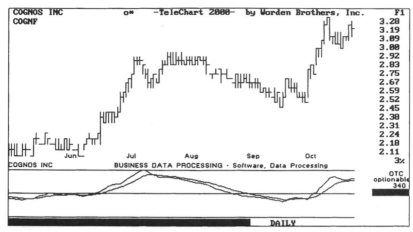

COGNOS INC   o*   —TeleChart 2000— by Worden Brothers, Inc.

FIGURE 12-5.   Cognos Daily Chart with MACD.

to make any really big money. Cognos was a timely buy in December 1993 and in December 1994. There was another buy signal on the monthly price line in May 1995 at $8.65. From there, the bull move traveled almost trouble-free to $34.75.

MACD and IBM

MACD on the monthly chart for IBM confirmed what OBV was saying (discussed in the previous chapter) and showed that this was no stock to own from 1987 to 1990 (Figure 12-6). The W and upward zigzag in price in late 1990, occurring in conjunction with the upward MACD crossover, might have suggested that this was a stock to buy. However, the feeble rise in MACD, followed by the savage monthly downside price reversal, should have indicated a quick exit from a bull trap (an apparently bullish breakout that fails). When MACD confirmed bearish action in price, the moving averages, and other indicators, there was no justification for continuing to own IBM. In the event, there was plenty of time for an orderly exit before the stock went into a further severe decline.

As we saw in the last chapter with OBV, there were signs that the plunge in IBM might have ended in a selling climax in mid-1993. In January 1994 fast MACD crossed above the slow. When the monthly price line made its next upturn in April, there was a prime opportunity to buy the stock at $26.50.

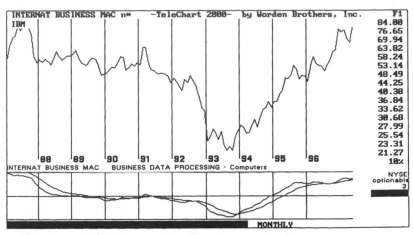

FIGURE 12-6.   IBM Monthly Chart with MACD.

Learn to Believe in MACD

Note that Cognos was an incomparably better and safer buy when it was going up than was IBM when it was going down. Never mind that Cognos was a relative junior and IBM the big blue chip.

When MACD is acting well and a stock is moving higher, believe in this indicator. The probabilities strongly favor a continuation of the trend until MACD and price action show real fatigue. Think in terms of having the kind of confidence an airline pilot has in the instrument panel when flying through the night. There can be many severe bumps on the way that do nothing to disturb the overall direction.

CHAPTER 13

The Building Blocks for Charts

Price Bar Action

This chapter takes a break from discussing technically generated indicators in order to look at individual price bar action. Even a single bar may show whether there is greater buying or selling pressure for that particular time period. Several bars taken together and put in the context of the larger picture may indicate the kind of momentum that leads to a more significant move in price.

For readers unfamiliar with the terminology of bar charts, this is the most basic evidence that technical analysts look at. (Some readers may already be familiar with the concepts in this chapter and the next one. Others may want to pass lightly over these important concepts and come back to them later, after reading more about the big picture to which they relate.)

The **basic bar** is the building block for all bar charts. It represents the range of trading for a certain period—a day, a week, or a month on its respective bar chart (Figure 13-1).

FIGURE 13-1. The Basic Bar.

The bar is set against a scale for calibration and has a notch on the right-hand side to indicate the final price at the end of the period. When there is a notch on the left side of the bar, it denotes the opening price for the bar.

The **closing price** is particularly significant, depending on whether it occurs at the top, bottom, or middle of the bar (Figure 13-2).

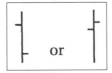

FIGURE 13–2. The Closing Price.

If the close is at the top, it suggests greater buying pressure. If the close is at the bottom, it suggests greater selling pressure. A close in the middle is neutral, but we assume that it has the same message as the previous bar's close.

An **inside bar** is one where trading is confined within the high and low prices of the previous bar (Figure 13-3).

FIGURE 13–3. An Inside Bar.

If traders cannot push out either the high or the low of the previous bar, assume that the heavy money is taking a rest.

An **outside bar** is one where price exceeds both the high and the low of the preceding bar (Figure 13-4).

FIGURE 13–4. An Outside Bar.

An outside bar is particularly significant if the close is at the extremity of its range or if it occurs on monthly or weekly charts. It suggests that weak short-term traders, those having a perspective no longer than the duration represented by a few bars, have been forced out of the market. Now the stock may continue in the direction of the strong close. If the range has been unusually great compared with the range of recent bars, the indication of direction from a strong close is additionally significant.

A **closing price reversal** occurs when price exceeds the previous bar's high and closes below the close of the previous bar. It also occurs when price exceeds the low of the previous bar and closes above the close of the previous bar.

A *downside reversal* (Figure 13-5) is the term for this reversal when it moves from a high toward the downside (the new indicated direction).

FIGURE 13–5.   A Downside Closing Price Reversal.

An *upside reversal* (Figure 13-6) occurs when price moves from a low toward the upside (the new indicated direction).

FIGURE 13–6.   An Upside Closing Price Reversal.

The closing price reversal is important. It suggests the possibility that the stock may be setting up for a worthwhile move. But there are many more reversals than important changes in direction, so you must consider one in conjunction with other indicators. It should not be used indiscriminately.

A **key reversal** is a combination of a closing price reversal and an outside bar. Price exceeds both the high and the low of the preceding bar, and the close is beyond the preceding high or low (Figure 13-7).

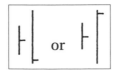

FIGURE 13-7.   A Key Reversal.

A **high/low reversal** occurs when price closes at one extremity of the trading range on one bar and at the opposite extremity on the next bar (Figure 13-8).

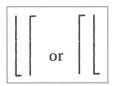

FIGURE 13–8.   A High/Low Reversal.

Although sometimes omitted from textbooks, the high/low reversal is particularly significant when followed by another high/low reversal or when one occurs shortly before or after a closing price reversal.

An **accumulation pattern** comprises a pattern of bars, each having successively higher lows and, ideally, also higher highs (Figure 13-9).

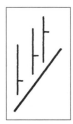

FIGURE 13–9.   An Accumulation Pattern.

During accumulation, persistent buying pressure finds buyers unable to buy as low as they could before, resulting in successively higher lows. It is likely that price can continue to move higher.

An accumulation pattern can be significant regardless of the closing price for the bar. It is valid on all charts.

A **distribution pattern** is the reverse of an accumulation pattern (Figure 13-10).

FIGURE 13–10.   A Distribution Pattern.

Sellers are able to sell only at successively lower prices as buyers become steadily less aggressive about how much they are prepared to pay, or as buying dries up.

A **consolidation** or **congestion area** occurs when price moves sideways. A wider band of equilibrium is often called a *trading range*.

A **gap** often occurs on daily charts. It is a blank space on a chart with no direct connection to the preceding bar or group of bars because no trading has occurred at the intervening prices.

As a rule, the bigger the gap, the more significant it is likely to be. All gaps show a surge in buying pressure when the gap is upward or in selling pressure when it is downward. Gaps often occur after news announcements that significantly change investors' views of a stock and set its price on a new course. They are particularly significant on the weekly chart when there is a change of perception between the close on Friday and the opening of the market on Monday morning.

We also consider that a gap occurs when the opening price gaps away from the previous close and never comes back to the previous close, even if there is not a complete separation between the bars. This is not a standard technical interpretation of a gap, but it is very useful.

When a stock has gapped up from a previous close, the gap is filled when there is a close at or below the price from which it gapped. A gap is tested when a stock returns into the gap, and even beyond the close from which the stock gapped, but does not fill it on a closing basis. The same applies in reverse when there has been a gap down.

Gaps represent levels of support or resistance. A stock often retraces and tests into a gap after the initial surge of buying or selling pressure abates. If the surge leading to opening of the gap is well-founded, the gap should remain open. After a stock has gapped up, new buying should come back for a stock as it settles back.

The daily bar chart for Eastman Kodak from December 1992 to August 1993 shows four different kinds of gaps, described below, although you may not necessarily know which is which until later (Figure 13-11).

A **common gap** can occur at any time. It has little significance by itself, but it is used in our Price Rules, described in the next chapter.

Often occurring within a congestion area, a common gap is generally filled within a few days by price moving back to establish a connection with the other bars on the chart. Of course, you never know

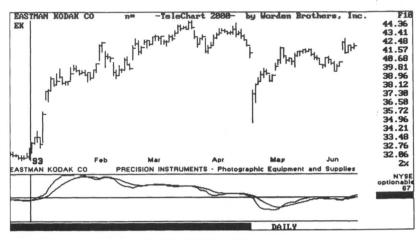

FIGURE 13-11. Eastman Kodak Daily Bar Chart.

until after the event whether this will happen or whether you are look-ing at the start of a breakout to a new price level.

A **breakaway gap** occurs when price breaks away from a congestion area and never looks back.

A breakaway gap is a reliable indicator of important buying or selling power. It suggests that a major move may be just starting. Although it can be alarming to see how far price has moved on the first day of a breakout, the rule of thumb is that the more powerful the breakout, the further price is likely to go and the more reliable the breakout is likely to be. Conse-quently, there is unlikely to be another chance to trade at a more favorable price and with a more manageable risk than there is by trading right away.

A **runaway gap** occurs in a stock that is continuing to tear away in a major run.

These gaps occur when a stock starts to go straight up or collapses downward. They are sometimes called *midpoint gaps* or *measuring gaps*. The idea is that they tend to show up around the midpoint of an appar-ently nonstop move. Nevertheless, this is only a rough rule of thumb for estimating how far a runaway move might go before it stops for breath.

An **exhaustion gap** occurs at the end of a substantial move.

You can never be certain until after the event whether a runaway gap is actually an exhaustion gap. An exhaustion gap occurs either when price gaps back the other way, leaving an island (the next defini-tion), or when the gap is filled by price closing below the bottom of the gap when the market is going up, or above the top of a gap when the market is going down. The expression *exhaustion gap* comes from the concept that the immediate buying or selling pressure is exhausted. These gaps often occur as a result of panic buying or selling. When the panic ends, the price can go the other way very fast.

Sometimes you may be able to make an intelligent guess to identify an exhaustion gap, when it occurs under circumstances where other indicators suggest the possibility that a top or bottom is being formed.

An **island** consists of one or more days of trading where there is a gap on the chart in both directions. It is often the ultimate manifestation of exhaustion at the end of a major move. It assumes greater significance when it comprises several bars. Then it signifies that the greedy or the desperate have truly finished doing the wrong thing.

Five consecutive closes in the same direction constitute a pattern of unusually persistent buying or selling and suggest that it is likely to continue. When this bar formation is wrong, it may be because it signifies exhaustion at the end of a major move or a major correction.

Always Follow the Footprints

It is always useful to look closely at a market's strength or weakness by examining its price action. Close inspection of individual bars and groups of bars often gives vital clues that confirm a direction or that warn of a possible change in direction.

A strongly rising market tends to have the majority of closes at the upper end of the range. It also tends to have a higher number of closes up than down. When the direction is up, individual advances are generally larger than individual declines.

A rising market that is tiring may show aberrational behavior, despite its ability to make gains in closing prices. For example, one downside reversal bar is likely to be a random aberration, especially if it has a small range. Several downside reversals suggest that sellers are asserting themselves. Gains early in the period are being consistently knocked down by sellers later on. Consequently, there is a high probability of at least a short-term correction, if not necessarily a change in the major trend. This interpretation is reversed when a declining market starts to show signs of buying pressure.

Gaps constitute one of the most obvious indicators of pent-up buying or selling pressure. One small gap within a consolidation area may mean nothing. They occur frequently and are usually filled soon; hence their designation as common gaps. The incidence of several gaps up indicates the release of pent-up buying power, suggesting a stock to own.

When there are several daily gaps down in a stock, it is highly likely that the stock will soon take a more substantial tumble. Downward gapping that leaves behind an island above the market is highly likely to signify exhaustion of the uptrend, at least for the intermediate term.

The next chapter looks at how groups of bullish bars develop a buy signal and how groups of bearish bars develop a sell signal.

CHAPTER 14

Price Rules

When to Pull the Trigger

The essence of timing is knowing when to buy or sell a stock or when to sell one short. This chapter describes price patterns or rules that call for action when other indicators confirm their buy or sell signal.

It is easy to look at a chart and get a general idea that you might like to own it. But should you buy it now or wait? Or should you have done it last week? All too often you can be overtaken by emotions. You want to see whether anything is going to happen before you make a move. But once the stock does move, is it then too late to buy? If you do buy, what is the risk of doing so just as a significant retracement begins? In the worst case, you may buy into a buying climax just as a major bull move comes to an end. Alternatively, you may buy a stock, expecting it to go up, but it never moves. On the other hand, you may own a stock that appears to be falling out of bed. Should you sell it today, or should you have sold it last week? Or should you hold it? It is all too easy to be driven by fear of losing a profit or of taking a bad loss and to sell out at the worst possible time.

Perfection in timing is unachievable. Nonetheless, the eight price rules described in this chapter come as close as possible to achieving timely entries and exits. They apply to charts for all time periods—monthly, weekly, daily, and for the very short-term trader, intraday. Although developed independently, they follow the same general principles as the ancient Japanese "candlestick" price bar patterns. Neither price rules nor candlesticks should be used as stand-alone indicators, although some people try to use candlesticks on their own. Both these approaches help in deciding when to buy or sell, provided they are related to the bigger picture.

Before presenting the price rules, the principles and conditions that govern them are described. Both buy and sell signals are illustrated, since it is just as important to know when to sell a stock, or when to sell short, as when to buy. The rules themselves are not cast in bronze, and they occasionally can be stretched if other indicators suggest that would be a reasonable course of action. (Occasionally, when the major trend is very strong, you might intentionally buy low or sell high before a price rule develops.) The most important thing is to understand what they are about.

Price Rule Principles

1. When random buying or selling occurs in the ordinary course of business, price charts show random patterns. When there is a persistent weighting of pressure toward either buying or selling, price charts also reflect this fact. One footprint in the sand says nothing. When a pattern of footprints starts to point the way, start looking for evidence that the trail may continue. Put another way, you want to buy strength and to sell weakness, but only when the probabilities favor continuation of either the strength or the weakness.

2. A close at the extremity of a bar's range suggests that the stock is likely to continue in the direction of the strong close. This is particularly so when there are several consecutive strong closes in the same direction.

3. Ideally, a price rule signal should be in force on the monthly and the weekly chart before buying or selling a stock.

4. A price rule signal must occur on the *daily chart* to buy or sell a stock.

   Completion of a price rule on the monthly or weekly chart delivers a signal in its own right, but this signal must be confirmed by a price rule signal on the daily chart.

5. It is important to act on a price rule signal as soon as it occurs. The best signals lead to price immediately following through. If you wait for more confirmation, it is almost certain that you will end up trading at a worse price. The risk of a retracement usually increases as the stock moves away from a price rule signal. Confirmations can sometimes be too much of a good thing once a stock starts moving.

   After completion of a buy signal, you can often buy at a lower price. However, the signals that let you do so are often the ones that fail. The best signals often lead to a profit right away. In the long run, it pays to act as soon as a strong price rule occurs.

6. This chapter primarily discusses price rules in terms of buying. However, they are also used to sell a stock that has run its course and for entering short sales.

Conditions for All Price Rules

1. To complete a price rule, the final bar has a close in the *top 25 percent* of the bar's range for a buy signal or in the *bottom 25 percent* for a sell signal.

2. A price rule may take longer to complete than the minimum specified time. Thus it could take four or five bars, rather than three, to complete a three-bar close rule (Rule 1). It could also take until the fourth or fifth bar to obtain a close in the top or bottom 25 percent of the bar's range, thereby completing the signal.

3. When price closes in the middle of the range, the result is neutral. Assume the same closing designation as for the previous bar.

4. When an emerging pattern is violated, start counting again at the beginning of the formation with a new bar 1.

5. When a price signal is completed (and other indicators confirm taking action), buy or sell right away. Do not chase entries unless there is a new signal.

Price Rules

1. The Three-Bar Closes Rule
A buy signal occurs on completion of two consecutive bars in which

FIGURE 14–1.   The Three-Bar Closes Rule.

price closes in the upper half of the range and the next bar closes in the top 25 percent of its range. A sell signal is the reverse.

2. The Reversal Rule

Shorten the proving time from three bars to two when either of the two bars is a reversal—closing price, key, or high/low reversal.

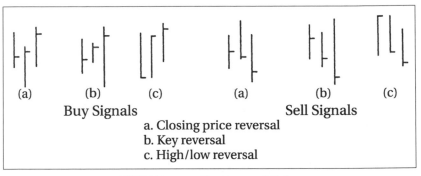

FIGURE 14–2.   The Reversal Rule.

3. The Gap Rule

Shorten the proving time from three bars to two when a gap occurs.

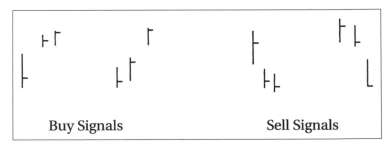

FIGURE 14–3.   The Gap Rule.

4. The Island Rule

Shorten the proving time to one bar when an island occurs.

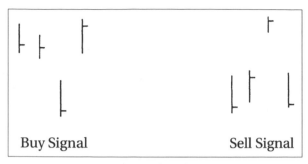

FIGURE 14–4. The Island Rule.

It is not necessary for closing price(s) within an island to be in the top or bottom of the range. An island may consist of one bar or many. However, the more time taken to form an island and the more symmetrical the gapping, the more likely it is that price has reached an important turning point and will continue in the direction of the new gapping. Islands often indicate absolute exhaustion of the previous trend.

5a. The Lindahl Buy Rule

Within *nine* bars from the bar of the *low* for the formation:

FIGURE 14–5a. The Lindahl Buy Rule.

1. Price must exceed the high of the bottom bar for the formation: (b) must take out the high of (a).

2. Price must then take out the low of the preceding bar: (d) must take out the low of (c).

3. To buy, price must take out the high of the preceding bar and close above the preceding bar's close and the current bar's opening price (e).

This formation may be completed in as few as three bars or as many as nine, depending on the number of intervening bars that do not contribute to development of the formation. Put another way, it is not significant when price exceeds previous highs and lows. There may be several neutral bars in between.

5b. The Lindahl Sell Rule

Within *eight* bars from the bar of the *high* for the formation:

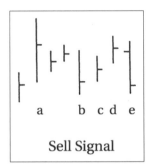

Sell Signal

FIGURE 14–5b.   The Lindahl Sell Rule.

1. Price must exceed the low of the top bar for the formation: (b) must take out the low of (a).

2. Price must then take out the high of the preceding bar: (d) must take out the high of (c).

3. To sell, price must take out the low of the preceding bar and close below the preceding bar's close and the current bar's opening price (e).

This formation may be completed in as few as three bars or as many as eight, depending on the number of intervening bars that do not contribute to development of the formation.

The commodity futures researcher Walter Bressert, our source for Lindahl signals, found that valid buy signals may require one more bar than is required to complete a valid sell signal. Some people find it difficult to grasp the detail of Lindahl signals. It may take time, but it is worth the effort. Lindahl signals are very reliable when other indicators indicate a turn in price. They also occur very frequently on stock charts of all durations. If you have difficulty learning to recognize Lindahl signals, think of them as looking like a miniature M or W formed by just a few bars.

6. *The Trend Continuation Rule*

Shorten the proving time to one bar when there is a single reversal bar in the direction of an established and unmistakable trend. A clear and unmistakable trend requires the 25- and 40-bar moving averages to confirm the direction on the monthly, weekly, and daily charts.

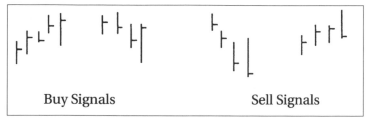

Buy Signals   Sell Signals

FIGURE 14–6. The Trend Continuation Rule.

It is psychologically difficult to chase a rapidly moving stock. This price rule provides the mechanism for buying with both a manageable stop loss and a high probability of making a profit right away. (The stop is just beyond the extremity of the price range of the entry bar, as discussed in Chapters 21 and 22.)

This price rule may also be used when other indicators suggest that a consolidation within a clearly established trend is ending.

7. *The Trend Reversal Rule*

Trade with the direction of a single, very big reversal bar, even though the trend appears to be in the opposite direction. Hence the name, *trend reversal.*

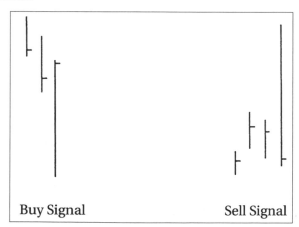

Buy Signal   Sell Signal

FIGURE 14–7. The Trend Reversal Rule.

This rule is useful for selling an existing position after a buying climax. The probabilities seldom favor using it to buy against the direction of an established trend.

8. *The Double Reversal Rule*

Trade on completion of a second reversal bar in the same direction within a period of six bars or fewer, whether closing price reversals, high/low reversals, or a combination. Both reversal bars should close in the top or bottom 25 percent, as appropriate, of the bars' ranges.

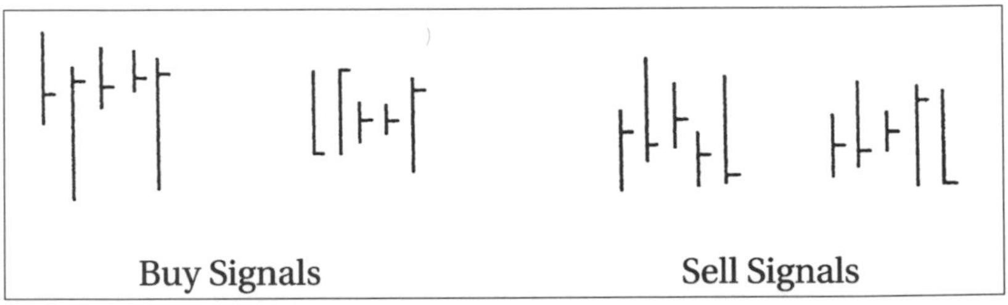

Buy Signals   Sell Signals

FIGURE 14-8.   The Double Reversal Rule.

As suggested by the name *double reversal,* this rule is a double trend continuation (Rule 6). Double reversals occur often and are very reliable. They also occur frequently in Lindahl formations (Rule 5).

When buying, the signal is much stronger if the second low is higher, and when selling, if the second high is lower—unless the second reversal is exceptionally powerful. The same goes for closes. The second one should ideally be higher when buying and lower when selling. Occasionally, this rule can be completed in as few as two bars. It is very powerful when the second bar completes a double reversal and is also a key reversal bar.

Illustrating the Price Rules

All the price rules except Rule 7 are shown on the daily chart for General Electric (Figure 14-9). The market simply never turned with enough vigor to illustrate a trend reversal.

The illustration for Rule 1 occurred after a Rule 2 (reversals) signal the previous day. The example for Rule 3 (gaps) is a contratrend signal, but it shows the idea very well. On the basis of closes, it is also a Rule 4 (islands) buy signal. Rule 4 (islands) is shown again the day after the

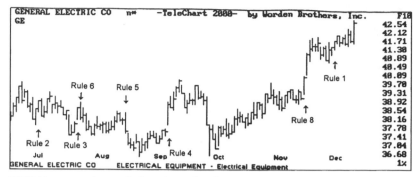

FIGURE 14-9.   General Electric Daily Chart with Price Rules.

price gapped up, leaving behind a massive fourteen-day island. Rule 6 (trend continuation) is shown on the basis of a single daily reversal in the direction of a trend assumed for this purpose to be down. Rule 8 (double reversals) is illustrated with a superb high/low reversal following a closing price reversal, which was also a key reversal two days earlier.

The monthly chart for IBM shows some prime months in which to buy or sell the stock using price rules (Figure 14-10). Note the huge monthly failure in February 1991, the high/low reversal that signified the total exhaustion of a bull trap. Also note the clear Rule 1 sell signal as the decline was starting to gather speed in 1992.

After the price bottomed in IBM, there were several excellent buy signals, beginning with a monthly Lindahl buy signal (in seven months) in February 1994. A second Lindahl buy signal (in nine months) occurred in April 1994. This signal was also a double reversal (Rule 8) signal.

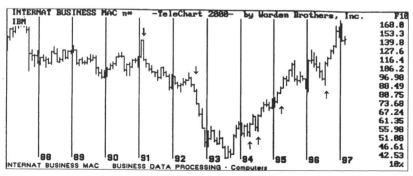

FIGURE 14-10.   IBM Monthly Chart with Price Rules.

A Lindahl signal on the monthly chart tends to be very reliable because it takes so long to form.

Note the huge outside up bar in August 1996. The low for the month was $89.13, and the close was at $112.13. If you were considering buying the stock, you might have thought the stock had traveled too far, too fast to buy at the end of August. Yet this exceptionally powerful Rule 6 signal, which paralleled a similar bar in January, showed that price should continue to move strongly up. In fact, it dipped only three dollars below the August close before surging to $166 over the next four months.

Not all price rule signals work, even when the trend is strong and other technical indicators are strongly confirming. All investment depends on the successful application of probabilities, which, by definition, can go either way. However, IBM shows how signals that follow through can take price a very long way in either direction. Note in particular the risk of continuing to own a stock when there is a monthly price rule signal to sell and the stock is in a downtrend. Applying the price rules and other methods in this book would have saved an owner of IBM stock from living through the price debacle in 1992.

The next chapter shows how using price rules and moving averages together can lead to identifying stocks with a high probability of immediate profit and a low risk of loss.

CHAPTER 15

Moving Averages: Use with Price Rules

A moving average provides another way to identify the direction of a trend. When it is pointing up, the trend is upward, and vice versa when it is pointing down. A moving average is a curved version of a trendline or a smoothed version of many price bars. It consists of the average of the closing prices for a designated number of months, weeks, or days.

Although moving averages are a lagging indicator, monthly moving averages serve extremely well to indicate the major direction of a stock. Sometimes a stock's monthly moving averages maintain a direction for many years. This long-term persistence generally occurs in stocks of companies operating in areas of the economy that are steadily growing and benefiting from a steady stream of innovation. They often occur in such areas as health care and computers, which are always innovating and growing with improvement in the human condition. The trends of stocks in cyclical industries, by definition, tend not to last so long, although stocks in any industry can move far enough for long enough to be worth owning.

When monthly, weekly, and daily moving averages for a specific stock show the same direction, the probabilities favor continuation of the major trend. When a stock trades *at or near* the rising moving averages, the time may be very favorable to buy (or to sell in a bear market). The risk is low relative to the potential reward.

When looking for a new upturn in a stock, it is generally better to wait until both price and the moving averages show signs of developing an upward rounding pattern. Getting in on the ground floor is a mug's game. Too many elevators remain interminably stuck at the ground floor or, worse, fall to the basement. An upward rounding pattern generally allows plenty of time to climb on board.

Settings for Moving Averages

Most effective for standard use are simple moving averages with settings of 25 and 40 as well as the 200-day moving average, which closely corresponds to the 40-week moving average.

Simple moving averages provide slightly longer-term perspective than weighted or exponential moving averages, which give more weight to nearby market action. The 25 and 40 settings are used by many technical analysts, so their effectiveness for potential support or resistance tends to be self-fulfilling.

Using two moving averages of different time periods makes it easier to interpret what is happening. Usually, but not always, the one of shorter duration turns before the longer one. Often, the longer-term one resolutely maintains its direction while the shorter one wobbles. When there is a conflict, it generally pays to heed the longer moving average.

Using Moving Averages

1. The 25- and 40-*month* moving averages indicate the direction of the major trend. On the monthly chart, the 25-month and especially the 40-month moving averages can show the same direction for many years. Flat and conflicting moving averages generally indicate a trading-range market and a stock to avoid, unless there is pronounced rounding that suggests a possible new trend.

   In a strong bull market the price of the stock should be above the uptrending 25-month moving average, and the 25-month moving average should be above the upward inclining 40-month average.

2. The 25- and 40-*week* moving averages indicate the direction of the intermediate trend.

3. The 25- and 40-*day* moving averages indicate the direction of the near-term trend.

Ideally, the moving averages for all chart durations should be pointing the same way when buying or selling a stock or selling short. In practice, the weekly and daily moving averages can chop around without signaling a trend change.

The 40-day moving average often serves as a pivotal level of support when looking to buy a stock at the end of an intermediate correction. Many investors watch price action at this level. As a result, strength coming back into a stack that has retraced to the 40-day moving average tends to become self-reinforcing. It seldom pays to sell a strong stock just because it has come back to the 40-day moving average or to a level just below it. Success or failure of a long-term uptrend in a strong stock is more likely to pivot at the 60-day moving average. Even then, however, selling on a failure at the 60-day moving average may be an exercise in selling at the worst possible time unless the monthly and weekly charts are also showing serious signs of fatigue.

4. The 200-day moving average, very nearly equivalent to the 40-week moving average, is widely regarded as a make-or-break level for a stock.

With so many people watching what happens at this pivotal level, its importance is significant. Either you buy at an excellent price or, if wrong, you can get out of a stock very soon and with a small loss.

The 200-day moving average is particularly significant for the Dow Jones Industrial Average. A crossover of this average has often signaled the start or the end of a major trend. As with many indicators, there have been more failed signals than successful ones from this primitive indicator. When it has been right, it has often been resoundingly right. Notable among the successful signals was the one occurring when the slide began from the 1929 market high. There were several upturns at or near the 200-day moving average for the Dow Industrials during the 1980s and 1990s. There were prime buying opportunities when retracements ended.

5. During price corrections the moving averages should act as support or resistance levels, as appropriate, and should also contain price on a closing basis.

   Moving averages act as a kind of equilibrium level. Price generally draws away from the moving averages and then comes back to a level at or near them. However long it takes, price and the moving averages generally meet or come close to each other from time to time. When a stock has moved a long way above the moving averages, it may be vulnerable to a retracement. However, moving averages say nothing about when a retracement might occur or how far a stock might have to settle back.

6. Generally, signals to buy or sell are particularly powerful when a stock is in an established trend and it has come back to a level at or near the moving averages when they are indicating a strongly trending market.

   The most powerful signals tend to occur on the relatively rare occasions when a strong stock comes back to its monthly moving averages. More frequent but timely and rewarding signals also tend to occur when a stock comes back to the weekly moving averages.

7. A price rule occurring with one or more of its bars touching a rising moving average often delivers an unbeatable combination of timeliness to buy or sell, along with moderate risk.

8. Moving averages show the approximate speed of a stock's advance or decline. When considering a stock with a well-established uptrend, it is helpful to get a rough idea what its annual rate of climb has been in the past. If all goes equally well in the future, the stock may continue to go up at approximately the same rate. When looking at a stock's rate of climb, you can generally see how important it is to buy when it is timely to do so. It is generally of much less use to look at the rate of decline in a bear market, because declining stocks sometimes do so in sudden plunges, and even those appearing to decline relentlessly can change their behavior at any time.

Microsoft and the Monthly Moving Averages

The monthly chart for Microsoft shows the 25- and 40-month moving averages in an apparently unstoppable uptrend throughout the period from 1988 to 1996 (Figure 15-1). Corporate developments continued to justify the overall trend of a rising stock price, with no serious sign that the overall trend was flagging. During the huge bull market of the 1980s and 1990s, there were numerous similar chart patterns in other stocks, with correspondingly favorable price action relative to their moving averages.

On the basis of the 40-month moving average, Microsoft was always a stock to buy during the 1990s—when there were signals to do so. The only caveat was that, ideally, you should buy it when the stock was not too far above the monthly moving averages.

At various times Microsoft traded an enormous distance above its 25- and 40-month moving averages. At its high in January 1992 the stock was trading around $41, while the 25-month moving average was only around the $21 level. It was always possible that the stock might keep on going, and indeed, that was probable over the long term. Nevertheless, a stock trading at twice the price of its 25-month moving average is likely to need a period of consolidation at some time. It might need a major retracement, which could be violent, before the probabilities favor a further immediate and substantial move higher.

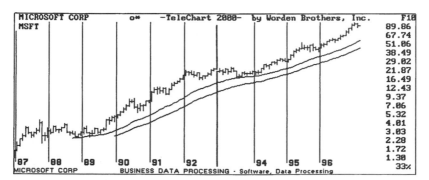

FIGURE 15-1. Microsoft Monthly Chart, with 25- and 40-Month Moving Averages.

Alternatively, the stock could simply go sideways until the moving averages have time to catch up, as occurred with Microsoft.

In this case, Microsoft stopped going up for a time in January 1992. The stock then went sideways in a relatively narrow range until the 25-month average caught up and there was a price touch in June 1993. This set the stage for the eventual decisive break to a new high in June 1994, when the stock began another new upward surge.

A monthly Rule 5 (Lindahl) buy signal occurred in March 1994, with its first bar touching the 25-month moving average. In May 1994 there was also a monthly Rule 1 (three-bar close) buy signal as the stock began its next big leg up.

Buy Off the Weekly Chart

If you missed buying Microsoft when the prime buying opportunity arose at the retracement to the moving averages on the monthly chart, all was by no means lost. The weekly chart shows how retracements to the 25- and 40-week moving averages also provided opportunities to buy a stock when short-term retracements had run their course (Figure 15-2). The stock pulled back to the weekly moving averages and then turned up again many times with price rule buy signals: in February 1995, September 1995, January 1996, and July 1996. Note how the upward crossover in MACD in February 1996 confirmed the resumption of upward momentum. The confirmation occurred after the stock had advanced by approximately $10, or 25 percent, from the correction low.

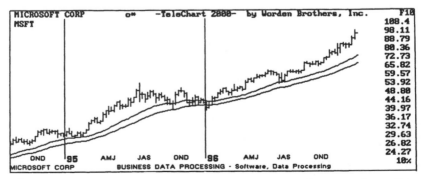

FIGURE 15-2. Microsoft Weekly Chart, with 25- and 40-Week Moving Averages.

If you owned the stock from lower prices, the 27-percent retracement between the high at $64.63 in July 1995 and the low at $40 in January 1996 could well have been worrisome had you arbitrarily bought at or near the top. It is important to recognize at the time what is clear to see after the event. Retracements even as great as 30 percent or so must be regarded as routine for such a strong stock. You can live with that in a stock that shows by the direction and speed of its moving averages that it may double or triple.

Buy Off the Daily Chart

The daily chart for Microsoft for 1996 shows the detailed picture of the stock's action during this period (Figure 15-3). The stock was a low-risk buy off the daily chart in early September, in mid-October, and also in December and in January 1997. The stock kept coming back to the 25- and 40-day moving averages and turning there.

When the stock turned with a price rule, after touching the moving averages, there was nearly always an immediate follow-through.

When You Should Wait to Buy

The search for ground-floor opportunities is always enticing. The challenge is to differentiate between those opportunities having potential worth the risk and going with stocks in an already established trend. The monthly charts for Schlumberger, the oilfield services company (Figure 15-4), and Imperial Oil Ltd., the big Canadian oil company and

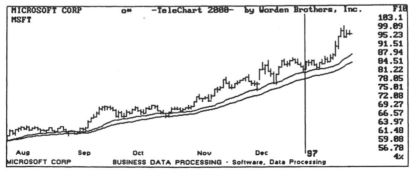

FIGURE 15-3. Microsoft Daily Chart, with 25- and 40-Day Moving Averages.

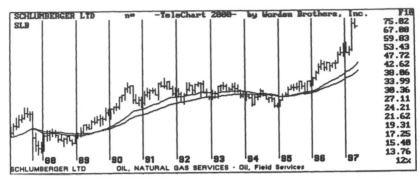

FIGURE 15–4. Schlumberger Monthly Chart, with 25- and 40-Month Moving Averages.

Exxon affiliate (Figure 15-5), provide examples of two stocks having the potential to make big moves in the future.

Imperial Oil shows an example of a classic stock to avoid through-out the period from 1991 to 1996. Price was decisively below its 25- and 40-month moving averages. In the meantime, the company was going belatedly through corporate restructuring and downsizing. Investors showed little interest until signs of better returns for shareholders began to become evident. There was no merit in being an early buyer of Imperial until the stock showed that it might be starting to move. Nor was there any merit in holding Schlumberger during the 1990s until the end of 1995.

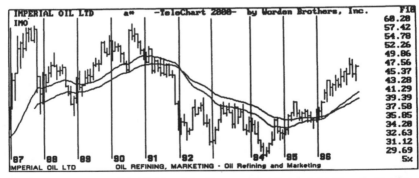

FIGURE 15–5. Imperial Oil Monthly Chart, with 25- and 40-Month Moving Averages.

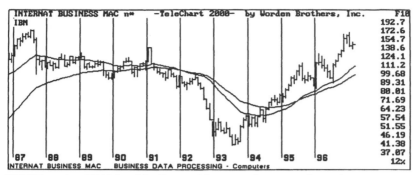

FIGURE 15-6.   IBM Monthly Chart, with 25- and 40-Month Moving Averages.

A Stock to Sell Short

Owning IBM for a long time after 1988 was clearly an exercise in fighting the last war (Figure 15-6). The stock was trending down. The 25- and 40-month moving averages were trending down. Most of the time, too, the price was below these moving averages.

Even the bear market rally in January and February 1991 was too abrupt to come close to bringing the 25-month moving average above the 40-month. Once that rally failed, the stock began to accelerate down, while delivering a superb sell signal for short-sellers in July 1992. The Rule 6 monthly downside reversal, occurring in conjunction with failure at the 25-month moving average, delivered a sell signal at $92.75. For the next six months the price went straight down without a single monthly bounce, delivering as good a short sale as one could ever normally hope for in a major stock, especially given the overall bullish action of the general market.

IBM selling just above $40 was very oversold when its 25-month moving average was just above $60. We now know that from this oversold condition, the stock began a new bull market.

The next chapter brings moving averages together with stochastics. This indicator shows how to measure an overbought or an oversold condition, when to buy in a bull market at the end of a downward retracement, and when to sell short when a bear market rally is cresting.

CHAPTER 16

Stochastics: Overbought/Oversold Indicator

When to Buy Low and Sell High

One technical indicator, stochastics, helps to achieve the elusive goal of buying low and selling high, although only in certain specific situations.

When a stock has gone up powerfully, this indicator has a very high or overbought reading, and vice versa when a stock has fallen sharply and stochastics are at an oversold level. There are often wonderful buying opportunities when a stock has sold off sharply but remains, in the big picture, in an uptrend. Similarly, there are often prime opportunities to sell short when a major bear market rally crests prior to resumption of the major downtrend.

Stochastics seldom help to identify tops in a stock that is in a major uptrend or bottoms in a stock in a major downtrend. An extreme reading may serve only to indicate the power of the trend, not that the stock is likely to make an imminent trend reversal. Stochastics can go to an overbought or an oversold reading and stay there for a very long time.

Setting for Stochastics

For the technically minded, stochastics show the relationship between the most recent close and the high-low range for a given period. They are similar to the relative strength index (RSI). Since RSI is based only on closing prices for a given period, it does not reflect the full range of price action. That information is useful in our core overbought/oversold indicator because we attribute so much importance to the range for a given bar. When there is a very powerful reversal, stochastics may show a turn that is not evident in RSI.

As with MACD, stochastics are plotted as a fast line, %K, and a slow one, %D. The fast line shows immediate responsiveness to price action; the slow, a more deliberate one. There is quite a wide range of settings that accomplish essentially the same results, although the main thing is to get used to working with what you see.

It is hard to improve on a setting in widespread use and which is often a default setting of 9, 3, 3S. Most software does not require the final S, since the fast variant is not in common use.

The setting expresses the following: %K, the fast line, is based on 9, the number of bars included in the calculations; %D is a three-day moving average of %K. The final 3 smoothes both %K and %D to produce the slow stochastics. The following are the parameters for using stochastics.

How to Use Stochastics

Stochastics are used in the same way on the monthly, weekly, and daily charts. This is not a stand-alone indicator. It must be used in conjunction with other indicators. The following are the specific applications:

1. A turn in %K, the fast line, is a signal to buy or sell.

2. When %K level is below 20, a buy may be shaping up. When %K moves above 20, there is a buy signal.

3. When %K level is above 80, a sell may be shaping up. When it moves back under 80, it generates a sell signal.
   %K crossing 20 or 80 should not be confused with %K crossing %D. Although in general these crossovers confirm what is happening, they occur too randomly to help with timing.

4. An overbought %K level above 80 counts as a negating indicator on the entry checklist to buy (described in Chapter 25). An oversold %K level below 20 counts as a negating indicator on the entry checklist to sell short (described in Chapter 31).
   An overbought or oversold level indicates that a stock may be vulnerable to a retracement. It is particularly important to heed

overbought or oversold readings on the monthly chart. Buying a stock with an overbought %K or selling one short when it is oversold may involve above-average risk, particularly when the stock is pressing against previous levels of support or resistance.

5. An overbought or oversold reading does not mean that you cannot buy or sell a stock. Extreme readings may be an expression of powerful buying or selling, particularly when a stock first breaks out of a consolidation or a trading range. %K will always show a high or low reading when the price of a stock moves to a new 52-week high or low. Then there may be a prime opportunity to buy or sell.

6. Ms and downward zigzags and Ws and upward zigzags in %K indicate the general momentum of a stock.

7. Stochastics often work extremely well when used in conjunction with moving averages. When there is a *very* low stochastics reading and price turns *up* at or near the rising moving averages, there is often a prime buying opportunity. When there is a very *high* stochastics reading and a price turns *down* at or near the declining moving averages, there is often a prime opportunity to sell short (or a prime opportunity to sell a stock that you should no longer own).

As with all indicators, but especially with stochastics, a good buy or sell signal may occur without stochastics in agreement. However, when stochastics agree with other indicators in confirming an entry or exit, the probabilities in favor of a successful trade increase substantially.

Stochastics Applied

The monthly chart for General Motors shows what many people expect of stochastics (Figure 16-1). The stock often turned up from oversold readings in stochastics and often turned down from overbought readings. Even so, market action was too erratic to have much confidence in arbitrarily buying low or selling high on the basis of stochastics alone. Sometimes the stock turned on cue, and sometimes it kept on going further.

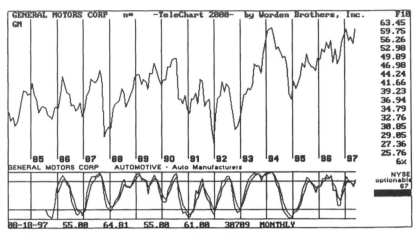

FIGURE 16–1.   General Motors Monthly Chart, with Stochastics.

The monthly chart for Coca-Cola shows most of what you can more usefully expect from stochastics (Figure 16-2). Starting in 1987, there is textbook negative divergence before the 1987 stock market crash. The small downturn in September occurred from a high lower than the one in March, creating in the process a textbook M. That in itself was not reason enough to sell the stock, but it delivered a warning that it was appropriate to look at market action on the weekly and daily charts.

After the October 1987 crash it took almost a year for stochastics to stabilize and to form a W. Note that the price of the stock came down

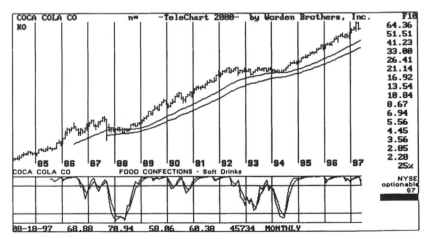

FIGURE 16–2.   Coca-Cola Monthly Chart, with 25- and 40-Month Moving Averages and Stochastics.

to the rising 40-month moving average but never closed below it. See how %K crossed back above 20, after forming a W, the month before the big surge in September that began the new bull market in the stock.

Once in motion again from the end of 1988, Coca-Cola's stochastics remained solidly overbought for the better part of four years. This was an indication of strength, not of vulnerability. The decline in stochastics below 80 in 1990 did not signal the end of the bull market. It merely coincided with corrections in the ongoing major bull market. Upturns in the single price line (not shown here) as well as upturns in %K provided superb buying opportunities.

Weakness in stochastics, with downward zigzags, during 1992 and 1993 suggested that you might have considered getting out of the stock for the time being, or at least not buying more. With relatively limited weakness in price and the 25- and 40-month moving averages steadfastly moving higher, there was really no reason to suppose that the long bull market in the stock was ending.

There was a very low stochastic reading at the end of 1995. In addition, by now the 25-month moving average had taken three long years to catch up with price. Mostly, the convergence occurred as a result of the moving average catching up, though the price of Coca-Cola stock came back just over 10 percent as well to help make it happen. When this happened, it was a wonderful time to buy the stock when the price turned up again. Here is a good example of how timing techniques help you to buy when it is timely to do so rather than to wait for months or years for the market to start showing that it appreciates the value of a stock.

This action in Coca-Cola shows how the convergence of price and the rising moving averages, when combined with a very low stochastic reading, often occurs at an unbeatable time to buy a stock. Similar prime opportunities often arise to sell a stock short in a bear market, when price catches up with the declining moving averages and there is a very high stochastic reading.

The weekly chart for Coca-Cola from 1995 to early 1997 shows the price of the stock working up alongside the 25-week moving average (Figure 16-3). There was a prime place to buy in January 1995 on the first pullback, even though the stochastics failed to go all the way down under 20. Subsequently, there were additional prime entry points. Whenever the price pulled back to the 25-week average and, in addi-

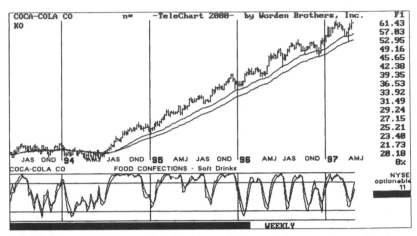

FIGURE 16–3. Coca-Cola Weekly Chart, with 25- and 40-Week Moving Averages and Stochastics.

tion, stochastics turned up from a level near or below 20, there was a prime buying opportunity on the next strong weekly price bar.

The daily chart for Coca-Cola in 1995 shows price plotted against the 25-, 40-, and 60-day moving averages as well as stochastics on the bottom of the chart (Figure 16-4). The chart shows that there were regular fluctuations that formed fairly regular monthly cycles. The stock advanced about 10 percent and then fell back a little less. At each crest

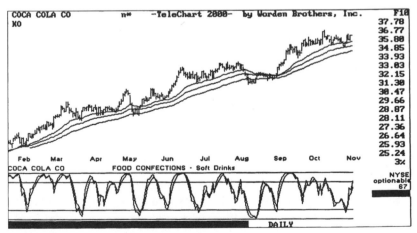

FIGURE 16–4. Coca-Cola Daily Chart, with 25-, 40-, and 60-Day Moving Averages and Stochastics.

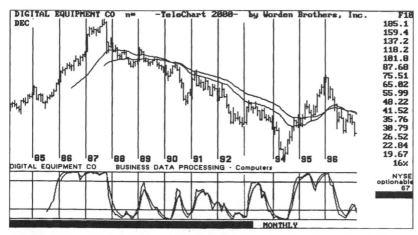

FIGURE 16-5. Digital Equipment Monthly Chart, with 25- and 40-Month Moving Averages and Stochastics.

the stochastics reached a high level, and at each valley a low level. When the price of the stock stabilized with stochastics at a low level, it was an excellent time to buy. With the wisdom of hindsight, you might think you should have sold out at short-term tops when stochastics peaked. The trouble is that you never know when the stock is going to keep on going, leaving you behind, as might have happened in June. It is very difficult to make more money by buying and selling within a major long-term uptrend than you would make by buying and holding throughout normal fluctuations. The secret is to know when technical action suggests that something more than a normal retracement may occur.

Note that Coca-Cola's retracement was barely contained by its 60-day moving average in May. A cursory glance at the weekly and monthly charts indicated that this aberration was not the end of the bull market in the stock. Even the low closes in August did not signify the end. On the contrary, the ultralow stochastics readings signified that in the short term, the stock was washed out. The second higher low about a month later was a very bullish confirmation that the stock had finished shaking the stock out of weak hands.

The monthly chart for Digital Equipment shows just how weak this stock really was. Oversold stochastics levels never correctly suggested the potential for any more than a bear market rally until the 1994 low

(Figure 16-5). On the other hand, the M formed by stochastics at the beginning of 1996 correctly confirmed the vulnerability of the stock to a retracement. In the event, of course, the retracement was rather more than that.

The next chapter illustrates other support and resistance levels where price is likely to turn.

CHAPTER 17

Trendlines, Channel Lines, and Linear Retracement

Drawing a Trendline

Trendlines, along with channel lines, their counterpart, stand the test of time. Since many investors use them, their effectiveness becomes self-fulfilling.

A trendline connects *lows* in a rising market and *highs* in a declining market. You can draw a tentative trendline when two identifiable highs or lows become established. The validity of a trendline is confirmed only when price returns to the assumed trendline for a third time or more, and again turns there or close to it. It is often tempting to assume a trendline developing on the appearance of every small blip in price action. However, most good trendlines require a significant length of time between highs and lows. By extension, the longer a trendline remains in force, the more validity it has.

Many software packages and chart services provide a choice between arithmetic chart scaling and logarithmic, and their respective impact on trendlines is significant. Arithmetic scaling treats all price action the same, regardless of the percentage of fluctuations. Logarithmic scaling produces charts that adjust for the proportion, or the percentage, of price fluctuations. Arithmetic charts are useful when there is no more than about a doubling in price from the low point on the chart to the high. Logarithmic charts are useful when larger moves are involved. Logarithmic charts are therefore generally more useful when drawing trendlines and channel lines for stocks. However, arithmetic charts are better for Treasury bonds and for commodity futures markets.

Drawing a Channel Line

After finding or assuming a trendline, find the most distant point from the trendline and draw a line parallel to it. There is then an upper and a lower line between which the stock should fluctuate.

The idea behind trendlines and channel lines is that price typically zigzags backwards and forwards between the trendline and the channel line. In a steadily trending market, price moves backwards and forwards while maintaining a steady overall direction. It is similar to the way a sailing boat tacks backwards and forwards while maintaining an overall direction that is a compromise between the two tacks. Hence the term *linear retracement.* A trendline is, in a sense, a form of moving average, for it shows both direction and speed.

For a strongly moving stock it is also worth drawing one or more additional lines parallel to the channel line, and at the same distance from it as the distance between the original trendline and first channel line. If the stock goes through a channel line, it is likely to fluctuate within a new range bounded by the original channel line and the next parallel and equidistant channel line. The original channel line becomes support and, in effect, the new trendline.

When a stock declines through an uptrend line in a bull market, the probabilities favor a downward extension. It seldom pays to hold a stock once it has decisively penetrated a clear uptrend line on the *monthly* chart. In the event that there is a false breakdown, sometimes known as a *bear trap,* you can always buy the stock back. However, the best stocks to own rarely violate major trendlines. Even a breakdown that appears to be an aberration may be a harbinger of trouble ahead.

Similarly, it seldom pays to continue holding a stock short once it has gone up through a major downtrend line.

The Dow Industrials and Linear Retracement

On the monthly line chart for the Dow Jones Industrial Average, there is a tentative trendline between the two points A and B from the 1982 low to the 1984 low (Figure 17-1). After assuming that potential trend-

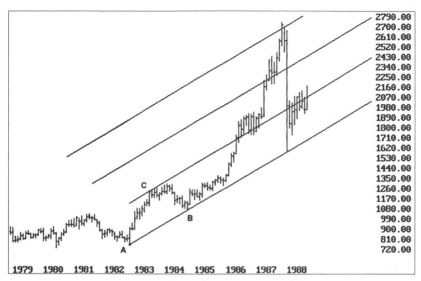

FIGURE 17-1. Dow Jones Industrial Average Monthly Chart, 1979–1988, with Trendlines and Channel Lines.

line, expect the channel line drawn from the high at C to contain upward price movement.

Note that lows during 1985 and 1986 came close to the uptrend line but not all the way back to it. It is a sign of a powerful market when the speed of the ascent is accelerating. The Dow accelerated to such an extent that it soared through its original channel line.

After the Dow went sailing on through the first upper channel line, that channel line then became the new trendline, the new line of lower support, the new line of support for retracements. Now a new parallel channel line became the new price target.

After a period of consolidation for almost a year, the Dow again started climbing fast and it soared through the next channel line target. As it did at the original channel line, it consolidated for several months, mainly above the channel line, before surging to the third channel line and its 1987 high.

When the stock market crashed in October 1987, the Dow found support exactly at the uptrend line originally assumed in 1984. It is remarkable that in all the frenzy of panic selling, it turned out that the decline held at exactly this support level. It is worth repeating the point that there is more involved than 20/20 hindsight in using trendlines and channel lines in practice. Since many investors use them, their effectiveness becomes self-fulfilling. It is reasonable to assume that there were traders looking to cover short positions, if not necessarily to buy, when the Dow was approaching its long-term uptrend line.

It is important to note that trendlines are significantly more reliable than channel lines. Markets often play with channel lines without reversing direction. However, it is always valuable to know where a channel line is so you can watch out for a potential retracement that goes beyond ordinary day-to-day fluctuations. It is also valuable to know that there is a higher risk involved in buying against an overhead channel line in a bull market or in selling against a lower one in a bear market.

Trendlines Drawn Off
Price Rules and Reversals

The monthly chart for General Electric shows how you can often draw trendlines off lows from the bottom of price rule formations and monthly reversals with the trend in a bull market (Figure 17-2). During 1987 there is an uptrend line, A-B, joining two upside monthly reversals in October 1986 and June 1987. Draw a trendline, while recognizing that the rate of climb was suspiciously steep. That steepness in itself should lead you to wonder about the stock's ability to continue rising so fast. When this uptrend line was tested and found wanting, you should have immediately looked at what was happening on the weekly and daily charts in case the stock started to fall apart.

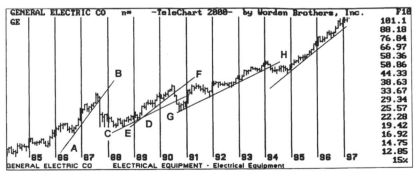

FIGURE 17-2. General Electric Monthly Chart, with Trendlines.

A potential, shallow trendline, C-D, began in 1988. Then the stock soon accelerated, permitting a steeper trendline, E-F, from the two monthly upside reversals in 1989 (the first of them a high/low reversal). Once this trendline was broken in August 1990, the stock fell a further 20 percent and took several months to stabilize.

With the November 1990 low in place, assume an uptrend line G-H. The distance between the two points strongly suggested that this was likely to be a trendline capable of remaining in good standing for a long time. When price broke through this uptrend line in early 1994, it did not signify the start of a slide in the stock. However, there was to be no further upward progress until it spent a full year digesting the previous gains.

The conjunction of price and a major long-term trendline is a critical time for a stock. On the one hand, buyers are eager to buy with a low risk at a level likely to contain the retracement. On the other hand, you have shareholders wondering whether or not the trendline will hold. Some potential buyers simply step up to the plate to buy when price touches the trendline or comes close to it. Before buying, however, it is better to see the ambiguity resolved with a strong price rule and confirming technical action from other indicators. Then there is less risk of the stock marking time while you wonder what to do with it. The probabilities favor a victory for buyers once the stock shows that it can start going again. Strong technical action at a trendline is likely to precede a powerful follow-through.

Of all the alerts for selling a stock, there are few as reliable as penetration of a trendline on the monthly chart. Obviously, you never know at the time which failures at a trendline will follow through or by how much. However, you can be certain that many other investors see the same breakdown. Some are likely to sell in case the ensuing decline becomes more serious, as occurred in October 1987. If you wait to see what is going to happen, you may find yourself selling out at the worst possible time, after price has slipped a long way. The likelihood of a significant decline is compounded when many potential buyers stand aside on seeing the price failing to hold up at the trendline. Then a stampede at the exit can cause a vacuum or an air pocket below the trendline.

Even the decline in General Electric during the second half of 1990 was worth avoiding. In July 1990 GE was far above its 25- and 40-month moving averages and vulnerable to a setback.

Occasionally, you find a chart where price comes back to the long-term uptrend so consistently and holds there so consistently that you wonder why everyone does not own the stock. From the 1986 low, Intel held on a monthly closing basis above the uptrend that established a total of five points of contact (Figure 17-3). It took from 1987 to 1995 before Intel reached the upper channel line drawn off the 1987 high, where sure enough, it had to retrace for nine months before the stock could start moving again. As with General Electric, the retracement from the channel line was moderate, with price coming back nowhere near the uptrend line. This lack of weakness proved to be an indication of the strength that took Intel on for a further doubling once it broke out again to new highs.

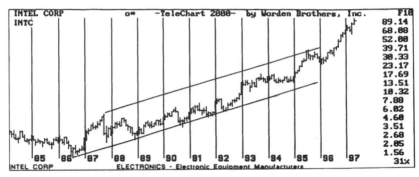

FIGURE 17-3.   Intel Monthly Chart, with Trendline and Channel Line.

The monthly chart for Unisys Corporation from 1987 to 1991 (Figure 17-4) shows how, during the earlier part of the decline, price retracements were contained by a downtrend line with essentially four points of contact. Then the rally early in 1990 failed to come close to this downtrend line. After this rally crested, you could draw a new and steeper downtrend line.

On the other hand, once the stock went up through the steeper downtrend line, in January 1992, it was possible that the bear market in the stock might be coming to an end. As often happens, however, the reversal of the downtrend did not mean that the stock was necessarily a good candidate to buy. It happens that the price went significantly higher for a time. It then went into a textbook sideways pattern, like the ones you always want to avoid.

The general principle seldom fails that a market requiring steeper

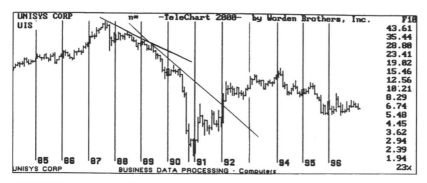

FIGURE 17-4. Unisys Monthly Chart, with Downtrend Lines.

trendlines should gather speed until a climax occurs—in the case of Unisys, a selling climax, because the trend was down. On the other hand, a stock requiring shallower trendlines is almost invariably one running out of momentum. A downtrend requiring shallower trendlines may be a market that is bringing in buyers attempting to find the bottom of the market in anticipation of recovery.

It should be self-evident that Unisys was not a stock to own when it was falling relentlessly, any more than were Digital Equipment and IBM when they were going down. However, you can be certain that some value investors were prepared to buy it. That's what makes markets.

Surprisingly often, stocks move up or down in zigzags contained within an identifiable range. You can make tentative projections ahead both for time and price, and you can estimate an approximate rate of climb from the point of contact with a trendline. The most reliable stocks to buy tend to be the ones making reliable fluctuations within the confines of a trend.

CHAPTER 18

Chart Patterns to Buy

The Long-Term Breakout

Sideways markets are paradoxical. On the one hand, you want to avoid buying a stock that is obviously going nowhere. On the other, to jump into a stock that suddenly springs to life after spending a long time going nowhere is often the best thing you can do.

There are several variations of the breakout from a long-term consolidation. Two variations occur frequently, are easy to spot, and have immense power when they work. These are the breakout from the long-term consolidation and the breakout from a reverse-head-and-shoulders pattern.

There is a reason for looking for breakouts. From a fundamental standpoint, what usually happens is this. A company churns away at work on a new product or a corporate reorganization. All the while, value is building, although it remains unrecognized in the marketplace. There is the *show me* syndrome. Investors want to see what, if anything, the company can really do. Early on, during the corporate progress toward success, a few value investors find the stock and buy it to lock away. They do not necessarily make the stock move. Sometimes they wait for a very long time for something to happen. Recognition may come slowly to the company and its stock, if it comes at all. The corporate developments that they anticipate may not come through, or only after much longer than they hoped. At last, there is enough critical mass of corporate success as well as enough critical mass of ownership by smart money. Then new buying pressure comes in to disturb the equilibrium of buyers and sellers. The stock appears on the list of actively traded stocks or on the list of stocks making a new 52-week high. Those are alerts equivalent to making it onto the *Billboard* chart. It makes people start to pay attention and to try to find out if anything is happening. Closer examination leads to more widespread appreciation in the form of buyers putting real money into the stock.

There is time enough to consider buying the stock now. If the company has laid good groundwork, its newfound success will not be an aberration that lasts only briefly. The stock may be the next Microsoft, McDonald's, or Wal-Mart. Investors climb on the bandwagon and the stock begins to surge. Everyone likes to buy a great stock early. It may seem as if the stock has already come a long way. However, buying early often means buying after a double in the expectation of it going on to double and double again. Then, the stock goes from wallflower to fashion plate.

By no means do all breakouts follow through. Nevertheless, some of those that do go on to great things make buying breakouts really worthwhile. The winners make huge money, while the losses are relatively small. If you double your money on half your purchases of breakout stocks and lose a third on the other half, on balance you make a lot of money. Besides, you may well be able to improve on those ratios. You can often tell at the time which are likely to be the best breakouts by looking at other indicators, notably OBV and MACD.

As a rule, the stronger the buying, the further the stock is likely to go when it breaks out. There is a rough rule of thumb that the target for a stock should be as far again as the range for the consolidation from which the stock breaks out. The longer the consolidation, or the more powerful the stock's history, the more likely the stock is to exceed that target.

Some Doldrums Never End

Sometimes a stock can be becalmed for years on end, trending between a floor below and a ceiling above. When a stock is trading within a range, as Homestake Mining did from 1986 to 1996, there is no prospect of making a big profit from the stock any time soon (Figure 18-1). You have to wait until it breaks out of its range. While waiting, you may as well not own it. Some people buy the stock before, as it approaches the high end of the range, in the hope that it may at last break out and follow through. Hope springs eternal that this time will be different and that a Homestake will finally break out as it approaches a previous high yet again.

During 1993 there was an immense surge in HM from the bottom of its range to the top. Despite the fact that this buying had a favorable impact on OBV, it was too much of a good thing. Without a base to act as a springboard, the stock ran into a concrete ceiling at previous resistance levels. Those who bought the stock the last time it took a run at the high were happy to sell when they could get their money back, and they clearly did so. Many people are programmed to get all or most of their money back out of a loser, however long it takes to nurse their loss in the meantime.

Then there are traders whose lifeblood it is (believe it or not!) intentionally to buy low and sell high within a trading range. Buy Homestake at $10 and sell it at $20. Then sell the stock short at $20 to buy back again at $10. Some of them make good bread-and-butter money from this kind of trading, but it is not the way to make big money in the long run.

Anyone can see from a chart where previous highs and lows are, and their buying and selling causes patterns of rallies and retracements to recur constantly—until something happens to disturb the

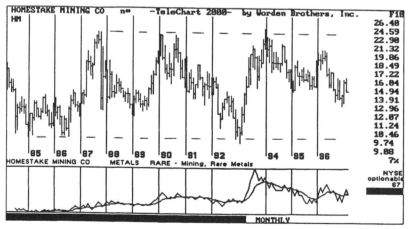

FIGURE 18-1. Homestake Monthly Chart, with Support and Resistance and On Balance Volume.

equilibrium. When you see a stock like Homestake in a trading range, avoid it like the plague.

If HM ever broke out above the $22 level, it should have a minimum price objective of about $34. In view of the length of the sideways action, the target, from a strictly technical standpoint, could be a triple or more. To judge by the chart as it now is, as well as the general apathy toward gold, it is hard to imagine HM ever breaking out of its lethargy.

There is no time limit on sideways market action. The price of Bank of England stock went more or less sideways for 150 years, sometimes doubling, sometimes halving, but never much more. That agony ended with nationalization in 1946.

Eastman Kodak Breaks Out

Most stocks in trading range require no more than a cursory glance to confirm that nothing is happening. Then you notice a pattern of higher lows beginning to form on the chart. Long-term moving averages begin rounding upward. OBV and MACD start strengthening.

All these things generally develop slowly. Once you identify a stock where it seems that something may eventually change, draw horizontal lines at previous highs and lows. It is important to draw these lines and to note the price levels where the stock stopped before. You need to know exactly where those people losing money in a stock can heave their collective sigh of relief and stop selling to get their money back. When a stock breaks out to a new high level, everyone is making money. The price will be held back by profit-takers but not by a hoard of people losing money in the stock. Then, the higher the stock goes, the more investors are likely to live by the rule of letting their profits run.

After the 1987 stock market crash, Eastman Kodak traded sideways between about $28 and $40 for five long years (Figure 18-2). In 1990, EK turned at the level of the 1986 low, and in 1991 the stock turned back down at the level of the 1989 high.

With a couple of higher lows in 1992, the stock was at last able to take a successful run at the two previous highs. After faltering, it broke decisively through the $40 level and stayed above it. The next challenge was the level of the 1987 high, at $55.87. It could hardly be considered attractive to buy Kodak in the low to mid-$40s for a maximum potential gain of $10 or so—unless something started to change.

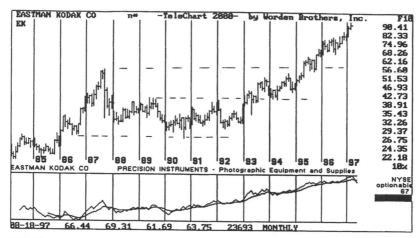

FIGURE 18-2. Eastman Kodak Monthly Chart, with Support and Resistance and On Balance Volume.

Note how the stock came back to the $40 level after breaking above that level and briefly reaching $50. This shows how resistance, once broken, becomes support. Anyone inadvertently short the stock from $40 now has the chance to cover the position close to break-even. Value investors have the opportunity to buy the stock low within the range and to wait patiently in the expectation of an eventual upside breakout. Kodak eventually rewarded those who bought low, but they had to wait a long time for the payoff.

There are three places to buy Kodak on the basis of its chart action. You might buy the stock when it made a significantly higher low in January 1995 and turned up at a point near the 25-month moving average. This anticipatory purchase might require patience, but now a technical case for owning EK was starting to emerge.

The next potential buy point was on the breakout above the 1987 high, which occurred in conjunction with superb confirmation by On Balance Volume. As often happens, particularly with a stock that has come quite a way quickly, Kodak had to consolidate just above the breakout level above the 1987 high. After six months of consolidation and on completion of a monthly upside reversal, the stock finally started moving.

After it has successfully broken out of its long-term consolidation, you can tentatively project how far the stock might go. From the 1987 high at $55.87 to the 1990 low at $26.62, the stock traded within a range of $29.25. Add that amount to the value at the 1987 high and there is a price projection of $85.12. In view of the length of time involved in Kodak's consolidation, that target might underestimate the stock's potential. After breaking out to new highs (and with the knowledge, incidentally, that there has been considerable corporate restructuring), it is possible that this venerable blue chip might come back into the sun.

Colgate Shows Emerging Strength

The chart for Colgate-Palmolive shows a stock much stronger than Eastman Kodak (Figure 18-3). It made its low in October 1987 and then began a steady climb back toward the 1987 high. Once it broke out above that high, it had to come back to test the breakout level. From there, it was ever on upward.

During the consolidation after the 1987 crash, Colgate had a range from top to bottom of $12.31, from $26.31 at the high to $14 at the low. Add $12.31 to the price at the top in August 1987 and you have the price target on the breakout. This level of $38.62 was achieved in March 1991. However, the stock was so powerful that it did not perceptibly falter on reaching this objective. It kept on going to $67.25 in April 1993.

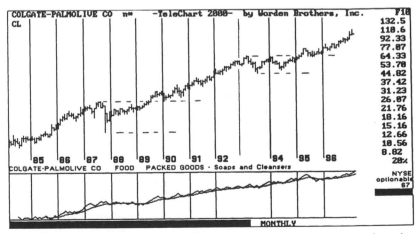

FIGURE 18–3. Colgate-Palmolive Monthly Chart, with Support and Resistance and On Balance Volume.

The ensuing retracement took the stock back to a low of $46.75 in August 1993, giving a range for the retracement of $20.50. The resulting target after the breakout was $87.75, achieved in September 1996.

Many investors using technical analysis, perhaps the majority, do not buy the first breakout; they wait for a return like the one made here by Colgate. You cannot count on that happening. When there is a breakout with other technical indicators strongly confirming, the probabilities favor buying right away. The very best stocks never make that retracement. So if you do not buy on the breakout, you get left behind. Those stocks that make the retracement generally do not cost you money, assuming that your entry price and the support at the breakout level are about the same. Note how OBV was steadily building from early 1989 as the stock was preparing to break out, continuing once the stock was into new high territory. It was not hard to live through the retracement.

It is worth looking at Homestake, Kodak, and Colgate together. You should be able to see that there is no reason even to consider Homestake interesting. Stay away! Kodak had been a dog and showed great promise that might or might not come through. It has possibilities but is not really exciting. Colgate, on the other hand, has an extremely powerful coiling pattern before the two breakouts that we see here. It was a screaming buy on both breakouts.

The Reverse Head-and-Shoulders

The monthly chart for Sears Roebuck illustrates the reverse-head-and-shoulders pattern (Figure 18-4).

This pattern offers a superior potential for gain with limited risk. The stock has been trading sideways for some time. Then it takes a plunge and rebounds to the level where it was previously trading sideways. Then it consolidates in a similar fashion to the previous sideways action before the plunge down to the low. If an upside breakout to new highs follows after completion of a big reverse-head-and-shoulders pattern, the probabilities strongly favor a substantial advance.

The difference between a reverse-head-and-shoulders pattern and a conventional sideways consolidation is that you assume that the

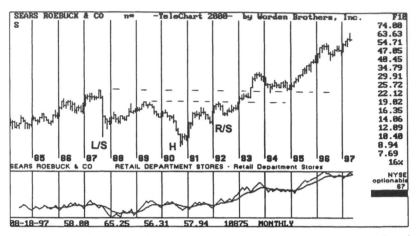

FIGURE 18-4. Sears Roebuck Monthly Chart, with Reverse Head-and-Shoulders and On Balance Volume.

stock has truly been through the wringer at the bottom. On the first low, the stock tested the mettle of patient shareholders. Many of those buy-and-hold, long-term investors still held onto the stock. Then there was a cathartic cleansing that wrung out many of the last diehards who bought high. They thought they were in for the long term, but the pressure of the final panic sell-off was too much. Now smart money could really start accumulating the stock with confidence. However, there is no point in trying to be smart too early. The best chart patterns can take many months and even years to develop, not just a few days or weeks after a selling climax.

The chart for Sears Roebuck shows how the stock tried to take a stand at the October 1987 low and that indeed it did make quite a recovery before faking out. The end of 1990 saw the selling climax that formed the upside-down head of the reverse head-and-shoulders. It took well into 1992, however, before you could begin to discern the head at the bottom and the left-hand shoulder formed by the 1987 low.

Given the length of the consolidation, there was a case to buy a small position on the breakout in early 1993 above the 1989 high. OBV was looking great, and you could not fault the good length of time the stock had spent working on development of a favorable chart pattern. Note that if you did not buy on the early 1989 breakout, there was never another opportunity to buy at such a favorable price. The stock never came back to test that breakout level.

Once through the 1987 high, there was a retracement back to the breakout level, but it did not cause damage to the technical picture.

Target for the stock after the break above the 1987 high was $38.44. In the event, the stock faltered well below that level, stopping at $32.36 in November 1993. That faltering was by no means the end of it. The stock went on to $65.25 at the top of the chart.

Here is an instance where you can look at a chart and think that you might have liked to buy the stock under $10 when it was making its low. However, successful investment is an exercise in buying and selling on the basis of probabilities. In addition, you cannot ignore time. The probabilities favor continuation of the motion when a stock is moving, and it favors continuing stagnation when it is not. Homestake shows how a stock can languish interminably in a sideways pattern. That is normality for sideways patterns, whereas the performance of Colgate-Palmolive is indicative of a stock likely to maintain its upward incline for the foreseeable future. Having started to show what it could do, Sears might be a stock at the beginning of such a move.

The Ascending Triangle

The ascending triangle is also a very powerful chart pattern when other indicators confirm. It generally occurs as a consolidation during the course of a major move or as one is just starting.

The chart for Hewlett Packard (Figure 18-5) shows a three-year consolidation from 1992 to 1994. Until the second half of 1994 the evidence was in conflict as to whether the next major move was to be up or down. There was a clear pattern of higher lows going back to the 1990 low and a less clear pattern of rising highs. On Balance Volume was strongly negative until October 1994. Then a crossover signal coincided with the breakout. Once HWP broke decisively above the highs of the consolidation, there was no looking back, and the price rapidly tripled during the next two years. This is the kind of move that makes market timing really worthwhile. The preceding three years of consolidation show how the royal jelly for a big move often needs time to cook.

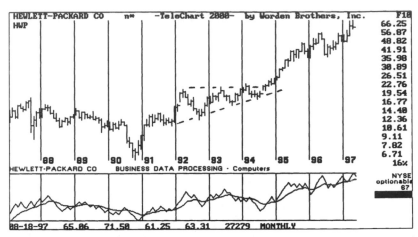

FIGURE 18–5. Hewlett-Packard Monthly Chart, with Ascending Triangle and On Balance Volume.

The chart for HWP is also interesting for showing a huge, if ragged, reverse head-and-shoulders with its head at the bottom at the end of 1990.

It is worth looking for all consolidation patterns. They come in every conceivable size and shape. The rule is that when a stock breaks out, it is likely to continue in the direction of the breakout when indicators like OBV and MACD confirm.

CHAPTER **19**

When to Look for Market Lows

Selling Climaxes and Double Bottoms

Although it is impossible to identify exact market tops and bottoms with acceptable consistency, some indicators help to identify bottoms soon afterwards. They consistently identified important lows soon after they occurred during the great bull market of the 1980s and the 1990s. Since they are based on good logic, it is likely they will continue to work in the future. Unfortunately, these indicators do not have a record of having much usefulness when the general market is cresting, but that does not detract from their usefulness soon after important lows.

The three indicators that suggest market bottoms are the Percentage of Stocks above their 200-Day Moving Average (TDA), the Zweig Breadth Thrust Index (ZBT), and Ticks. The first two are available on the *TC 2000* software program, and they are both used on monthly charts. They set up the conditions for the other indicators in this book to identify when it may be timely to buy stocks. The ticks indicator is generally available with services providing continuous market data during the day. It is used on the daily chart and gives a closer view than the other two longer-term indicators. The ticks indicator is a more directly useful indicator in its own right, and it is most useful when major turns happen fast, that is, within a few weeks.

Stocks Above Their 200-Day Average (TDA)

TDA is shown as a monthly bar chart that is plotted against a line chart for the Dow Jones Industrial Index (Figure 19-1). There is a conjunction of major lows in price, from which major advances followed. This indicator shows when stocks are really washed out. The table below shows the readings for TDA at historic lows from 1987. When TDA reaches 30 or lower, start to look for an end to the overall decline of the market.

November 1987	3
August 1990	19
April 1994	28
November 1994	23
September 1998	23

There have been few times when TDA has been much below 40 when the overall market was not at or near a low. A partial exception occurred in 1994. The Dow made a higher low in November when TDA made a lower low than the one in April. In the intervening seven months, stocks drifted sideways, but with very good base-building prior to the subsequent powerful advance. Of course, even five out of five samples do not provide enough evidence for long-term statistical reliability but, since we know the concept makes sense, TDA still looks good.

FIGURE 19–1. Monthly Chart for Stocks Above Their 200-Day Moving Average and the Dow Jones Industrial Average Line Chart.

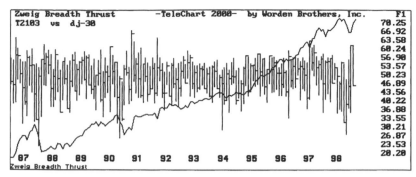

FIGURE 19–2. Monthly Zweig Breadth Thrust Indicator and Dow Jones Industrial Average Monthly Line Chart.

The Zweig Breadth Thrust Indicator (ZBT)

ZBT is also shown here as a monthly bar chart that is plotted against a line chart for the Dow Jones Industrial Average (Figure 19-2). This indicator is based on the ratio of stocks going up versus those going down.

As with TDA, there were pronounced lows in 1987, 1990, and 1998.

Compare the two indicators and price for the Dow in 1994. The Dow and ZBT made their low in April. Both completed a W with a higher low when they turned up in December. TDA made a substantially lower low in November. When it turned, however, it did so with immense power.

Ticks As a Selling Climax Indicator

The ticks indicator shows at any given time the number of stocks selling on an uptick minus the number selling on a downtick. The number is constantly updated during market hours in response to every trade in every individual stock. Normally, the net difference, the tick reading, fluctuates between plus or minus 500 or so. Short-term traders look to buy at bottoms when the reading is between minus 500 and minus 1000, and they look to sell when the reading is above plus 500, depending in both cases on market conditions.

Figure 19-3 shows on top the Standard & Poor's 500 daily bar chart from July 1998. Below is the daily bar chart for ticks. Each bar for ticks

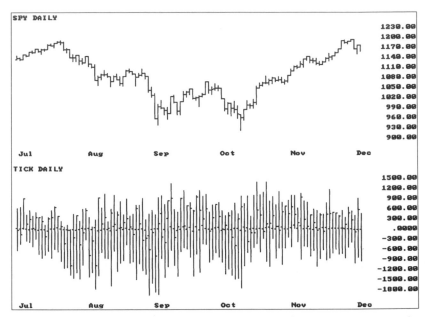

FIGURE 19-3. Daily Standard & Poor 500 Daily Cash Chart and the Daily Ticks Bar Chart.

shows the entire range of readings for that day. As with a price bar chart, each bar has a notch for the opening and closing ticks reading at the start and finish of market hours.

A reading of –1500 or lower generally occurs in conjunction with a selling climax. However, the heavy selling may go on for several days and may continue far longer than you expect. You don't want to be trying to catch a falling rock. As with other indicators, however, this one becomes really useful in conjunction with the concept of zigzags. First, ticks should make one climactic low when panic selling washes stock out of weak hands at the worst possible price. Then, some time later, there should be a second selling climax when the maximum minus reading for ticks does not exceed the previous one.

The point about zigzags is, of course, that you don't know you have one starting until the evidence has fallen into place. There is no point in trying to guess that you have in place an exact bottom when the first climactic sell-off appears to have run its course. The probabilities are overwhelming that the market will have to make at least one more test of the bottom. There is time enough then to test the water, after you can see a higher low in selling pressure.

Here is the record of maximum minus readings going into the September 1, 1998, low:

August 27	−1982
August 28	−1596
August 31	−1856
September 1	−1932

After September 1 the market stabilized. It was not clear whether there had been enough of a washout to establish a base or whether the general market would make a further leg down. On October 8 there was another climactic selling wave, with many indexes and many individual stocks going below their September 1 lows. However, the lowest reading for ticks that day was −1738, a significantly smaller negative number than occurred in August and September. When that selling climax ran its course, which did not take long, the result was the kind of W formation we look for in price and other indicators.

In addition to looking at the daily range for ticks, it is also useful to look at the reading at the end of the day. When the daily close is strong, it shows that buying pressure, at least for that day, exceeds selling pressure, as it does with price rules. A strong daily upside reversal in ticks suggests the likelihood that price will continue upward the next day, and vice versa for a downside reversal. The significance of this interpretation increases when there is a succession of strong closes.

S&P made its low on October 8. That day, the daily bar for ticks registered a massive upside key reversal despite the fact that S&P closed down for the day, although near its daily high. Even more significant is that the preceding day's bar for ticks was also an upside reversal despite the relatively weak close in S&P.

It is worth noting that most of the highest daily tick readings were comparatively low ahead of the market decline that began in July. There was never any heavy buying pressure at any time of day during this period when the overall market was setting up for a tumble.

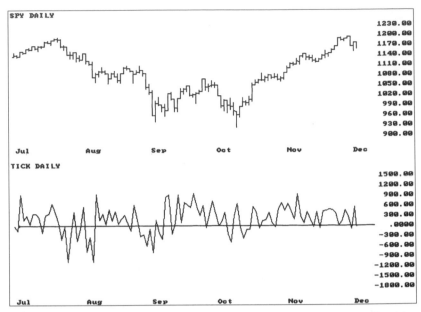

FIGURE 19-4. Daily Standard & Poor 500 Daily Cash Chart and Daily Ticks Line Chart.

The Line Chart for Ticks

Figure 19-4 shows the same cash chart for S&P plotted against the line chart joining daily closes for ticks. Across the middle of the chart is a zero baseline; closes above have a positive reading, and there is a minus reading for closes below. Normally, there should be more positive closes in a bull market and more negative closes in a bear market. Note that even during the 20 percent decline in the S&P from its August 1998 high, there were relatively few days when ticks closed with a negative reading.

The secondary low for ticks on October 8 suggested not only that the heavy weight of selling had finished but also that new money was buying. Now the bull market could resume.

Major bottoms occur so seldom that it is not practical to stay out of the market and wait for them. Nonetheless, when market conditions suggest that a general decline has run its course, you can sometimes buy stocks at excellent prices. Once you identify the possibility of an important low in the market, buy stocks that have held up well during the decline rather than the ones most beaten up. Stocks that have held up best are by far the most likely to recover soonest and most strongly and then to go on to make new highs. They are also the least likely to go down if the market has to make another test of the low. A very strong stock can quickly double or triple when coming out of a major market low, but one that is depressed may gain just a few percentage points. There may be valid fundamental reasons for its poor performance, and recovery in price may only be grudging as disappointed investors sell just to get their money back at break-even.

It is worth repeating: Buy strength, not weakness!

What Else You Need to Know

CHAPTER 20

Interest Rates

When Interest Rates Drive Stocks

It is essential to know what interest rates are doing, particularly when the stock market in general appears to be very high or very low.

Risk-free returns from Treasury bills and low-risk returns on Treasury bonds compete with expected returns from owning stocks. Therefore, when interest rates are high and especially when they are rising, it is less attractive to own stocks. Consequently, there is a shift out of stocks and into Treasury bills and bonds. Even when business conditions are good, this shift may alter the balance of supply and demand so that stocks start going down, adjusting their relative value versus the risk-free alternative. Rising interest rates raise one of the major costs of doing business, so profits may suffer. And the attractions of owning stocks suffer two blows at once.

When interest rates are rising, you must beware the saying: Don't fight the Fed! The U.S. Federal Reserve raises interest rates to fight inflation, to maintain the external value of the currency when it is under pressure, and to control the level of business activity when the economy overheats. Higher interest rates can amount to the same thing as a war on share prices. When the economy is doing well, stocks can handle a moderate rise in interest rates. In fact, a moderate rise in interest rates may provide just enough of a setback in prices to provide a buying opportunity. However, stocks can take only so much of the

Fed's medicine of raising interest rates before investors see that the relative value of stocks is out of line. Then they sell.

When interest rates are low, and particularly when they are declining, all investments except cash and Treasury bills tend to become more attractive. The builder of an apartment building requires a lower return in order to be able to pay the mortgage and make a profit. Similarly, most businesses become more active and more profitable. What is good for profits is good for stock prices. Earnings may be very depressed, and for many companies nonexistent. However, smart money starts to smell recovery before it starts. When there is no one left to sell and it is a buyer's market, low interest rates attract smart money to venture into stocks.

Bonds Versus Stocks

Figure 20-1 shows the 30-year U.S. Treasury bonds from mid-1978 to the end of 1989. When the price of bonds goes up, interest rates go down, and vice versa. The more a bond costs, the less it yields. A bond's interest rate remains constant, unlike stock dividends, which can rise or fall depending on profits.

Figure 20-2 shows the Dow Jones Industrial Average for the same period. From about 1960 to mid-1981, owning bonds or any other

FIGURE 20-1. U.S. 30-Treasury Bonds Monthly Chart, 1979–1989.

fixed-interest investment was a disaster. High inflation meant that the purchasing power of both capital and income was going down the drain. Hardly surprisingly, bonds were in a major bear market that lasted for decades.

Profits continued rising for many companies during the 1970s. Although yields on stocks were only about half what they were on bonds, stock dividends were increasing and slowly narrowing the adverse spread versus bonds. Nevertheless, most stocks went sideways despite the steady growth in their underlying value, as the chart for the Dow shows. The Dow does not show that this was a marvelous time for stock pickers and for corporate raiders. With many companies selling far below their breakup value, buying carefully selected stocks was the proverbial steal.

A major new bull market in stocks began once bonds made their eventual low in 1981. It was held back as interest rates rose again in 1984. Then stocks merely faltered. The Dow declined from a closing high of 1276 to a closing low of 1104. A decline of 13 percent is mildly uncomfortable, but it does not necessarily begin a new bear market.

When bonds were soaring in 1985 and 1986, stocks really took off. They continued their flight to much higher levels even as interest rates started heading sharply higher in 1987.

FIGURE 20-2. Dow Jones Industrial Average Monthly Chart, 1979–1989.

Eventually the conflict between rising interest rates and rising stock prices did in the stock market. The October 1987 stock market crash should not have surprised anyone aware of the potential impact of higher interest rates when facing off against the highest stock price valuations since 1929. Owning stocks during the first nine months of 1987 was an exercise in fighting the Fed if not initially, an exercise in fighting the flow of money into stocks.

When the stock market crashed, the Fed moved aggressively to lower interest rates. The bond market soared by 7 percent in a single day. Stability returned almost at once to the stock market, although it took time to resume its advance. Many people, notably the wave theorists, said the world was revisiting the Great Depression and an equivalent bear market in stocks. This was no time for that theory. The Fed was on side and so was the economy. As almost always, it was time to ask the question: What are stocks really doing? Is buying pressure or selling pressure the stronger?

With the economy still expanding, as it was not in October 1929, stocks slowly regrouped and began to build the foundation from which to recover the ground lost in the crash. In due course, the majority of stocks went on to new highs far above the 1987 peak.

Figures 20-3 and 20-4 show bonds and stocks from 1987 to 1998. Most of this time was good for stocks except for an interlude of a few

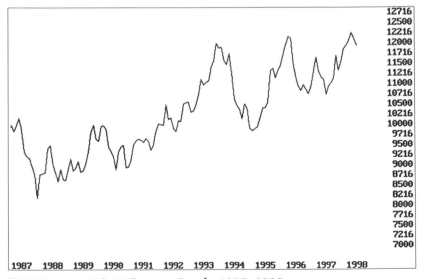

FIGURE 20-3.   U.S. 30 Treasury Bonds, 1987–1998.

FIGURE 20-4. Dow Jones Industrial Average Monthly Chart, 1987–1998.

months in the second half of 1990 and another one of about 18 months starting in early 1994. Notice how bonds sold off in 1990 and also how they nose-dived from the end of 1993 to the end of 1994. During 1994 higher interest rates kept a lid on stock prices, much as occurred during the late 1970s. Once the pressure was off, stocks could move higher again.

Cause and Effect Reverse

Popular wisdom has it that declining interest rates are invariably good for stocks. There are times when popular wisdom is wrong. Interest rates usually drive the economy and, by extension, the stock market. Nevertheless, there are times when the economy drives interest rates, and not the other way around. This reversal generally occurs when a long-term capital investment boom finally ends.

The most conspicuous and long-drawn-out example is the 15-year bear market in stocks between 1881 and 1896 that occurred in conjunction with declining interest rates. Railroads lowered the cost of transportation by 95 percent compared with the horse and cart, and they made fortunes for many of those who built and owned them. However, there was economic devastation when the economy choked on overcapacity. When the corresponding excess of debt to finance railroads imploded, economic depression followed.

Similarly, a massive capital investment boom crested in the summer of 1929. By October the very high-priced stock market collided with the knowledge that business was no longer booming. After the crash it took years for stocks to recover. Interest rates were low enough. From October 1929 to the summer of 1932, the annual rate for overnight money declined steadily until it reached a low of just one-half of one percent. The Fed was aggressively trying to expand the money supply, but there were no takers in the depressed economy. There was an extreme excess of capacity in almost every industry. Why build a new factory if the ones already built can't sell enough to make a profit?

The classic modern example of a reversal of the normal relationship between interest rates and stocks occurred in Japan after 1990. The economy crested in 1989, choking on an excess of capital investment and a boom in the price of stocks and real estate that far exceeded what happened in the United States in 1929. When the bubble burst, the economy imploded. The Japanese stock market continued to make new lows for almost a decade after the 1989 high, despite short-term interest rates below 1 percent.

The Asian crisis that began in 1997 was also caused by an excess of capital investment. The world market could not absorb all the corresponding new production. The collapse of the Asian economies laid waste the banking industry. So loans were often unavailable to finance the exports that might have kept viable factories running. So more factories went bankrupt, putting further pressure on the banks. As almost always happens when a bubble bursts, the economic downturn fed on itself. The virtuous circle turned vicious, causing immense hardship for those least able to look after themselves.

No doubt, the demise of the Japanese boom and the Asian economic collapse were to provide a marvelous opportunity to buy stocks, but only when they started to show stability and when buying pressure for stocks could be seen to have staying power. Ironically, one of the signals for buying stocks when a depression is ending is when interest rates start rising from an exceptionally low level. That shows that there is again a demand for money, which comes from people interested in buying and building things again.

Why Capital Investment Booms Go Bust

There are reasons for long-term capital investment booms, and there are also reasons why they tend to end badly. There is an economic law that the more profitable an opportunity, the more it attracts investment. In the face of competition from more modern factories, even old and established factories have to invest to stay competitive. The capital investment laws have a multiplier effect on all business activity as the workers employed building new plant spend what they earn, generating more demand in the process. In due course, however, the economic law prevails that the more investment a business opportunity attracts, the more certain it is that the resulting overinvestment will eventually make everyone's investment unprofitable. Oversupply drives down prices below the cost of production. A new upturn can begin only when enough unprofitable capacity has been retired so that demand finally catches up with supply. Reduction of capacity often occurs as a result of bankruptcies. Bankruptcies and loan defaults hurt the banks, sometimes putting them out of business too, and almost invariably leading them to cut back on new loans. The result is a further slowing of the economy as bank loans are available only to the few remaining borrowers of unqualified creditworthiness. They may not need bank loans.

This process of contraction is the creative destruction by which capitalism renews itself. The real pain passes in due course in a free economy. In a heavily regulated economy or a communist one, the cleansing process is more painful. The excesses become that much greater before the overinvestment and malinvestment collapses under its own weight. The prime example of this phenomenon is the collapse of the economies of the former Soviet Union in the 1990s after the fall of communism. The situation in Japan in the 1990s was similar, but for cultural reasons rather than political ones.

Even in a capitalist economy there is a natural tendency toward rigidity and toward malinvestment. Few governments and central banks can resist the allure of easy money and interest rates lower than economic conditions warrant. Low interest rates therefore lead to more investment than would occur if the market were left to its own devices. Artificial growth of the money supply, fueled by central bankers keen to see prosperity continue, is the cause of malinvestment.

Artificial growth of the money supply equates to inflation. It may not show up in consumer prices, but it amounts to much the same thing if it shows up as an asset inflation, such as an extreme rise in the price of stocks and real estate. Artificially plentiful money also leads to malinvestment, which is productive capacity without economic justification. That leads to destruction of capital and a decline in real incomes, regardless of whether prices rise or fall. The preceding boom begets the ensuing bust, and the implosion of a virtuous circle turns vicious.

CHAPTER 21

How to Manage Your Capital

Risk Versus Reward

Before looking at stops and how and when to sell, let's take a break to look at the challenge of capital management.

Investment in stocks should form part of an overall financial plan. Depending on your circumstances, that may mean setting up a regular savings plan or setting aside capital all at once. Either way, it means setting up a budget as you would for any business venture. As with any business, you make capital investments, in this case by buying stocks or bonds. You also need to keep a reserve of working capital. You have to provide for unforeseen expenses or for significant new opportunities, ones unforeseeable when making your initial investments.

You expect profits, of course. However, you must also prepare to accept losses as well. As when setting up a clothing store or any other business, it is inevitable that some stock has to go out on sale, and some at prices well below cost. The same thing happens in all business. No business is a one-way street to moneymaking. It is enough to make good profits overall.

Ideally, losers go out at prices near where you place the initial stop-loss (discussed in the next chapter), but even with the best planning, the occasional bad loss occurs. It is important to internalize a state of mind that accepts the fact that some losses are a cost of doing any business of any kind, in the stock market as in any other aspect of life. In the overall scheme of things that does not matter as long as there are major successes that more than offset the inevitable losses. Running profits and cutting losses should mean that some winners return huge profits, many times what you invest. You do not need many big winners to pay for the inevitable losers and to make big profits on balance.

Don't Invest All at Once

Never put a large amount of money into stocks all at once. There is hardly a more important rule than that. There is too high a risk of buying at a top, only to see the entire portfolio going down right after you buy. Statistically, the likelihood of buying at a long-term market top is small. Major tops do not happen often. Nevertheless, there is a great likelihood of buying at an intermediate top because things always look best at tops.

We have seen what happened in 1987. If you placed a large amount of money in stocks or mutual funds in August, you would have lost much of your capital at the bottom of the crash in October. From the top in August 1987 the Dow Jones Industrial Index fell from a high of 2735 to a low of 1592, a decline of 42 percent. If you invested total capital of $100,000, at the bottom you lost $42,000—42 percent of your money in just two months. That the market came back after the 1987 decline is irrelevant. It does not always come back, and, indeed, many individual stocks continued down after the crash. Murphy's Law suggests that some stocks you own will be among those that do not come back.

It is an absolute certainty that in future, there will be stock market declines similar to the one in 1987. Some will be more severe, and some will last much longer. So you don't even want to think of having all your investments going down the drain simultaneously from the top of the market.

Keep Capital in Reserve

There is a strategy for avoiding the disaster of investing all your money at or near the top of the market, and it is not simply to diversify into different stocks and stock mutual funds. They are mostly variations on the same theme. The only meaningful way to handle the risks of the stock market is to invest only a part of your capital in stocks and to hold a cash reserve. Unless there is serious inflation, which is unlikely in the United States, there is almost no risk in holding cash or cash equivalents like Treasury bills.

Buy bonds sparingly and only when they are going up (and interest rates are declining), or at least when they are relatively stable. Bonds are really worth owning only when they are in a bull market or when you need a regular income. You run the risk of tying up capital without having the flexibility of cash on hand with which to buy stocks. Buy bonds for retirement income when you are retired.

What Gerald Loeb Did

It is worth taking a leaf from the book of a great investor of the early twentieth century, Gerald Loeb. He never put at risk in stocks more than a portion of his capital, and he never bought on margin (using borrowed money). Despite his knowledge and closeness to market action, he thought there was too much risk of being wrong. He always kept substantial cash reserves, even during the roaring bull market of the 1920s. He aimed to find a small number of stocks with the potential to make very big gains. However attractive the prospects, he never invested more than a third of his money in any one stock. Then, if it went down instead of up, he had the cash and the flexibility with which to grasp new opportunities when they arose. Even more important, it was easy to take losses on the investments that failed to perform as expected. Losses never seriously dented his capital, but big gains often added to it enormously.

Loeb was delighted to put just 10 percent of his capital into one prime investment and see it double or triple in a year. In the unlikely event of losing all of that 10 percent, his overall capital was essentially unimpaired. On the other hand, tripling 10 percent of his capital gave him an annual return of 20 percent overall for the year, assuming no return at all on the balance of his capital. In his book *The Battle for Stock Market Survival,* Loeb was adamant that you must at all times maintain a cash balance so you can grasp new opportunities when they arise. That is impossible if you are always fully invested in stocks, and especially if much of your portfolio is under water.

Loeb often invested on the basis of good information, and he generally put a huge amount of money into just a few stocks at any given time. In this respect he was a precursor of Warren Buffett, intentionally not diversifying beyond what he could follow closely. He differed from Buffett, however, in that he was seldom a long-term investor.

You may never succeed in finding a single stock that triples in a year, and there is little point in looking for these stocks intentionally. The rule is that looking for long shots does not work over time. You have too high a percentage of losers, unless you are exceptionally lucky. Luck is different from probability theory. You cannot count on it with acceptable consistency as a useful component of the process of making investment decisions. Luck generally comes to people who are already doing the right things; chance follows design. Buy a stock with the potential to double within a few years and you are likely to buy the occasional one that takes off like a rocket.

Have Your Cake and Eat It Too!

Here is how the compromise of more conservative capital allocation can work when combined with buying strong stocks.

Consider, for the purpose of illustration, that you had $100,000 to invest in 1988. You bought five stocks, like Microsoft, Intel, and Coca-Cola, which you identified as technically strong and having the potential for major long-term capital gain. You invested the other half in the money market. With this division of assets, you retained a high level of liquidity, although forgoing the potential for maximum reward. Assume that there was no capital gain on your investment in the money market. Between 1988 and 1996, even assuming imperfect timing when buying, your stocks went up by six times, at an average rate of about 25 percent annually, to a 1996 value of $300,000. (This was a rate of gain at the lower end of what actually happened in the strongest stocks.) The total value of your entire portfolio rose over the eight years to $350,000. It rose at an average annual rate of about 19 percent. That is about in line with what the major stock indexes did in the same period and about what the best money managers achieved with their entire portfolios invested in stocks. In the meantime, you had only half your capital at risk.

Now assume the worst case, that you invested your capital at the start of a bear market. Instead of going up, the stocks in your portfolio halved in value, declining from $50,000 to $25,000. That is unlikely to happen using market timing techniques. Nevertheless, make the assumption. You might have selected stocks badly. You might have had a market accident that wiped out one or two of your stocks completely. You might have failed to find a single worthwhile winner.

Invested only half in stocks and half in the money market, the total value of the portfolio is still $75,000, comprising $50,000 in the money market and a stock portfolio worth $25,000. The overall portfolio value has sustained a loss of 25 percent, despite the very poor performance of the stocks. With $50,000 in the money market, you still have in hand money for a rainy day and a treasure chest with which to buy more stocks when the market starts going up again.

Routine Retracements and More Serious Ones

The next chapter discusses the stops that cut a loss when a stock stumbles as soon as you buy it. If the stock falls back by more than a routine retracement, you get out. That means defining what is or is not routine. Then you have to build into your capital management plan an allowance for the certainty that some stocks fail to perform as expected and have to be sold out at a loss. Depending on the volatility of a stock, you have to allow for fluctuations against you of at least 10 percent of the price you pay, but generally not more than 30 percent. A standard budget to allow for a retracement in a major stock should be about 15 percent.

If you invest $100,000 all at once, the chances are that you will be budgeting for stop losses that together put about $15,000 at risk. You have to assume the worst case: that every one of your selections is stopped out. If your total capital is $100,000, that is quite a serious loss. If you do not use a stop and have no mechanism for selling out of losing stocks, your loss could theoretically consume all of your capital. On the other hand, if you start with total capital of $100,000 and initially invest only $30,000, perhaps $10,000 in each of three stocks, you are likely to incur a risk of losing $4500 in the event that all of the three investments fail. That represents 15 percent of the $30,000 actually invested out of your $100,000 capital. A loss of that amount should not impair your ability to come back at the market with complete peace of mind.

Once the stocks you buy start going up, then you can venture a little more money into one or two more stocks. Ideally, you should be working with profits, incurring risks no greater than would put you back to the amount of money you started with. Once you get ahead substantially, you can tolerate greater fluctuations and truly live by the maxim of letting profits run.

Give Winners Room to Breathe

There has to be a trade-off between giving a stock room to breathe and living through a huge reversal. Any fluctuation back to an identifiable previous low, plus a small allowance for aberrations, may be normal backing and filling. All investments fluctuate and must be allowed to do so, but only within reason. Allowing stocks less room to fluctuate than 10 or 15 percent before you dump them is a strategy that incurs many unnecessary and debilitating losses. However, giving a stock too much room to fluctuate makes recovery difficult. Remember that it takes a 100 percent gain to recover from a 50 percent loss.

The mutual fund industry is correct insofar as it advises investors to accept the fact that stocks can go down as well as up (although they neglect to tell you anything about the difference between acceptable and unacceptable fluctuations). There is no getting around the challenge that any stock may set back quite a lot without violating a long-term uptrend. You have to accept that it is impossible to invest for gains of 100 percent or more in the long term without making allowances for as much as 30-percent setbacks on the way. Under normal circumstances in a bull market few stocks in your portfolio should all retrace simultaneously by so much. Nevertheless, that can and does sometimes happen. You must prepare for the real possibility of it happening by not going in too deep all at once.

Don't Average Down!

Logically, you might want to buy more of a good stock if it goes down, not throw in the towel. In the jargon of the industry this is called "averaging down." The mutual fund industry constantly recommends this approach to investing on the grounds that you cannot expect to time the market. Since, or so they maintain, the long-term direction of stock is always upward, averaging down means that you make more money in the long run.

For all practical purposes, averaging down is a loser-play. This logic is absolutely not recommended because of the risk of doubling a loss rather than doubling a profit.

Remember the futures trader's adage: Never add to a losing position! It seldom pays to depart from the principle of running profits and cutting losses. Buy more of a stock that is making money, not one that is losing.

When you buy a stock, ideally, it should go up right away. Realistically, that happens only about half the time. Sometimes you have to be patient. Capital management is also a function of patience. Even the strongest bull markets falter and sometimes fluctuate violently.

Think Positively in a Bull Market

Sometimes, it is fairly clear that the stock market is going up and that you have a solidly based bull market. Then you can be a little more venturesome than at times when there is ambiguity. You might go to as much as 75 percent or so of your money in stocks. Nevertheless, you still need to maintain a cash reserve. You don't want to find yourself living through a normal setback only to find that you could not buy more stock even if you wanted to, but on the contrary, find yourself pressed by a margin call.

Margin is the money a broker will lend you to buy more stocks than you can pay for outright. You can normally borrow half the cost of stock you buy. If the stock goes down instead of up, the broker will call for more money if the loan exceeds 60 percent of the value of the stock. You can meet a margin call either by paying in more money or by selling stock. Selling stock may be an exercise in selling out at the worst possible time so that you lose money even though you are right on the stock.

When you identify a bull market and you see a stock going up, think positively. It is logical to ask the question: If I would like to own a stock, why don't I? If you see a Microsoft, Intel, or a Coca-Cola, it is not logical to wish you owned it and not do something about it. The chances are that if the stock looks as if it is going up, then it will go higher still. Don't just lament the lost opportunity and do nothing about it.

Ideally, you should look for a logical place, an entry signal to buy after a retracement. If the stock is really strong, then it is likely better to spoil yourself by just going ahead and buying a very small number of shares rather than not buying it at all. If you have a $100,000 account, it is not too serious to find $5000 to buy a strong stock right away, even without an entry signal. You just don't want to have several impulse buys on the go all at once that are not making money.

Think Defensively in a Bear Market

The other side of this coin is that you must be prepared to bite the bullet in a stock going against you. If you wish you didn't own a stock because it never stops going down, then sell it. As a rule, it practically never pays to hold a stock for recovery when the general trend for stocks is down. The probabilities are that a loss will become greater. The bigger the loss, the greater the likelihood of it becoming bigger still. In the event of a rally, you may be tempted to hang on only to see the stock fall below the level where it first started troubling you. It is better to live by the saying *first loss is best loss.* Like a toothache, a brief period of suffering soon ends once you get rid of the bad tooth. Then you can make new decisions objectively.

Remember the dynamics of a bear market. Once a bear market becomes entrenched, buyers hold off in anticipation of lower prices. More and more investors want to cash in their profits while they still have them, and they are relentless sellers. Those who bought stocks with borrowed money have to sell because their market value no longer supports the loans taken out to buy them. As prices sink lower, despair becomes the counterpart of the previous enthusiasm, and selling pressure swamps buying power.

It is relatively easy to live through a moderate decline of 10 or 20 percent, or through a decline of short duration like the crash of 1987. However, the normality of bear markets is that they are a slow and grinding process, and that is painful to endure. Inexorably declining stock prices lead to inexorably rising desperation. Mutual funds experience net outflows of money instead of net inflows. So mutual fund managers sell stock to meet redemptions, and their stock sales drive prices ever lower. A bear market creates a vicious circle. You absolutely do not want to be invested in stocks during a full-fledged bear market.

The upside of bear markets is that eventually they provide the opportunity to buy the best stocks at wonderful prices. Only those who have cash can profit from that opportunity. Plan to be one of them.

Separate Income from Capital

It used to be that there was income and there was capital. You could spend income, but it was a cardinal sin to spend capital. Spending capital was like eating your seed corn for the next crop. So it was a cardinal sin to live off capital. This approach is still valid.

Reality for pension funds, for most family trusts, and for many other investors is that people need income to live on. The capital and income returns from investment should therefore be separated. It is, of course, true that you can draw off money from either capital or income. The staff of life stands better when you live on income and leave capital to do its work. When the perspective is for retirement in years ahead, then the bias can be toward capital gains. When you need to increase income, then look for higher-yielding stocks that also have the potential for capital gain. When personal or general economic circumstances warrant, shift some money out of lower-yielding stocks and into bonds and higher-yielding stocks, preferably selling weaker stocks to do so, rather than selling winners. You may not make superior capital gains in higher-yielding stocks and bonds, but the risk of losing either capital or income is generally lower. It happens surprisingly often that higher-yielding stocks also make superior capital gains, so you can sometimes have it both ways, often with lower risk.

If you plan to supplement income with realized capital gains, the result may be that you find yourself going through a time when there are no capital gains. Then you lose both ways, selling the capital that should be generating income. That is an exercise in killing the goose that lays the golden eggs.

Capital Management Summary

Here is a summary of the main points to remember when bringing decisions to buy or sell together with the amount of money available to do it. The list includes points already discussed as well as some new ones that can be handled in point form.

1. It is too risky to put a large amount of capital all at once into stocks, or into any other form of long-term investment. Start small and add to your winners while weeding out your losers. Put another way, fools and their money are soon parted.

   It can be very difficult psychologically to sell out an individual stock, let alone a major portfolio of stocks (or bonds), when your investments are hopelessly under water.

2. Keep a cash reserve. However favorable the market conditions and however well your stocks are acting, there will always be rainy days when you need cash for something else. Also, there will always be new and better opportunities for which you need money.

3. Do not buy too many different stocks. It is not necessary to diversify by owning, either directly or through a mutual fund, a large number of different stocks. Aimless diversification merely increases the likelihood of investing in fewer great stocks. That is the downfall of many mutual funds. Real diversification involves diversification between entirely different asset classes, between stocks and bonds or cash equivalents like Treasury bills and the money market.

   Warren Buffett achieved success for Berkshire Hathaway by investing huge amounts of money in a relatively small handful of stocks. It can be enough, even for someone investing tens of millions of dollars, to own as few as a half dozen prime stocks as long as the market in them is reasonably liquid.

4. Run your profits and cut your losses! There is no way to put it better than to repeat this old chestnut.

5. Responsible capital management requires that you sell when the technical case for owning an individual stock, or for the market generally, is no longer favorable. It is infinitely easier to accept losses when they are small, when they represent a manageable proportion of your portfolio. Then you have the means to come back at the market again, with both cash and peace of mind. Remember how much money you can make when you are right!

6. Do not trust a mutual fund to preserve your valuable savings during a bear market.

Remember what the fund managers themselves say: "*We are not market timers . . . It's not our job to sell out during a bear market. We are always more or less fully invested all the time . . .*" Remember what they have in fact done in sector-specific funds they manage during bear markets in those sectors.

7. During a general bear market, put your money into cash equivalents like Treasury bills until the storm blows over. The return always seems inadequate, but unless you are among the few prepared to sell stocks short, you are only looking for a parking place. The alternative, investing for the long-term and staying in stocks during a bear market, is to go down with the ship.

8. International investment may well *not* constitute diversification.

   The world economy is increasingly interdependent. The United States has the world's strongest and most open economy, and for the most part, the best investment opportunities. In addition, you can keep track of what your stocks are doing. International diversification may appear attractive. Nevertheless, there are more companies with a growth rate of 50 percent or higher in the United States than there are in all the rest of the world put together. Weaker economies can catch cold without infecting the United States. When the United States catches cold, other economies may get double pneumonia.

9. Don't be afraid to come back to the stock market after taking a bad loss or when all about you is doom and gloom.

10. Separate capital from income.

    Think in terms of spending income, if you want, or reinvesting it. Selling capital to live on or, worse, borrowing against your capital to live on may mean that you have neither capital nor income. Living off capital is like gambling with the rent money. You may be able to do it very successfully for a time. In bad times, however, the pressure to make money may guarantee that you lose it. The futures trader has a valuable saying: You can't trade scared money! Trying to find surefire winners because you need to make money virtually guarantees that you will in fact buy losers, not winners.

Capital management is an essential component of the investment business. You must buy stocks when it is timely to do so, after working out how much you can sensibly afford to buy, given that the investment may not be successful. You must sell stocks when it is timely to do so, bearing in mind the duty to conserve capital for the long term. In sum, you must manage your capital responsibly, as if it were an independent business.

The next two chapters discuss how to distinguish between setbacks that are acceptable and those that are not, and how to use stops to protect your capital.

CHAPTER 22

Protect Capital with a Stop-Loss

The Initial Protective Stop (IPS)

This chapter discusses one of the most important challenges facing the stock trader: stops—starting with the *initial protective stop* (IPS).

The stop, or the *stop-loss,* as it is often called, serves to limit your loss if a stock that you buy goes down instead of up. Say that you buy a stock at $10. You decide that you are prepared to lose $2. Then you prefer to sell and start again rather than ride the stock down to $5, or however much more it may drop than the $2 allowance for which you budget. The stop-loss provides the means of protecting your capital from ruinous losses. Remember that it takes a gain of 100 percent to recover from a 50 percent loss, but it takes a gain of only 25 percent to recover from a loss of 20 percent.

You can also use stops to protect profits when a stock goes up. This is the *trailing protective stop* (TPS), discussed in the next chapter. Say you buy that stock at $10 and it goes up to $20. Then you fear that it might make a round trip back to what you paid for it. You enter a TPS to protect some profit, leaving the stock room to move, and let the profit run so that it may double again. You might place the TPS at $15. Then you protect a profit of $5 rather than give back all of the $10 profit, or worse, see a profit turn to a loss.

Why You Need a Stop

Always place an IPS as soon as you buy a stock. If you do not know where to place the stop, then you should perhaps not buy the stock at all, or you should buy only a very small number of shares to start with. Capital conservation requires putting a handle on potential losses, if only for disaster insurance. Counting gains, otherwise known as counting chickens before they are hatched, does not, by any means, always work. You cannot count on it working. You can expect the best only if you prepare for the worst. Murphy's Law works often enough without asking for the additional trouble of inviting a bad loss that you cannot afford to take.

As discussed in the previous chapter, you might think that you should buy more of a good stock when it retraces to a better price than you paid initially. This logic proves wrong such a high percentage of the time that, for all practical purposes, you should discard it totally.

If you buy two stocks and one goes up and the other down, buy more of the one that goes up, not the one that you can buy cheaper. The first is what winners do. The second is a standard loser-play.

Apart from the practical problem of risking a doubled loss when doubling up on a loser, there is another problem. Psychologically, it is much more difficult to take a big loss than it is to take a small one. Even under the best of circumstances, when you think you have the best possible information, there will be times when you miss some vital piece of the jigsaw puzzle. Many a stock that looks great goes down instead of up. Sometimes there may be nothing wrong with the company or its stock. It is just that the stock has become too expensive and its high price attracts more sellers than buyers. Sometimes you inadvertently find a stock like Digital Equipment that never stops going down once corporate business problems and bad technical action become entrenched. Even in normal times, there are many Digitals. In a full-fledged bear market, most stocks are Digitals.

How to Set the Initial Protective Stop

Some successful stock traders simply allow a stock to retrace by 10 percent or so and no more. If it goes down that much, they sell the stock and try again. This is better than averaging down, for it imposes a discipline that prevents bad losses. However, it is better to place stops on the basis of what constitutes an acceptable technical retracement.

As long as a stock remains above the technical formation that activated the initial entry, the probabilities remain favorable. Any retracement is likely no more than a routine consolidation, even if the price goes all the way back to test the low. If the price level below the entry formation is violated, it means that the probabilities in favor of the stock going up have dissipated—at least for now. It is probably better to sell the stock and stand aside, or to look for another one performing better. Many investors find it very difficult to be disciplined about selling a loser, but there is consolation. Remember how much money you can make when you are right!

The previous chapter emphasized the importance of not putting a large amount of money into the market all at once in case you find yourself inadvertently buying at the top of the market. The same principle applies to buying any individual stock. You have to ask the question: What am I going to do if the stock fails to meet my expectations? Placing the stop is half of the answer. Being prepared to accept the outcome in the event the stop is hit is the other half.

There is always a small risk of a sudden lunge beyond your stop level before your stop is hit, so that you get a much worse price than you expect. Most of the time you can expect to be filled near your designated stop price. So you know before you buy the stock approximately how much money you are budgeting in the event that the stock's performance fails to work out as expected. You can see the range of the market action that leads you to buy the stock and identify the bottom of that range. Measure the distance between your buying price and the bottom of the range and you can see how much to allow for an acceptable fluctuation, plus a small allowance for aberrations. Now you can budget for an acceptable loss per share in the event that the stock falls instead of going up.

Then you have to internalize psychologically the prospect that you may lose money instead of making a profit. If you prepare yourself for losers, the winners will look after themselves.

The IPS in Practice

In practice, the best way to buy a stock is to have the monthly, weekly, and daily charts all lining up, as discussed in Chapter 23. Assume a decision on the basis of the monthly chart to buy Wal-Mart Stores at the end of October 1993. As it happens, you pull the trigger at the beginning of November when the actual entry comes through (Figure 22-1). Then you can place a stop under the formation that justifies the decision to buy. When taking a long-term view, the low dictated by the *monthly* chart is the one that you do not want to see exceeded. Occasionally, you have the monthly, weekly, and daily charts all dictating the same place for the stop.

There were some reasons not to buy WMT. They included a negative reading for MACD and a distinctly lackluster pattern for OBV. Nevertheless, there were also some positive indications that this might be the time to buy a stock that had previously done so well and might get going again soon. The stock had come back to its rising 40-month moving average, and stochastics had reached a maximum oversold reading. That is often an excellent place to buy when the stock turns up again. Even if you are wrong, there is a wonderful reward-to-risk ratio, and the stop is normally very manageable. In addition, there was a

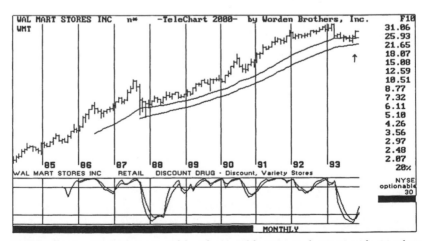

FIGURE 22–1. Wal-Mart Monthly Chart, with 25- and 40-Month Moving Averages and Stochastics.

superb double monthly upside reversal, although one where the second low was lower than the first.

Assume that you buy WMT at $28.25 on November 11, using the daily chart to pull the trigger (Figure 22-2). The low for the retracement on the monthly chart from which the stock rebounded was at $23. Any penetration of the $23 level suggests at best that the stock may not go up after all. It may be going into a trading range, or it may start a more serious decline, possibly even toward the 1990 low at $12.50. If the recent low is exceeded, you are flying blind as far as the downside risk is concerned.

A stop at $22.75, under the monthly low, guarantees a minimum loss of $5.50 per share, or about 20 percent of your money invested in this stock. That might seem like a nasty loss relative to the value of the investment, and it would be hard to take if you put into Wal-Mart all of your available capital. After all, a loss of 20 percent is as much as many people make in profit in a good year in a bull market. On the other hand, if the stock did well, it could advance by $5.50 per share in a month or two. At $28.25 the stock is down from $34 at its high, and the decline down to $23 could be enough of a correction. Add the amplitude of the correction from $34 down to $23, or $11, to the high and you have a potential target for the stock of $45. So you risk $5.50 versus

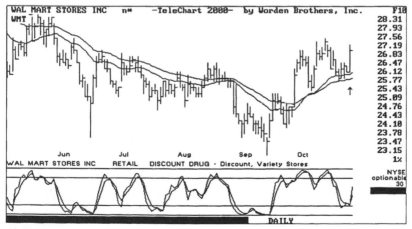

FIGURE 22-2. Wal-Mart Daily Chart, with 25- and 40-Day Moving Averages and Stochastics.

a visible potential of $16.75, and probably much more if the stock keeps on going. Not a bad proposition at all, but you cannot be complacent. You still need a stop.

For the longer term the speed of the moving averages from 1990 suggests that the stock has been advancing at a rate that triples the price in three years. Continuation of that rate of advance could take the stock up again by a further three times from the recent low of $23. Therefore, buying Wal-Mart at $28.25 for a potential advance in three years to $69 amply justifies risking a loss of $5.50 per share. Risking $5.50 per share is nothing compared with risking $14.50 per share down to the 1990 low. That represents a loss of 54 percent of your investment, not just 20 percent. You can reasonably expect to find many stocks that will recover a 20 percent loss quite soon. Finding a stock that will more than double within a reasonable time so as to recover a 50 percent loss is a much more substantial challenge.

So you buy Wal-Mart at $28.25, investing, for the sake of argument, 10 percent of your available capital. If the stock performs as expected over the long term and goes to $69, you make a gain of 144 percent over the three years, or almost 2.5 times your money. That gain alone would lift the value of the entire portfolio by almost 14 percent. If the stop is hit and you sell out at $22.75, the overall loss for the portfolio is less than 2 percent. The ratio of reward to risk is very good, and the risk justifies the investment.

When you buy Wal-Mart at $28.25, the broker enters the stop-loss order to sell if the stock goes down to $22.75. If the stock hits that price, it is automatically sold at the best price available at the time. The stop is placed on a "good-till-canceled" (GTC) basis and remains in force until one of two things happens: Either you are sold out or you cancel the stop. The protection of your investment in this stock is in place. Now you have no need to agonize over what to do if the stock starts slipping. You have quantified the risk that you are prepared to take and have budgeted for the potential loss as a routine cost of doing business. You know for certain that some investments just do not work, but in advance you never know which. This may be one of them. You also know that on balance, the gains should far exceed the losses. In choppy market conditions, you may have a fair number of stocks sold out at the stop-loss point, but in a strong bull market you should lose very few.

You may not sell a stock on a stop-loss order at exactly the designated price. There is always a spread between buying prices and selling prices, so in practice, you are likely to be filled at a tick or two below the designated price. In an active stock like Wal-Mart and under normal market conditions, you are likely to be filled on the stop order at $22.75 or $22.62.

That cost of doing business pales beside the risk of carrying WMT down by an unquantified amount below $20. In the event of bad news or a sharp general decline in the market, it can happen that you sell out a stock at a price far below your stop. If WMT suddenly announced a loss instead of an expected profit, the stock might open trading one day at $18, rather than near the designated stop price of $22.75. When the stock trades through a stop price, that amounts to the same thing as hitting the price. You still sell out at the best available price, however low. While this may seem like a disaster, the rule is that the worse a stock does, the worse it is likely to continue doing. A sudden plunge in price almost invariably occurs for a good reason. It is far more likely that the decline will continue than that the stock will recover quickly. There are, of course, exceptions, and many stocks open sharply lower only to recover smartly. On balance, however, it is better to live with the market saying: First loss, best loss.

The Weekly and Daily Charts for Stops

Sometimes you have to look to the daily or the weekly charts for stops. This happens when a stock has gone a long way and particularly when a stock is overbought by such measures as distance above the moving averages. Sometimes the level for a stop dictated by the monthly chart is simply too rich. So you have little choice other than to find a better place. When a stock is moving very fast, stops dictated by the daily chart are almost invariably better than ones dictated by the monthly chart.

The daily chart for WMT shows our entry above an identifiable consolidation, with a corresponding identifiable low at $25.75 on October 27. There is also the earlier identifiable low on the daily chart from two weeks before at $25.37. You could consider placing a very tight stop at, say, $24.75. That would mean placing the stop below two identifiable lows, with the second one so close adding weight to the validity of the stop level. In this instance, our choice would be to use the monthly low as the stop point. We know that we really like this stock and do not want to part with it unless something is truly going wrong. Note that the daily chart as printed appears to suggest quite a wide range in price. That is partly the result of price expanding to fill the available space on the screen. The monthly chart shows that a decline back to the $23 level is really noise on the line in the bigger picture for this stop.

As it happens, Wal-Mart hit $22.75 in May 1994, and the stock was sold out accordingly. In the event, this was a reasonably good thing to happen. Figure 22-3 shows how market action unfolded over the next three years. Although the stock eventually rebounded back to the original buying price and went half a dollar higher in July 1995, market action showed that this was no longer a prime stock to own for the time being. The 25- and 40-month moving averages rolled over, and at best, the stock was now in a sideways market. At worst, there was the prospect of WMT going into an extended bear market. In this case, the stock went only a little below $20 during its extended consolidation. That is not the point. The stop averted three years of agony. If you kept the stock, the result, at least on paper, was a temporary loss of several dollars more than the level where the stop was set, and there was no meaningful recovery for a long time. A paper loss is still a real one. So

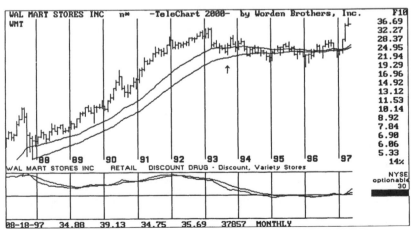

FIGURE 22-3. Wal-Mart Monthly Chart, with 25- and 40-Month Moving Averages and MACD.

the decline in the value of your investments, even when only tempo-rary, still represents a real loss at the time. It also represents a loss that can become greater just as readily as it can turn back toward a profit.

Mind Good-Till-Canceled Stops

There is an important additional point to mention about stops. A good-till-canceled stop means what it says. It remains in force either until the market fills your order or until you cancel it. You can end up selling a second time a stock that you sold a long time ago. Then you have to buy the stock back in order to close out your inadvertent short position. If you always use stops, it is easy to remember to cancel them when you sell a stock in the ordinary way.

Do not underrate the importance of using an IPS. Some investors have the saying: No one ever went broke taking a profit! That saying is a loser-play. It should be reversed: You never go broke taking a loss—when you can afford to take it! Let your profits run and make some huge profits that pay for the inevitable mistakes and for the losses in stocks that just do not perform as originally expected. With good capi-tal management and a good system for buying stocks, you can take many small losses before they make a serious dent on the value of your portfolio.

CHAPTER 23

Stops for Protecting Profits

The Trailing Protective Stop (TPS)

The trailing protective stop (TPS) moves up behind the price when a stock starts to make money. The challenge is to try to stay in strong stocks like Intel or Microsoft but to get out of a Digital or a Micron Technology before you lose all your profit, or worse, see a profit turn to a loss.

There is always a conflict between giving a stock too much room to move and too little, given that all markets fluctuate, moving erratically from one level to the next. It would be easy to know what to do if these fluctuations were less erratic. You could simply sell at the top of a band and buy at the bottom. However, the best stocks go up more than you expect, often charging through expected upper limits. So trying to sell high frequently gets you out of the strongest stocks prematurely. Then you have to pay a higher price to get back in than you sell for, if you ever do buy back. A very strong stock may also fluctuate significantly. It is by no means unusual for a stock to set back by 30 percent without damaging an uptrend. Once you get out, the strongest stock often seems the most difficult to buy back, although that is often the best one to buy. So you want to stay with strong stocks and sell them only when serious damage is done to an uptrend.

On the other hand, the weakest stocks often go up less and go down more than you expect. They may not reach overbought objectives, so the discipline of selling high may lead to selling your best stocks and keeping the mediocre ones. Here too, the TPS does its job. It is far more likely that a structurally weak or mediocre stock will be kicked out than that you lose a high flyer.

In sum, there is always the dilemma that if you give a stock too much room to move, you give back all the profit if the stock goes into a significant swoon or changes direction altogether. On the other hand, if you give a stock too little room to move, you never stay in the market for the major moves that make investment really worthwhile in the long term.

Fortunately, there is a compromise available between these two unsatisfactory extremes, and it is sufficiently reliable to balance the probabilities in the investor's favor. Logical chart-point stops placed consistently will see you through in the long run. As we saw in Chapter 8, a bull market should make successively higher highs and successively higher lows. When this pattern is violated, you have to question whether there still is a bull market. The trailing protective stop establishes the basis for identifying unacceptable fluctuations, and serves as the mechanism for setting the stop that sells out a stock accordingly.

There are other means of selling high and of selling a stock showing signs of running out of steam. In any case, the TPS, as disaster insurance, is not a bad compromise when used as the only mechanism for selling a stock that starts to act poorly.

There are three different kinds of trailing protective stops. No single one applies all the time because of the wide variety of different market action that can occur.

Note that stop price levels should always be adjusted by downward rounding so that they are placed slightly below round numbers, particularly below obvious ones such as $10 or $20. (The reverse applies when protecting a short position; the stop is placed *above* an obvious round number.)

1. The Higher-Low Stop

The higher-low stop follows the upward zigzag of a bull market on the monthly chart, using the principles for bull market designation described in Chapter 8. When using this as the only means to sell a stock, it is generally better to act when the monthly *closing* price exceeds the stop point. There are often aberrational plunges that wash out weak holders. Then price comes back and resumes its advance. When market conditions are generally favorable, you lose fewer great stocks by making a decision just once a month than you do by inviting the market to hit a stop in the course of a random intramonth fluctuation.

To find the chart-point for the higher-low stop, identify the last or the highest *intramonth* low on the monthly line chart where there is also an upturn in the monthly price line. The intramonth low within that consolidation may occur a month or two earlier than the month with the lowest closing price. Switch back to the monthly bar chart and find the intramonth low within the formation in case it is not the same as the one generating an upturn on the single-line chart.

Having found the intramonth low before the last monthly upturn, calculate a 5 percent allowance for an aberrational setback. This is the level for the higher-low stop. Sell out if the stock closes at the end of any month below the stop price level.

Table 23-1 shows an example of the calculation.

It always seems like a lot to give back $21.50 a share or more when you use this means of selling a stock. Bear in mind, however, that you own the stock in the expectation of it going eventually to $150 or $200. If you bought it at $45, it is not serious to give back 25 percent or so from its best level reached. The point is that the probabilities favor upward continuation once a consolidation is completed unless market action shows that something may be going wrong with that assumption. When you own a stock selling for more than you paid for it, let the price fluctuate as it may during the course of the month. The higher-low stop will not protect you from a big sell-off during the course of the

TABLE 23-1

Current price	$109.00
Closing price low (before the last upturn in the monthly price line)	$100.00
Intramonth low during the retracement	$ 92.50
5-percent allowance from $92.50	$ 4.60
Stop price (rounded)	$ 87.50

month. However, sometimes other indicators may tell you that you no longer want to own a particular stock, or to be in the market at all.

The Higher-Low Stop in Practice

The monthly line chart for Microsoft shows a stock that you might think you should always want to own (Figure 23-1). That perception is partly a function of how any chart looks when the price goes a long way from the bottom left-hand corner of the chart to the top right-hand corner. The chart makes you see through rose-colored spectacles the fluctuations and sideways patterns on the way. There were times when the stock rested for quite a long time. Then you could just as well have been out of the stock and looking for a time to buy as when it showed signs of waking up again.

Assume that you bought Microsoft at $4.40 in September 1989, when the stock surged to a new high after going sideways for more than two years.

Place an IPS at $3.20. This stop allows for much more leeway than many traders allow. In this case, it is 27 percent of the value of the stock. However, the breakout is powerful. So a retracement, if it happens, is more likely to provide a buying opportunity than to suggest that the purchase was a mistake.

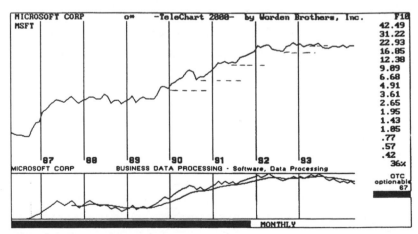

FIGURE 23-1. Microsoft Monthly Line Chart, with Higher-Low Stop Levels and On Balance Volume.

This entry also proves the adage that the more powerful the signal, the more likely the stock is to go to a profit right away. By extension, the more powerful the signal, the less likely it is that there will be a significant retracement, even though the disaster-insurance stop has to be placed distant.

Table 23-2 below shows how the higher-low stop moves as the price of Microsoft rises. Figure 23-2 shows the monthly bars, unlike Figure 23-1, which joins the monthly closing prices. The bottom of the bar represents the formation low in the table.

There were several occasions during the course of the advance from September 1989 to August 1993 when Microsoft retraced intramonth by more than 10 percent. The retracement in August 1990 was a seemingly huge 37 percent, from $8.98 to $5.65. Yet this big retracement did nothing to damage the powerful uptrend. A stock on its way to doubling, tripling, or more often has retracements of about a third or so without reversing direction.

Just because you sold out the stock in August 1993 does not mean that this was the end of opportunities to own this stock. There were opportunities to buy it back around May of 1994 when it showed that it was likely to get going again.

The remedy for handling the volatility that accompanies such a powerful stock is not to pass on buying it. It is to invest only as much as your financial and psychological resources can handle when the fluctuations are against you.

TABLE 23-2

Date	Monthly Close	Formation Low	5% Allowance	Stop Price
11/3/89	4.35	3.84	0.19	$ 3.65
9/5/90	6.56	5.65	0.28	$ 5.37
5/6/91	11.43	10.34	0.52	$ 9.82
5/4/92	19.01	17.84	0.90	$16.94
12/31/92	21.34	21.31	1.07	$20.24
8/2/93	Stopped out at $18.19			

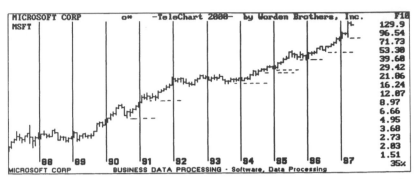

FIGURE 23-2. Microsoft Monthly Bar Chart, with Price Reversal Stop Levels.

2. The Price Reversal Stop

Place a stop just under the most recent monthly closing price reversal or high-low reversal. This stop is given to the broker on a good-till-canceled basis, unlike the trend reversal stop. The stop is activated any time the price of the stock hits the price. Because of the reliability of support under monthly reversals, you can count on stops at that level doing their job at any time during the month. If the stop level is penetrated, it could mean that there will be a further substantial and rapid decline.

Sometimes a stock is too strong to make identifiable lows on the monthly line chart that are a remotely reasonable distance from the previous low. When a stock has run away to a double without an intervening monthly correction, you do not want to leave a stop so far below the market that you give back all the profit. Particularly in junior and more speculative issues, there is a great risk that what goes up can go all the way back down again.

The theory of reversals is that you are entitled to assume that market action at the low has shaken out the stock in weak hands. Now with the stock in stronger hands, the price should stay above the level where it washed out and turned up again. (Completion of an upside reversal often provides a prime buying opportunity, with the expectation that the price will continue higher right away.)

When a stock is moving fast, the upside reversal stop is also useful with upside reversals on the weekly and daily charts, particularly when the upside reversal is also a key reversal.

The Price Reversal Stop in Practice

Table 23-3 shows how the price reversal stop moves on Figure 23-2, as the price of Microsoft rises.

It so happens that Microsoft never activated a monthly price reversal stop during the entire seven-year period covered by the above table. This is an amazing manifestation of the power of this stock.

There were two notable occasions when retracements threatened these stops. In August 1991 the price threatened the stop placed at $9.80 in April, dipping to $10.10 after reaching for a high at $13.07 in May. The July retracement penetrated below the bottom of the upside reversal, but price held above the pivotal $10 level.

In January 1996 the price retraced just below the $40 level and tested the stop placed at $39.75 in October. Again, the round number provided pivotal support, although not without a tiny blip below. This occurred after the price had reached for a high of $51.69 in November.

3. The Trendline Stop

The trendline stop is more subjective than the two previous stops. Unfortunately, of course, there is no totally objective means of buying and selling that beats working within the guidelines of good logic. It is worth recalling the saying of Paul Getty, once the richest man in the world, that you have to be right in business only 50 percent of the time

TABLE 23-3

Date	Monthly Close	Formation Low	5% Allowance	Stop Price
11/2/90	7.23	$ 5.95	0.10	$ 5.85
4/5/91	12.24	$10.34	0.55	$ 9.80
8/31/93	18.78	$17.60	0.35	$17.25
8/1/94	26.69	$23.44	0.20	$26.75
3/1/95	31.63	$29.13	0.38	$28.75
10/27/95	50.00	$40.19	0.44	$39.75
8/12/96	62.63	$53.75	1.00	$52.75
7/18/97	140.50	$87.50	1.00	$86.50

in order to be successful. When Paul Getty was right, he did very well indeed.

The trendline stop comes in three flavors, each requiring additional homework when the alarm goes off:

1. Sell on a monthly close below a long-term uptrend on the monthly or weekly chart.

2. When, during the course of the month, a stock has violated a long-term uptrend on the monthly chart, refer to the weekly and daily charts to consider an intramonth exit.

3. When a stock is extremely overextended and you suspect a buying climax, use trendlines on the weekly chart to identify when to get out. Sometimes action on the daily chart, such as islands suggesting exhaustion tops, may show a bubble bursting.

Find the best uptrend line available, generally the one drawn on the bar chart and joining lows at the extremity of each retracement, not closes.

In the early stages of a bull market, it can be difficult to assume any uptrend line. Generally, it takes at least six to eight months from an identifiable low before there is a reasonable likelihood of identifying a second low that will stand the test of time. Despite the many and obvious conflicts when trying to identify a trendline that should contain retracements, this approach often provides the least imperfect means of judging when to protect profits and avoid losses.

When market action is ambiguous, look at the indicators on the weekly and daily charts. You might, for example, want to sell a stock without delay if there is downward gapping or if there is a clear pattern of numerous adverse reversals on the daily chart. On the other hand, you might want to stay in a stock that is oversold on the daily chart when price on the monthly chart is at or near the uptrend line.

The Trendline Stop in Practice

Figure 23-3 shows the monthly bar chart for Microsoft with the two best available trendlines. By mid-1992 there was a superb three-point trendline based on points of contact on retracements (or almost for the third, in 1991). Soon after validation with the third upturn, the price of the stock proceeded to wander through the uptrend line. There was no dramatic sell-off as there often is when a trendline is broken. However, the break signified that the momentum had gone out of the trend. Sure enough, the price proceeded to go sideways for a further year and a half before it resumed its climb.

It was a judgment call whether or not you moved to sell the stock after the steeper trendline was broken. There was no great advantage to owning the stock until other indicators showed that the consolidation might be ending, with renewed expectations of the price going up.

The second long-term trendline outlived the duration of the chart. The brief penetration in December 1995 led immediately to a monthly upside reversal, and the stock was on its way again.

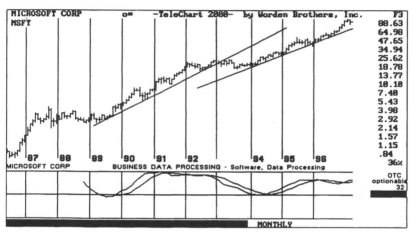

FIGURE 23-3.   Microsoft Monthly Chart, with Trendline Support Levels.

Stops When You Really Need Them

The monthly chart for Micron Technology shows the stock immensely strong in the first half of 1995 (Figure 23-4). There were many reasons, such as the bulge in OBV and known huge overvaluation to the point of absurdity, to suggest that the stock was vulnerable to a major setback.

The weekly chart allows you to draw an uptrend beginning with the low from the breakout in February 1995 at $22.75 (Figure 23-5). The August 1995 low at $55.25 is more than double the price at the February low. Although only a second point of contact, it provides a reasonable basis for assuming a valid trendline, given the prodigious strength of the stock.

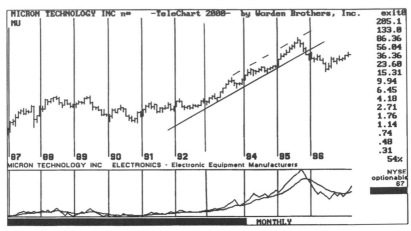

FIGURE 23–4. Micron Technology Monthly Chart, with Trendline, Channel Line, and On Balance Volume.

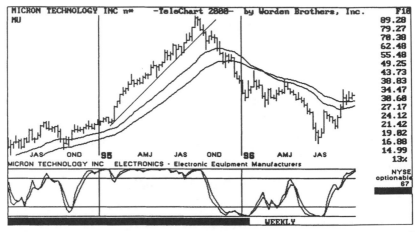

FIGURE 23–5. Micron Technology Weekly Chart, with Uptrend Line, 25- and 40-Week Moving Averages, and Stochastics.

It is worth noting the weekly upside key reversal ending on September 5, 1995. In a healthy bull market, that should signify a cleansing from the market of stock in weak hands, and then the price should continue significantly higher. In a stock seeming to many to be inordinately expensive, this action may show that short-sellers tried to knock the stock down and failed, at least for the time being. Their time perspective is often quite short when a trade goes against them, and they take a small loss quickly. In doing so, they can create an upside reversal on the daily chart. Whatever the immediate cause of the turn-around, the logical place for a tight stop is underneath the low of the weekly key reversal, at $67.50.

The daily chart shows in detail how Micron Technology began to unravel (Figure 23-6). The way to get out was to use the trendline stop in conjunction with weekly and daily price action. The stock had soared, with numerous runaway upside gaps during August and September, largely fueled by short-covering. In hindsight you can see that the final gap up in September, with the close for the day at $87.25, was an exhaustion gap. The stock went on for four more days before making a downside reversal at the very top.

The gap down on September 15, with the close at $86, is most significant. It left behind a seven-day island top. The stock fell rapidly from its high close at $94.37 to the retracement low on October 9 at $65. The next day's violent upside reversal set the stage for a failure swing. The price then fell below the 40- and 60-day moving averages, which, although still rising, were now rolling over. Once the price turned down again at the end of October, there was no longer any case for owning this stock. A sale around the $65 to $70 level might seem late in relation to where the top was, but it protected you from the decline below $20 that was to unfold over the next few months.

If you buy stocks like Micron Technology at a good price, it matters relatively little in the long run whether you get out at the equivalent of

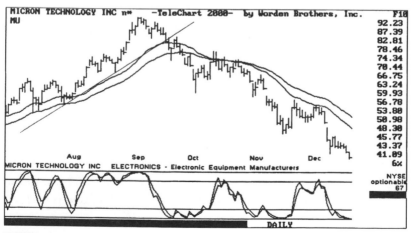

FIGURE 23–6. Micron Technology Daily Chart, with Trendline, 25- and 40-Day Moving Averages, and Stochastics.

Micron at $60 or $85. As we have said several times, perfection is impossible. The important thing is to be prepared to buy when the technicals are favorable and to sell when they turn against you. It's the declines from $95 to $20 that can kill your success, not whether you merely double your money instead of tripling it when the time comes to leave the party.

Many, many people expect a stock to go on forever, despite evidence to the contrary. Having given back one-third of the value that was once there in Micron Technology, you might want to wait until the stock returns toward its high. Remarkably, often it just does not happen that a stock goes back to its high once the back of a bull run is broken, and it did not happen in this stock. Greed and lack of discipline can all too easily allow a big profit to evaporate or turn to a loss. When the technicals turn against a stock, the probabilities turn against the justification for owning it. Staying in is gambling.

Although it is seldom advisable to sell short a stock making a spike top, it was worth knowing that many short-sellers were lying in wait for Micron Technology.

Be Prepared to Buy Back

It is essential never to regard any stock as a one-trade deal. If you sell a stock on a stop or for any other reason, then buy it back if it turns around and generates a new buy signal. There is a high probability that the stock for which you once did successful homework will deliver the goods again. Buying and selling stocks is always an imperfect art, and one of the most conspicuous imperfections is the inadvertent selling of a stock that you still want to own. Never mind! That is better than incurring the risk of staying wrongly in a Micron Technology or a Digital Equipment when the new trend is down. Whether a new buy signal comes sooner or later, it is imperative to discard the psychological difficulty involved in going back into a stock that you previously owned.

You may buy and sell a really good stock like Microsoft or Micron Technology several times over a number of years. If you have to buy back a stock for more than you sold it for, it probably means that it is going higher still. It is almost certainly a better buy than the stock that appears to be just starting to move up. Say it again: Buy the strongest stock, and sell the weakest!

CHAPTER 24

Finding the Best Stocks

Where to Start Looking

There are, of course, two ways of finding stocks to consider buying. You can start by looking at market action, or you can start with the story, which may include conclusions based on fundamental analysis. You can buy stocks successfully by relying only on favorable market action, but it can help to know whether the story makes sense—what you might call the sex appeal factor. Buying stocks without any regard to the technicals is like buying cows in the moonlight. It can be done, often very successfully, especially in a bull market. Nevertheless, you are not playing with the full deck of cards when you do so. For example, it has often happened in the past that a stock has a wonderful story and continued to pay a good dividend, yet it lost 75 percent of its value. On the other hand, the complete lack of a dividend or the foreseeable prospect of receiving one does not prevent a stock going up by many times. It is worth repeating the axiom that it is better to buy a poor or an unknown stock when the timing is right than it is to buy a great stock when the timing is wrong.

There are plenty of standard technical alerts. Many computer software programs automatically set off some of them, but in general you need to have the stock active in your computer before it can happen. It is not practical for most people to have more than a couple hundred or so stocks active in the system. So keep your ears and eyes open for stocks that may be worth looking at. Once you decide to examine a stock, get enough data for a comprehensive review. Several years' worth is good. A decade or more is better. You do not want to find yourself making a decision to buy a stock while inadvertently ignorant of the fact that its current price is at or near a prominent high from a few years before.

There are three sections here describing stock alerts, some of them confirmed by statistical analysis done by Jim O'Shaughnessy for his book *What Works on Wall Street* (McGraw-Hill, 1996). The first covers technical alerts. The second covers fundamental or value-oriented concepts that have been shown to work over the long term. The third covers fundamental or value-oriented concepts that have been proven to be loser-plays. They should not necessarily deter you from buying a stock, but it is valuable to know which popular ideas have not worked over the long term.

Technical Alerts That Work

1. Buy Strength

Statistical evidence proves the general principle—the principle upon which this book is based—that buying strength in stocks is the single most successful strategy, and as a general principle, the more strength the better.

It also shows that you can reinforce your success by buying value as well as strength. Jim O'Shaughnessy found that you get exceptional performance in the long run from the stocks that have gained the most in the prior year and in addition have the fundamental background of a price-to-sales ratio below one. Under certain circumstances, such as during a raging bull market, it may not be possible to find any stocks that fulfill both conditions.

2. Monthly Reversals, Double Monthly Reversals, and Lindahl Price Rules

Any monthly upside reversal in the direction of a strong and established trend generally provides an excellent signal to buy a stock, and vice versa when selling short in a bear market. A Lindahl price rule (Rule 5) and a double reversal price rule (Rule 8) are particularly powerful indicators of the potential for a stock to make a substantial move.

A single monthly reversal *against* the direction of the major trend may mean nothing when the overall chart for a stock is strong. A Rule 5 or Rule 8 signal against the direction of an established trend may well mean that the stock is due for a rest. Depending on other indicators and general market conditions, it may be signaling that the stock is preparing to reverse direction.

3. 52-Week Highs and Lows

When a stock makes a new 52-week high after resting, there is a high probability that the consolidation has ended and that it will provide a springboard for the stock to move higher.

It is important to try to catch a stock as early as possible after a 52-week breakout. The later you leave the entry, the greater the retracement that you may have to live through before the stock goes on again. Worse is the possibility that you might buy at the high for the immediate move and get taken out by the initial protective stop.

The new 52-week high alert does the job of recognizing that you can be continuously looking back a year and can buy a stock in the early stages of a potentially big year ahead.

You should never own a stock making a new 52-week low, but you might well consider selling it short.

New 52-week highs and lows are published in major daily and weekly newspapers.

4. Gaps and Islands

A stock that gaps shows that it has blown the gasket of normal day-to-day trading action. One gap in isolation within a consolidation may mean nothing. When, however, it fits in with other timing indicators and a stock moves to a new high or low, it may suggest a call for action. Buy when the stock gaps up. Consider selling a stock that you own when it gaps against you. When a market gaps down that has recently gapped up, there is a high probability of at least an intermediate trend reversal.

5. 50-Percent Retracements

Look for retracements within an established trend to retrace 50 percent of the previous move from bottom to top in a bull market, and vice versa in a bear market.

Many investors look at Fibonacci ratios to guess how far a retracement might go. In round numbers the percentages are 38, 50, and 62 percent. If a stock retraces more than 62 percent, it is likely to go the rest of the way back to where it started. If you know you want to own a stock (or to sell one short), you can sometimes trade into a 50-percent retracement without even waiting for a price rule to develop. Then you can sometimes enter at an excellent price with a very manageable stop.

6. Volume Surges

A surge in volume, whether daily or for the week, means that a stock has become the focus of new buying or selling pressure. When the surge occurs in conjunction with an upward move in price, there is a high probability that big money is anxious to press the market to buy stock. It can be just as significant when there is a sudden surge in selling pressure. A volume surge often occurs in the early stages of a major move. It is generally obvious from market action whether there is a surge in pressure to buy or to sell. Volume surges also occur at the end of a major move as a result of a terminal buying frenzy or a panicky selling climax.

Newspapers print a list of the most actively traded stocks. Sometimes this can be the tip-off to check out the technicals.

7. Five Days Up or Down

A stock that goes up for five consecutive days is obviously being bought aggressively by people unwilling to wait for the price to subside after initial buying interest. The same applies in reverse, when there is persistent selling.

When the technicals fall in line, don't be deterred from chasing a stock on the sixth or seventh day. You should get on board a rapidly moving market as soon as possible, if you are ever going to. Otherwise, there may not be another timely signal such as a reversal with the trend, for some time. By then, the price may have moved a long way.

Sometimes the price of a stock may go in the same direction for five consecutive days at the end of a major move. There is usually other evidence of a buying or a selling climax.

8. Big Gainers

Stocks making big daily and weekly gains are always worth looking at. One day's big gain may mean little, but several days of strong action or a big weekly gain may be a prelude to more big weekly gains. Look for big daily and weekly gains to tie in with potential monthly reversals with the trend.

9. Stochastics Crossovers

Some software programs, such as *TC 2000,* give an alert when stochastics cross above the 20-percent line or below the 80-percent line.

When crossing above 20 percent, this alert can be useful for buying a temporarily oversold market as it resumes an established uptrend. When crossing below 80, it can be useful for selling short a temporarily overbought market in an established downtrend.

This alert is seldom helpful in identifying tops in a bull market or bottoms in a bear market. However, it is worth keeping an eye on it if other indicators are leading you to expect a major top or bottom.

10. 40-Day Moving Average Crossovers

Like stochastics crossovers, this alert is generally most useful after a retracement when buying in a bull market, or selling a short position in a bear market. The probabilities favor a continuation in the direction of the moving average unless it appears to be changing direction in a slow-motion rollover.

On its own, an adverse crossover of the 40-day moving average does not constitute a signal to sell a stock. However, it serves as a warning that you should examine the technical case for staying with it.

11. Stock Group Subindexes

Stock group subindexes provide a shortcut to finding areas of the market where there are stocks with superior prospects for gains. They also show where there are stocks with little or no prospect of outperforming the market generally, or which, on the contrary, may be candidates for short sales.

A comparison of the Worden subindex for international oil companies (Figure 24-1) versus the subindex for domestic oil companies (Figure 24-2) shows that the internationals have by far the stronger chart pattern.

British Petroleum (Figure 24-3) is at a much more advanced stage of development than Atlantic Richfield (Figure 24-4). BP is the stock to buy, not Atlantic Richfield: Buy the strong and sell the weak.

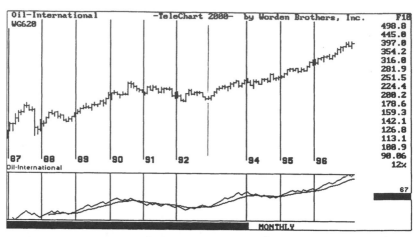

FIGURE 24–1. Worden International Oils Monthly Chart, with On Balance Volume.

At the other end of the spectrum, look at the Worden subindex for steel companies (Figure 24-5). This chart looks really, really bad. Individual stocks within the group are likely to invite short sales.

12. Time Cycles

There is a marked tendency for all markets to establish a rhythm, with several simultaneous beats, depending on the length of the cycle.

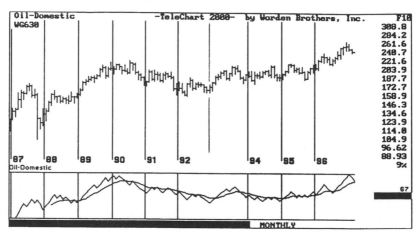

FIGURE 24–2. Worden Domestic Oils Monthly Chart, with On Balance Volume.

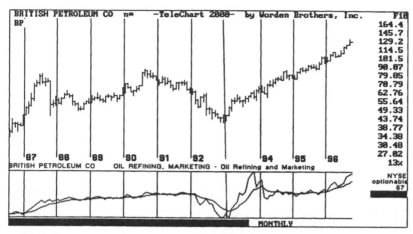

FIGURE 24-3.   British Petroleum Monthly Chart, with On Balance Volume.

Cycle theory looks for regularity between lows, but with wandering highs in between. In a strong market the upward side of the cycle lasts for most of its duration, with only a small downward correction if there is one at all. On the other hand, in a very weak market most of the time is spent with the price declining and only an occasional upward blip. The risks are notably lower when buying soon after an expected cycle low, particularly one for a longer-term cycle. The risks are correspondingly higher when approaching the likely downside of a long-term

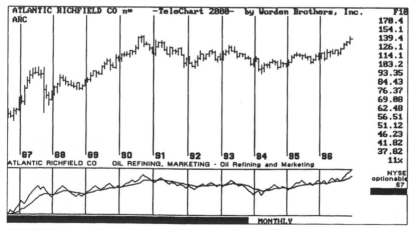

FIGURE 24-4.   Atlantic Richfield Monthly Chart, with On Balance Volume.

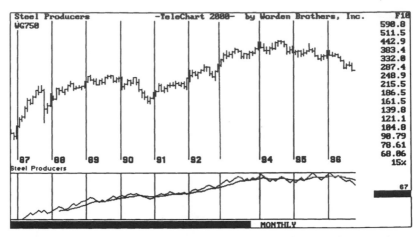

FIGURE 24–5. Worden Steel Producers Monthly Chart, with On Balance Volume.

cycle or during the course of one, which is generally obvious at the time.

You can often see how a stock goes up for a week or two and then comes back for a week or two, making lows at intervals of about a month or so.

Most markets tend to have a conspicuous annual low, and the most common time for an annual low for stocks is in October or November.

Stocks tend to make lows every four years in accordance with the so-called Presidential cycle. The idea is that U.S. Presidents try to roll out goodies toward election time and to deliver less welcome medicine in between, and that stocks respond accordingly.

The Presidential cycle can be found throughout the twentieth century. There were major identifiable lows in 1970, and then in 1974, 1978, and 1982. One was due in 1986, but it came a year late. When it came, it did so with a vengeance, taking the market hard down in one of the greatest crashes of all time. The four-year low in 1990 came at the end of a barely perceptible bear market that lasted less than four months. There should have been a four-year cycle low in 1994, but it too was barely perceptible. Instead of making a clearly identifiable low, stocks merely consolidated in a sideways pattern for most of that year, although bonds sold off hard.

Fundamental Alerts That Work

1. Earnings Gains for Five Consecutive Years

The general principle holds that companies doing well are likely to continue doing well and vice versa for companies doing poorly. The market is rightly prepared to pay a premium for consistency. Nevertheless, you should beware of getting carried away with an excess of enthusiasm for growth, as we have seen with Wal-Mart in the 1990s and Coca-Cola from 1939 to 1959.

Depending on overall market conditions, enthusiasm for growth should normally be tempered with the condition that a stock worth buying on the basis of past growth in earnings should not have a price-to-sales ratio higher than 1.5. Also, the price-to-earnings ratio ideally should not exceed the expected growth rate for corporate profits.

All valuation criteria should be considered in relation to the prevailing fashions of the market, whether stocks are very much in favor or out of favor. In the past, huge overvaluations have led either to huge profit growth or else, eventually, a huge decline in the stock price.

It is easy to notice big gains in currently reported profits when looking at the newspaper. This information can be extremely misleading, although a lot of people act on it. The bigger the reported gain, the more likely it is to include some nonrecurring profit. Also, the bigger the reported gain, the more likely the news is to have been built into the current price of the stock.

Several chart services provide good fundamental data, including earnings and dividends plotted against price. The Value Line Investment Survey, available in many libraries, combines useful fundamental information in conjunction with recommendations for timeliness.

2. High Dividends

A strategy based on buying the ten highest-yielding stocks in the Dow Jones Industrial Average is one that works. For 25 years to 1995, it consistently outperformed both the Dow as a whole and the S&P 500 Index. This is a wonderful strategy for trustees who have to combine paying income to current beneficiaries with preserving and enhancing the value of capital for the future. You are entitled to ask why it is so difficult for money managers to implement it.

A higher current dividend yield sometimes occurs when there is a risk of the dividend being cut or eliminated. However, that risk can be lessened by spreading the exposure to it across a number of dividend-paying stocks. A combination of looking for high dividends and using timing indicators is likely to produce very good results in the long term.

Dividends are worth having and are worth looking for, particularly as a defense against bad times and bad turns in the market.

3. Look About You!

Look around and see which businesses seem to be doing well. You may get an idea about a company from visiting a shopping mall or staying in a good hotel or going to Disneyland. Then follow up your impressions with a look at the technicals for the stock. There is a high probability that they will confirm your sense for a conspicuously good business.

Certain areas tend to stand out as offering long-term potential. Sometimes that potential becomes considerably overpriced, but you still have to buy the market leaders, the Microsofts, not the Digitals. All kinds of technological innovation are likely, on balance, to provide opportunities for superior growth and therefore for rising stock prices. On the other hand, a mature company that refines sugar is normally less likely to be in the forefront of new technology or to have exceptional growth prospects. Then, too, it is worth recalling author Peter Drucker's observation that more money has been invested in computer technology than the total combined profits to date from the industry. Similarly, in the early 1990s total accumulated losses for the U.S. airline industry exceeded all of the equity ever invested in it.

4. Read the Financial Press

Many financial publications discuss stocks and the companies behind them. *Barron's* is a particularly good source of good ideas. Nevertheless, it is amazing how often the good idea behind a stock does not yet fit the technical picture. It frequently happens that some guru has a favorite stock that has a wonderful story; however, the technical case stinks. It may not continue stinking forever, though. Sometimes good ideas that start with lousy technicals can be marvelous buys when the technicals finally come on side.

5. Remember That Times Change!

This is really more of an alert for you personally than it is for finding stocks. Remember that every industry has had its day in the sun and that every industry, however successful, has its day in the shade. Success leads in due course to overinvestment in new capacity. Lack of profits leads to underinvestment, scarcity, high prices, and opportunity. Even the most dilapidated rust-belt company can come back strongly after a long period of hard times, when competitors have fallen by the wayside and hard times have imposed the need for efficiency. Even the most prosperous company can fall by the wayside if it fails to keep up with the times.

Banking was once regarded as one of the stodgiest of industries, and also the most accident-prone. Initiative tended only to lead to disastrous lending and overexposure to every newly fashionable deadbeat cause, whether the oil industry, real estate, or less-developed countries. In the 1990s the industry is probably sitting on a time bomb of credit card debt and automobile leases. However, banks are among the biggest beneficiaries of computer technology, and their stocks became market darlings as a result.

Remember how Chrysler nearly went down, while General Motors was solid? There was big money to be made in Chrysler stock as the company recovered, but little in GM.

Similarly, General Public Utilities stock collapsed after the Three Mile Island nuclear accident in 1979. Over the next fifteen years, the stock advanced twentyfold from its low, with many buy signals confirming the advance all the way.

Fundamentals That Don't Work

1. Low P/E Multiples

Contrary to popular wisdom, statistical evidence shows that the best-known value approach works poorly. It does not pay to look for a low price-to-earnings multiple except, to a limited extent, when this approach is applied to large-capitalization stocks. Even then, it tends to be a loser-play unless applied in conjunction with timing techniques. As a general rule, it does not pay to buy what looks cheap. The best stocks always look expensive.

2. Buying Low

Buying the losers of prior years simply because their price is low is an all-time worst possible loser-play, unless you find a loser that is truly staging a turnaround, like Chrysler or GPU when they looked as if they might go under. Even then, there will be plenty of time to see strengthening market action as it starts developing. The rule is that companies doing poorly continue to do poorly. Stocks that go down, go down for a reason. They generally do not make significant and worthwhile price gains until business recovery in the company itself is well advanced.

3. High Valuations

Buying stocks having the highest market valuations seldom works well in the long term. These valuation criteria include stocks having:

> The highest price/sales ratios
>
> The highest price/book ratios
>
> The highest price/earnings ratios
>
> The highest earnings gains in the previous year

High valuations did not stop valuations going ever dramatically higher during the 1990s. It became the rule that the biggest gains occurred in stocks already having the highest valuations. The justification often seemed to be that investors were prepared to pay immense premiums for an established franchise. Nevertheless, this approach has not worked well in earlier times, as it did not for Coca-Cola from 1939 to 1959.

There are, of course, always exceptions to every rule and for every alert. Above all, times and fashions change.

Bringing It All Together

Entry Checklist: Bringing the Signals Together

M ost people find it difficult to pull the trigger to buy or sell; it is difficult to be completely objective, either hoping too much or fear-
ing too much without good reason to act. Using a checklist
imposes discipline and helps to avoid oversights. That is why airline
pilots use them, even though they make thousands of flights over the
years.

Often the greatest stocks to buy appear to involve a high risk
because they have moved so far in a short time. Many people find it difficult to buy a stock that has gone up by 20 or 30 percent in a surge.
Others cannot resist buying a stock that seems to be running away,
although the prime entry point has long been left behind. Naturally,
you do not want to buy a stock only to see it come all the way back
again. Nevertheless, the one that shows that it can go higher is most
likely to go on higher still. The stocks that go on to double or triple or
more should take care of the inevitable losses many, many times over.
It is all too easy to buy a dog of a stock because you think there is a low
risk. In fact, there may be a high risk and no corresponding upside
potential to offset the risk.

No system is perfect. An entry checklist using the indicators described in this book provides the best available compromise between
knowing that a stock can move and knowing that the reward-to-risk is
favorable relative to a reasonable stop-loss. For easy use, photocopy
the Entry Checklist to fill a full-size sheet (see Table 25-1).

Your entry checklist has three columns, one each for monthly, weekly, and daily indicators. The monthly list provides the essential information for the big picture—whether you want to own the stock at all. The weekly checklist confirms the intermediate picture. Ideally, the monthly, weekly, and daily chart patterns should all simultaneously confirm whether the stock is a buy now, but the main thing is the monthly chart for the big picture and the daily chart for an actual entry signal. At different times every variation in chart patterns can happen, so there is still an element of judgment required in many situations. Simultaneous new buy signals on the monthly or weekly list at the same time as a daily buy signal indicate that the probabilities are strongly favorable for the stock to start making money right away.

Place a ✔ beside an indicator when it confirms a buy and leave a blank when it is negating it. Below the list of confirming indicators is a list of negating indicators to make sure that there is not a weight of evidence against the decision. You might think it would be obvious not to buy a stock going down instead of one going up. Not so! A lot of people do it. Remember that someone has to take the other side of every trade. Otherwise, you cannot do business!

There should normally be about twelve or more confirming indicators across the board. There should not be more than one or two negating indicators. There should be almost nothing ambiguous or contradictory about the best stocks to buy.

It is generally best to make out one or two checklists in addition to making out one for the specific stock that you are considering. Go through the entry checklist for at least one of the major stock market indexes as well as for a sector index, if available. It may also be worth making out the entry checklist for more than one stock in a market group.

When one stock comes in with more positive indications than another, go with that one. It seldom pays to depart from the rule that you should buy the strongest stock and sell the weakest. The strong stock may double from its current price level, even if it seems already to have done a lot, while the laggard goes up by only 50 percent. The psychology of expecting laggards to catch up is generally a loser-play over the long term.

ENTRY CHECKLIST: BUY

Stock	Price	Date	
Confirming Indicators	**Monthly**	**Weekly**	**Daily**
1. W/Zigzag Line			
2. 25 Bar MA			
3. 40 Bar MA			
4. OBV 1			
5. OBV 10			
6. Fast MACD			
7. Slow MACD			
8. %K Turn			
9. %K Level (under 20)			
10. Price Rule			
11. Turn at MA/Trendline			
12. Key Reversal			
13. Double Reversal			
14. Chart Pattern			
15. Gap			
16. Island			
17. Market Conditions			
18. Value			
TOTAL			
Negating Indicators			
1. Adverse W/Zigzag Line			
2. Adv. 25 MA			
3. Adv. 40 MA			
4. OBV 1			
5. OBV 10			
6. Fast MACD			
7. Slow MACD			
8. %K Level (above 80)			
9. Resistance			
10. Channel Line			
11. Adv. T-Line Cross			
12. Value			
TOTAL			

Confirming Indicators

1. **W Formation/Zigzag Line.** There is no more powerful indicator of a bull market than an upward zigzag on the monthly line chart, or of a W to indicate the potential start of an upward zigzag. For all practical purposes, the probabilities seldom favor buying a stock unless there is an upward zigzag or a new W.

   A stock that has gone through a big correction within the major trend may actually have a negating zigzag on the *daily* chart. Severely oversold stochastics should offset this negativity.

2. **25-Bar Moving Average.** The 25-*month* moving average should show an upward direction, and ideally, this average, as well as price, should be above the 40-*month* moving average.

   The 25-week and 25-day moving averages ideally should confirm when you buy a stock, but they may not necessarily do so when the stock is extremely oversold in the short term.

3. **40-Bar Moving Average.** The 40-month moving average should, for all practical purposes, always be pointing up when you buy a stock. A wobbling 25-month moving average may show aberrations, but the primary indication of market direction by the 40-month moving average seldom fails unless the price has advanced a long way above it.

4. **OBV 1.** The direction of the simple unsmoothed line for On Balance Volume shows the immediate weight of buying or selling pressure in a stock. This line is particularly bullish when it defines its own upward zigzag pattern.

   There are two conditions in the action for OBV that you have to be careful with. When OBV 1 has moved a long way from its 10-bar moving average, it may indicate a buying climax rather than the kind of persistence that keeps a stock moving steadily higher. You also have to beware when price moves to a new high but OBV makes a lower high.

5. **OBV 10.** The smoothed OBV line takes the wrinkles out of the ebb and flow of supply and demand. It shows persistence more reliably than does OBV 1. You want it to confirm direction.

Although not required for the checklist, OBV generates a buy signal in its own right when it crosses over its 10-bar moving average. It is particularly significant when the crossover occurs after a period of rounding by the two OBV lines.

6. **Fast MACD.** Fast MACD should be pointing upward for a confirming indicator when buying a stock.

    Sometimes this is a lagging indicator, and an upturn may occur after other indicators fall into place. Nevertheless, you can generally tell whether fast MACD is in the process of rounding up and likely to turn up.

    As with OBV, beware of buying a stock when MACD fails to make a higher high along with a higher high in price. It may be showing flagging momentum. The result may either be that the stock fails to follow through or that it is unable to move up significantly until MACD comes decisively back on side.

7. **Slow MACD.** Slow MACD should be pointing upward when buying.

    Some of the biggest and best moves start from the time when fast MACD crosses the slow and they both begin a steady upward progress.

8. **%K Turn.** This indicator should be pointing up to confirm a buy.

    Unlike MACD, the fast stochastic %K is a fast-acting indicator. When a stock is underway, %K should show the likely direction of price, regardless of whether it is at a high or low level. Flagging action in %K may indicate that a stock is in need of a rest and may be vulnerable to a retracement. It does not by any means suggest an impending trend reversal, for which many indicators need to fall into place.

9. **%K Level.** This indicator should currently be or have recently been below 20 to confirm a buy, thereby indicating the likelihood that a correction has been completed.

    When %K is at a level below 20 in a bull market, you may want to buy a stock before %K turns up. It may be enough that the stock has finished an intermediate correction or is imminently about to do so.

10. **Price Rule Signal.** You need to have a new price rule on the *daily* chart to pull the trigger to buy a stock.

Ideally, there should be a clear price rule signal in force on the monthly chart and on the weekly chart when buying a stock. In practice, it is often enough to get a general impression that bars on the weekly and monthly charts are generally favorable, with closes mostly in the upper end of their respective bars.

11. **Turn at MA/Trendline.** There is a positive indicator when, after completing a retracement, the price stops and turns at a level at or near the 25 and 40 moving averages, or at a clear trendline.

There is high probability that the moving averages will contain the retracement. Therefore, a price rule signal at that level is much more likely to succeed than one occurring randomly.

The 25 and 40 calibration may seem random. However, the probabilities tend to be more favorable on retracements to these levels for two reasons. First, they show that the stock is not exceptionally overextended and vulnerable to a retracement. Second, many traders watch the 25 and 40 moving averages, so their effectiveness in containing retracements tends to be self-reinforcing.

12. **Key Reversal.** Count a favorable indicator for a key reversal.

A key reversal with a strong close powerfully contributes to the probability of a stock continuing in the direction of the close. An upside key reversal provides the visible means of showing that weak holders have been flushed out at a bottom and that strong money has come in to buy.

Key reversals on the monthly and weekly charts tend to show strong newfound power in a stock, especially when there have recently been one or more additional upside reversals.

A key reversal occurring in conjunction with a buy signal on the daily chart increases the probability of a stock moving to a profit right away. A key reversal on the daily chart in a rapidly moving stock may provide a prime entry, and do so in conjunction with a manageable stop placed below the low of the day.

13. **Double Reversal.** Count a favorable indicator with this occurrence.

A double reversal in the direction of an established trend and occurring within a few bars is as powerful as a key reversal, if not more so. The two reversals indicate cleansing of the market of weak holders and preparation for a strong upward move. A double reversal is much more powerful than a single one occurring at random.

14. **Chart Pattern.** Count a favorable indicator when a stock is breaking out of a trading range or is completing a reverse head-and-shoulders pattern.

15. **Gaps.** Count a favorable indicator when there is an upward gap on the weekly or daily chart.

    Gaps on the weekly chart tend to have more significance than you might expect because of so many people who make their investment decisions over the weekend.

16. **Island.** Count a favorable indicator when the price has gapped down and then gapped up. Best of all is when there are several days of market consolidation underneath the market prior to a sharp upside resolution of the standoff between buyers and sellers. This can be one of the best indications to show that a retracement has ended.

    On the other hand, an island above the current price that results from downward gapping may show that the stock has exhausted its upside potential. Any consolidation below an island may simply be the harbinger of a further significant decline when new buyers find they are wrong.

17. **Market Conditions.** It is essential to look at the bigger picture for the market generally, for interest rates and for the group index for the stock that you are considering.

    When the stock market generally is going either sideways or down or is at a very high level, be careful. Depending on your interpretation of a necessarily subjective array of considerations, it means that you should buy lightly, not that you should pass when there is a strong signal to buy a specific stock.

    In a general bear market, be wary of buying any stock of any kind in any company. It is extremely rare to find one of the 10 percent of stocks that are going up in a general bear market, but it can occasionally happen.

18. **Value.** The best stocks generally have an external reason to buy them—the sex appeal factor. You like the product. Or you think what they do seems to fit into the general pattern of society's needs or desires, such as for health care or hamburgers. If a business looks busy and prosperous, the chances are that it is well run, that it makes money and that its stock will perform well. You don't have to be an accountant to sniff out a great business, particularly if the technical patterns on the charts look good.

Negating Indicators

1. **Adverse W/Zigzag Line.** It practically never pays to buy a stock unless there is an upward zigzag or a newly forming W on the monthly line chart. Lack of this confirming indicator amounts virtually to a total trade embargo.

   The weekly and daily charts may not have an upward zigzag pattern after a severe retracement. The main thing is to have a strong monthly chart pattern confirming a major uptrend.

2. **Adverse 25-Bar Moving Average Direction.** A downward incline in the 25-bar moving average counts as a negating indicator.

   Many stocks take off before the 25-month moving average turns up, but the probabilities are not favorable for a sustained move, and the risk of a major retracement, if not outright failure, is high.

   As with an adverse W, lack of this confirming factor almost amounts to a trade embargo.

3. **Adverse 40-Bar Moving Average Direction.** A downward incline in the 40-bar moving average counts as a negating indicator.

   Ideally, price should be above the 25- and the 40-month moving averages several months, say five or more, unless there is a very pronounced rounding by both price and the moving average.

   An adverse close below rising 25- and 40-bar moving averages may simply express a very oversold condition in a bull market.

4. **OBV 1.** When OBV 1 points down, count this indicator negative.

   The direction of the On Balance Volume single line should

be pointing upward or making no more than a small downward incline in an overall bullish pattern. Also, a new high in price should be accompanied by a new high in OBV.

When OBV 1 is extremely overextended, this indicator may be showing signs of climactic buying, rather than the kind of steady and persistent buying that confirms the strength of the stock.

5. **OBV 10.** Count this indicator negative when OBV 10 is pointing down.

   Ideally, OBV 1 should be above OBV 10. A single and short-lived adverse crossover of OBV 10 may mean little. When OBV 1 is persistently below OBV 10, the probabilities are that the stock is being sold and that a decline in price may go further than you expect.

6. **Fast MACD.** Count it a negating indicator when fast MACD is pointing down.

7. **Slow MACD.** Count a negative indicator when slow MACD is pointing down.

8. **%K Level.** Count a negative indicator when fast stochastic %K is above 80 or higher.

   . This condition often occurs when a stock is overbought and vulnerable to a retracement. It also occurs, however, in the fastest-moving markets and when a stock first breaks out of a consolidation. Therefore, a high %K level may be a sign of market strength. So you have to interpret this overbought level in the context of specific market action at the time.

9. **Resistance.** Resistance counts as a negative indicator when a stock is approaching a historic high where it previously turned down and began a *major* correction. It is easy to fear that the most recent high on the *daily* chart may signify a more durable top when no more than a temporary correction has occurred. Look for resistance on the monthly and weekly charts, for levels that have truly rebuffed attempts by the stock to go higher.

10. **Channel Line.** Count this indicator negative when a stock is pressing against an upper channel line. Then there is a high probability of a retracement back to the uptrend line.

11. **Adverse Trendline Crossover.** Count as a negative indicator when price is below a clearly identifiable uptrend line. That means that the market has lost its immediate upward momentum. A strong stock should not require ever shallower trendlines.

12. **Value.** Count this indicator negative when there is no known fundamental value in a stock or there have been poor earnings results. Even the most ardent technician and antivaluation investor should have some general awareness of the difference between a Dow stock and a speculative new issue with no financial history. If the technical picture is good enough, the best thing may be just to buy a small number of shares rather than pass on buying the stock altogether.

Stops

Don't buy a stock without knowing where to place the stop! Remember that a 50-percent loss requires a double to get your money back. A loss of 20 percent requires only a 25-percent gain to get back to where you started.

CHAPTER 26

Case Study: Buy Into an Established Trend

O n April 13, 1995, the monthly chart for Citicorp shows the kind of established trend that generally provides for the best combination of safety and a high probability for success (Figure 26-1). This case study covers the initial entry, using the Entry Checklist on page 251. Once CCI was on its way, there were numerous new entry signals for many weeks afterwards, both from the weekly chart and the daily. As soon as a correction ended, even one lasting only a day or two, you could again buy the stock.

The Entry Checklist for Citicorp

Monthly Confirming Indicators

1. **W Formation/Zigzag Line.** Yes. The stock has been a buy on the basis of the monthly line chart since the price exceeded, with a new high close, the June 1992 monthly closing high of $20.37. This occurred with the January 1993 close at $26, which completed a W formation where the higher high came first.

2. **25-Month Moving Average.** Yes. From early 1992 the 25-month moving average has confirmed a bull market.

3. **40-Month Moving Average.** Yes. The 40-month moving average has confirmed a major bull market from the time of its upturn in early 1993, after rounding out for about a year.

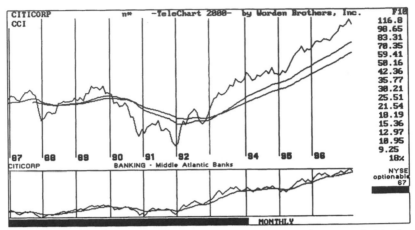

FIGURE 26-1. Citicorp Monthly Line Chart, with 25- and 40-Month Moving Averages and On Balance Volume.

4. **OBV 1.** Yes. OBV showed some selling in late 1994, with completion of a small M. It then reversed with a small W in the first quarter of 1995. The second low is significantly higher than the first.

5. **OBV 10.** No, but not strongly negative. This indicator counted as mildly negative until the monthly close for May 1995 when OBV 1 grudgingly topped OBV 10. The crossover could reasonably be anticipated in April, given the double bottom in OBV 1.

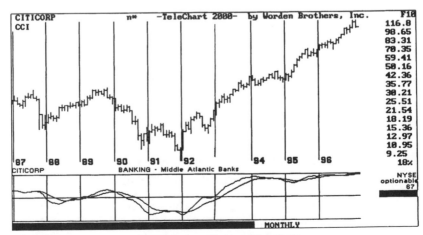

FIGURE 26-2. Citicorp Monthly Bar Chart, with MACD.

6. **Fast MACD.** No. Fast MACD was hard down throughout 1994 and did not even go flat until April 1995. Count this indicator negative until May, although it is acceptable to anticipate an upturn in April, given the preponderance of other bullish indicators.

   On the monthly chart MACD is a lagging indicator. Ideally, it should show signs of flattening to suggest that it can turn up. Once turned, it usually maintains momentum for a very long time.

7. **Slow MACD.** No. Count a negative reading. If you waited for the MACD crossover in July, you missed a major move. On the other hand, once there was a crossover, the probabilities favored a further substantial continuation of the uptrend.

8. **%K Turn.** Yes, with a new upturn constituting a signal in its own right. Count %K negative until April. Then count it very positive with the W double bottom. In a trending market the first turn in %K often gives a timely entry signal at an excellent price.

9. **%K Level.** No. Count this indicator neutral. It does not give a positive reading after being oversold, below 20. Nor is it negative as a result of showing an overbought reading above 80.

10. **Price Rule.** Yes. Count a Rule 1 price rule in effect from March. This was the fourth consecutive month with the close in the upper half of the monthly range, which adds conviction to the buy signal.

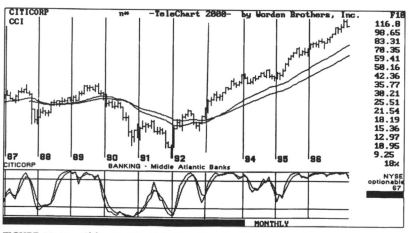

FIGURE 26-3.   Citicorp Monthly Bar Chart, with Stochastics.

11. **Turn at MA/Trendline.** Not applicable for the moving averages. There is no relevant trendline.

12. **Key Reversal.** Not applicable.

13. **Double Reversal.** Not applicable.

14. **Chart Pattern.** Yes. Count as positive. There is a powerful reverse head-and-shoulders bottom, with its head at the end-1991 low. The stock looks capable of going a very long way after making such a substantial low. The consolidation during the last eighteen months has occurred well above the 1987 and 1989 highs, making a very bullish right shoulder. This pattern should support a good move from here.

15. **Gap.** Not applicable.

16. **Island.** Not applicable.

17. **Market Conditions.** Yes. The major stock market indexes have been consolidating throughout 1994, carving out chart patterns quite similar to the one for Citicorp. If the market as a whole starts moving up, then CCI should participate fully. Count this indicator positive.

18. **Value.** Yes. Count this indicator positive. After the bank's brush with death in 1991, the probabilities favor recovery for profits and the condition of the balance sheet, assisted by a favorable interest rate environment.

Monthly Negating Indicators

1. **Adverse W/Zigzag Line.** Not applicable.

2. **Adverse 25 MA Direction.** Not applicable.

3. **Adverse 40 MA Direction.** Not applicable.

4. **OBV 1.** Not applicable, but not exactly confirming strongly.

5. **OBV 10.** Mildly negative.

6. **Fast MACD.** Negative, but potentially turning.

7. **Slow MACD.** Negative.

8. **%K Level.** Not applicable.

9. **Resistance.** None. CCI has cleared all significant resistance.

10. **Channel Line.** Not applicable.

11. **Adverse Trendline Crossover.** Not applicable.

12. **Value.** Covered on the monthly list.

The confirming indicators are so strong that there is little risk in overriding negative to neutral readings for OBV and MACD.

Weekly Confirming Indicators

1. **W Formation/Zigzag Line.** Yes. The stock is a buy the week of April 6, 1995, when the weekly price line completes a W. (There are minor aberrations on the *TC 2000* historical charts, since they show completion of monthly and weekly bars on days that do not always coincide with the end of the month or week. For our purposes, the last day of a month or a week are significant. They are days of reckoning when short-term traders and market-makers decide whether they want to continue carrying on their books a long or a short position in a stock over the weekend or into the next month.)

2. **25-Week Moving Average.** Yes. Confirms with gentle upward round and a small W, which is great.

3. **40-Week Moving Average.** Yes. Confirms, with the same positive indications as the 25-week.

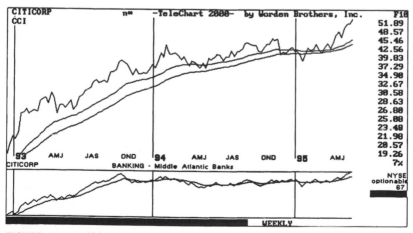

FIGURE 26–4. Citicorp Weekly Line Chart, with On Balance Volume.

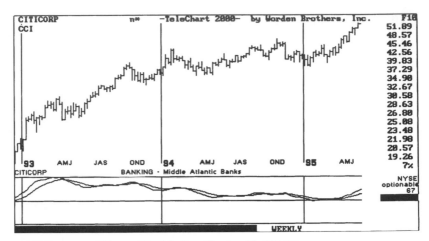

FIGURE 26–5.   Citicorp Weekly Bar Chart, with MACD.

4. **OBV 1.** Yes. OBV confirms with a small W.

5. **OBV 10.** Yes. Confirms with an OBV 1 crossover, though it is not looking conspicuously strong.

6. **Fast MACD.** Yes. Confirming beautifully.

7. **Slow MACD.** Yes. Confirming with superb rounding.

8. **%K Turn.** Yes. Count %K positive, with a good W pattern.

9. **%K Level.** No. Count negative. Bear in mind that an overbought

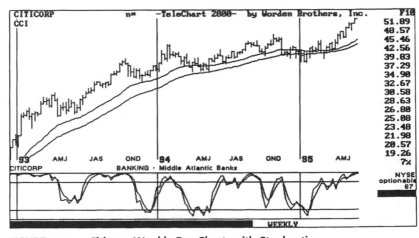

FIGURE 26–6.   Citicorp Weekly Bar Chart, with Stochastics.

stochastic reading is often a sign of strength, not of vulnerability, particularly when a stock is at or near a new high and when other indicators, such as MACD, confirm strongly.

10. **Price Rule.** Yes. Count a Lindahl price rule (Rule 5) on April 13, which could not be better.

11. **Turn at MA/Trendline.** Yes, perfect!

12. **Key Reversal.** Not applicable.

13. **Double Reversal.** Not applicable.

14. **Chart Pattern.** Yes. Count positive. The weekly chart is completing a small reverse head-and-shoulders pattern over the past five months.

15. **Gap.** Not applicable.

16. **Island.** Not applicable.

17. **Market Conditions.** Covered on the monthly list.

18. **Value.** Covered on the monthly list.

Weekly Negating Indicators

1. **Adverse W/Zigzag Line.** Not applicable.

2. **Adverse 25 MA Direction.** Not applicable.

3. **Adverse 40 MA Direction.** Not applicable.

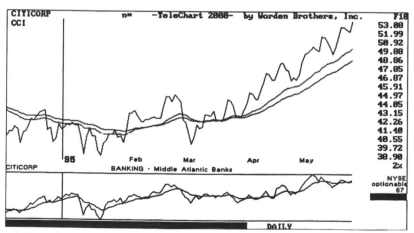

FIGURE 26-7. Citicorp Daily Line Chart, with On Balance Volume.

4. **OBV 1.** Not applicable.

5. **OBV 10.** Not applicable.

6. **Fast MACD.** Not applicable.

7. **Slow MACD.** Not applicable.

8. **%K Level.** Count negative. However, the reading probably denotes strength, not weakness.

9. **Resistance.** None. CCI has cleared all significant resistance, although it needs to follow through above the November high.

10. **Channel Line.** Not applicable.

11. **Adverse Trendline Crossover.** Not applicable.

12. **Value.** Not applicable.

Daily Confirming Indicators

1. **W Formation/Zigzag Line.** Yes. The daily price line has been gathering strength with a wonderful upward zigzag since the beginning of March.

2. **25-Day Moving Average.** Yes. Confirms with a strong upward acceleration.

3. **40-Day Moving Average.** Yes. Confirms, with the same positive indications as the 25-week.

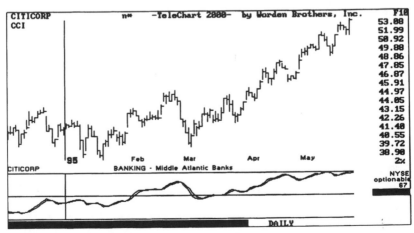

FIGURE 26-8. Citicorp Daily Bar Chart, with MACD.

4. **OBV 1.** Yes. OBV confirms with an erratic upward bias.

5. **OBV 10.** Yes. Confirms, although surprisingly grudgingly.

6. **Fast MACD.** Yes. Confirming beautifully.

7. **Slow MACD.** Yes. Confirming beautifully, with superb rounding.

8. **%K Turn.** Yes. Count %K positive, with a good W pattern.

9. **%K Level.** No. Count negative. As noted on the monthly checklist, an overbought stochastic reading is often a sign of strength, not of vulnerability, when other indicators confirm strongly.

10. **Price Rule.** Yes. Count a Rule 3 price rule, with a small gap up on April 13.

11. **Turn at MA/Trendline.** Yes, perfect!

12. **Key Reversal.** Not applicable.

13. **Double Reversal.** Not applicable.

14. **Chart Pattern.** Yes. Count positive. The daily chart is making a small W.

15. **Gap.** Yes, on April 13, the entry day.

16. **Island.** Not applicable.

17. **Market Conditions.** Covered on the monthly list.

18. **Value.** Covered on the monthly list.

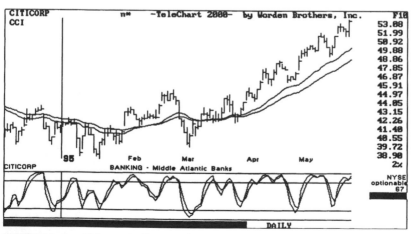

FIGURE 26-9. Citicorp Daily Bar Chart, with Stochastics.

Daily Negating Indicators

1. **Adverse W/Zigzag Line.** Not applicable.

2. **Adverse 25 MA Direction.** Not applicable.

3. **Adverse 40 MA Direction.** Not applicable.

4. **OBV 1.** Not applicable.

5. **OBV 10.** Not applicable.

6. **Fast MACD.** Not applicable.

7. **Slow MACD.** Not applicable.

8. **%K Level.** No. Count negative. However, the reading almost certainly denotes strength, not weakness.

9. **Resistance.** None. CCI has cleared all significant resistance.

10. **Channel Line.** Not applicable.

11. **Adverse Trendline Crossover.** Not applicable.

12. **Value.** Not applicable.

It might have been tempting to buy CCI at various times before April 13, 1995, when the stock seemed on several occasions to be poised for an upward surge. However, the monthly chart was a bit slow in coming on side and even then it came in that day with only nine confirming indicators and three negative. While it is true that OBV 10 and MACD are sometimes slow to confirm, ideally, they should at least show that they may be preparing to come on side, as they were here. In the meantime, the weekly and daily indicators were turning overwhelmingly favorable.

There is an element of arbitrariness in selecting April 13, 1995, for this case study. There are often many, many days when the indicators come together to buy a stock during the course of a bull market. On April 13 there was a particularly impressive conjunction of favorable monthly, weekly, and daily indicators. Once the stock started moving and confirming the uptrend with the surge to new highs, you could buy the stock on completion of any new upturn after a retracement. Note particularly the four-day island from which the stock gapped up on May 4.

Setting Stops

For a buy on April 13 at $46.25, look at the intramonth low from which the monthly line chart last turned up. It is at $39.62. The best

ENTRY CHECKLIST, CITICORP: BUY

Stock CCI	Price $46.25	Date 4/13/95	
Confirming Indicators	Monthly	Weekly	Daily
1. W/Zigzag Line	✔	✔	✔
2. 25 Bar MA	✔	✔	✔
3. 40 Bar MA	✔	✔	✔
4. OBV 1	✔	✔	✔
5. OBV 10		✔	✔
6. Fast MACD		✔	✔
7. Slow MACD		✔	✔
8. %K Turn	✔	✔	✔
9. %K Level (under 20)			
10. Price Rule	✔	✔	✔
11. Turn at MA/Trendline		✔	✔
12. Key Reversal			
13. Double Reversal			
14. Chart Pattern	✔	✔	✔
15. Gap			✔
16. Island			
17. Market Conditions	✔	✔	✔
18. Value	✔	✔	✔
TOTAL	**9**	**13**	**14**
Negating Indicators			
1. Adverse W/Zigzag Line			
2. Adv. 25 MA			
3. Adv. 40 MA			
4. OBV 1			
5. OBV 10			
6. Fast MACD	✔		
7. Slow MACD	✔		
8. %K Level (above 80)	✔	✔	✔
9. Resistance			
10. Channel Line			
11. Adv. T-Line Cross			
12. Value			
TOTAL	**3**	**1**	**1**

you can do is to put the stop at, say, $38.75, which budgets for a potential loss of $7.50 per share, or 16 percent of its value. A stop set that distant might seem rich on activation of the stop. Nevertheless, the probabilities in favor of a successful trade are very good, and the stop is more for disaster insurance, not because you expect to sell the stock there.

CHAPTER 27

Case Study: Buy a Long-Term Breakout

The monthly chart for Schlumberger shows the stock going sideways interminably for five long years, from 1990 to the end of 1995 (Figure 27-1). There is a prime opportunity to buy the stock on the upside breakout at $35.82 on February 9, 1996, as we see from using the Entry Checklist on page 261.

Here is an example of the merits of bringing together the disciplines of value analysis and market timing. It helps to know that SLB is inherently a much more interesting company than General Motors, Homestake, and a multitude of other lackluster stocks. The company has the reputation as one of the best oilfield drilling and service companies. It is well-managed, and profit growth has generally been excellent. However, low oil prices led to a general lack of enthusiasm for any oil or oil-related stocks, including this one. Nevertheless, lean times have made the company ever more efficient, as indeed they have made the company's clients, the oil producers.

Toward the end of 1995 it looked as if the stock might be starting to come to life. Entering 1996, things really start to look interesting. After being a stock to avoid for so long, there is a possibility that the long consolidation may lead to a breakout and therefore to very much higher prices in due course.

The Entry Checklist for Schlumberger

Monthly Confirming Indicators

1. **W Formation/Zigzag Line.** Yes. The monthly price line completes an interesting W in January 1996, at a very high level compared with previous zigs and zags. It is easy to be deterred by the most bullish patterns and easy to be tempted by the least bullish ones. The much higher low is a strong sign of strength, what we want most of all when looking for stocks likely to go to a profit right away.

2. **25-Month Moving Average.** Yes. The 25-month moving average has been slowly rounding upward for nine months, with price holding above the average.

3. **40-Month Moving Average.** Yes. Much the same as for the 25, with the 25 now above the 40.

4. **OBV 1.** Yes. OBV shows a wonderful upward zigzag.

5. **OBV 10.** Yes. If there were any doubt about OBV 1, it should be dispelled by the textbook upward incline in OBV 10. OBV is screaming that this stock is under accumulation.

6. **Fast MACD.** Yes. Beautiful!

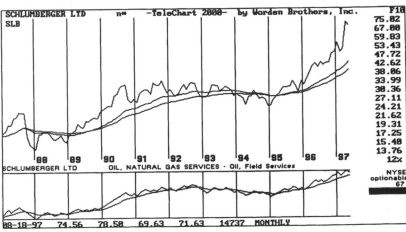

FIGURE 27-1. Schlumberger Monthly Line Chart, with 25- and 40-Month Moving Averages and On Balance Volume.

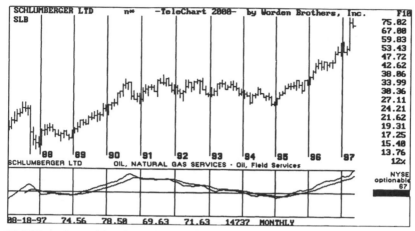

FIGURE 27-2.   Schlumberger Monthly Bar Chart, with MACD.

7. **Slow MACD.** Yes. Excellent! The way MACD has turned suggests that the stock may maintain its upward momentum for a very long time.

8. **%K Turn.** Yes. Count %K positive, and note the upward zigzag, although at rather a high level.

9. **%K Level.** No. Count this indicator negative. However, the high level is probably an expression of power rather than vulnerability, given the excellent configuration of other indicators.

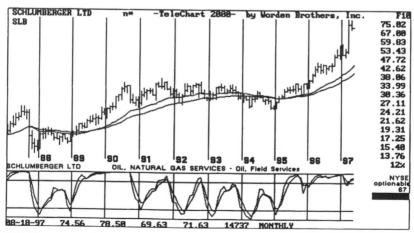

FIGURE 27-3.   Schlumberger Monthly Bar Chart, with Stochastics.

10. **Price Rule.** Yes. Count a Rule 2 signal for January.

11. **Turn at MA/Trendline.** Yes. A textbook turn at the moving averages when the stock tested down in October.

12. **Key Reversal.** Not applicable.

13. **Double Reversal.** Yes, a double high/low reversal, with one in November and another one in January.

14. **Chart Pattern.** Yes. Count as a positive indicator. This looks like a textbook breakout from a long-term consolidation.

15. **Gap.** Not applicable.

16. **Island.** Not applicable.

17. **Market Conditions.** Yes. The major stock market indexes have been strong through 1995 and look likely to continue strong.

18. **Value.** Yes. Count this indicator positive. Schlumberger has long been considered a great stock, and it could flourish again with very little encouragement.

Monthly Negating Indicators

1. **Adverse W/Zigzag Line.** Not applicable.

2. **Adverse 25 MA Direction.** Not applicable.

3. **Adverse 40 MA Direction.** Not applicable.

4. **OBV 1.** Not applicable.

5. **OBV 10.** Not applicable.

6. **Fast MACD.** Not applicable.

7. **Slow MACD.** Not applicable.

8. **%K Level.** Yes, but unlikely a cause for concern.

9. **Resistance.** None. SLB is breaking above all resistance, going at last to a record high.

10. **Channel Line.** Not applicable.

11. **Adverse Trendline Crossover.** Not applicable.

12. **Value.** Not applicable. No problems with this stock.

The confirming indicators are so strong that there is little risk in overriding negative to neutral readings for OBV and MACD.

Weekly Confirming Indicators

1. **W Formation/Zigzag Line.** Yes. The weekly price line has been quite turbulent, but it looks as if the face-off between buyers and sellers is about to be resolved decisively with an upward zigzag.

2. **25-Week Moving Average.** Yes. Confirms with a strong and accelerating upward slope.

3. **40-Week Moving Average.** Yes. Confirms with the same positive indications as the 25-week.

4. **OBV 1.** Yes. OBV confirms with a strong upward zigzag.

5. **OBV 10.** Yes. Confirms with a crossover and a conspicuously strong upward slope.

6. **Fast MACD.** Yes. Confirming beautifully.

7. **Slow MACD.** Yes. Confirming beautifully.

8. **%K Turn.** Yes. Count %K positive, with a good W pattern.

9. **%K Level.** No. Count negative. Bear in mind that an overbought stochastic reading is often a sign of strength, not of vulnerability, when other indicators such as MACD confirm stirringly.

10. **Price Rule.** Count a Rule 1 on February 9.

11. **Turn at MA/Trendline.** Yes, a perfect turn at the 25-week moving average!

12. **Key Reversal.** Not applicable.

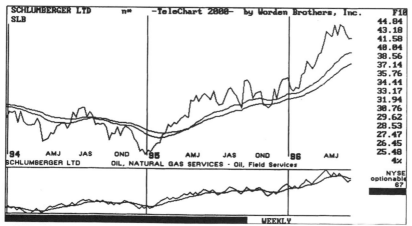

FIGURE 27–4.   Schlumberger Weekly Line Chart, with On Balance Volume.

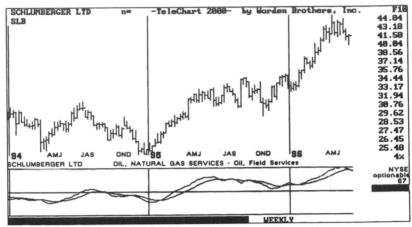

FIGURE 27-5. Schlumberger Weekly Bar Chart, with MACD.

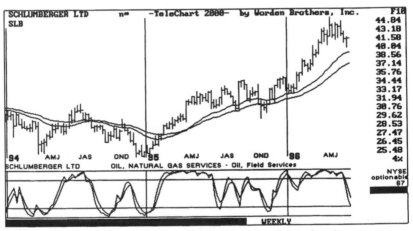

FIGURE 27-6. Schlumberger Weekly Bar Chart, with Stochastics.

13. **Double Reversal.** Not applicable.

14. **Chart Pattern.** Yes. Count as a positive indicator. The weekly chart is making a small W after completing a miniature reverse head-and-shoulders pattern over the past five months.

15. **Gaps.** Not applicable.

16. **Islands.** Not applicable.

17. **Market Conditions.** Covered on the monthly list.

18. **Value.** Covered on the monthly list.

Weekly Negating Indicators

1. **Adverse W/Zigzag Line.** Not applicable.

2. **Adverse 25 MA Direction.** Not applicable.

3. **Adverse 40 MA Direction.** Not applicable.

4. **OBV 1.** Not applicable.

5. **OBV 10.** Not applicable.

6. **Fast MACD.** Not applicable.

7. **Slow MACD.** Not applicable.

8. **%K Level.** Count negative. However, the reading probably denotes strength, not weakness.

9. **Resistance.** None.

10. **Channel Line.** Not applicable.

11. **Adverse Trendline.** Not applicable.

12. **Value.** Not applicable.

Daily Confirming Indicators

1. **W Formation/Zigzag Line.** Yes. The daily price line was struggling during January. It now seems to be shaking off its lethargy ahead of a potential upward surge.

2. **25-Day Moving Average.** Yes. Confirms with a strong upward acceleration.

3. **The 40-Day Moving Average.** Yes. Confirms with the same positive indications as the 25-day.

4. **OBV 1.** Yes. OBV confirms with an erratic upward bias.

5. **OBV 10.** Yes. Confirms strongly.

6. **Fast MACD.** Yes. Confirms strongly.

7. **Slow MACD.** Yes. Confirms strongly.

8. **%K Turn.** Yes. Count %K positive, with a good W pattern.

9. **%K Level.** No. Count negative. The overbought stochastic reading is a sign of strength, not of vulnerability, when other indicators such as MACD confirm strongly.

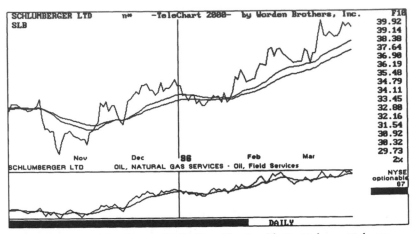

FIGURE 27-7.   Schlumberger Daily Line Chart, with On Balance Volume.

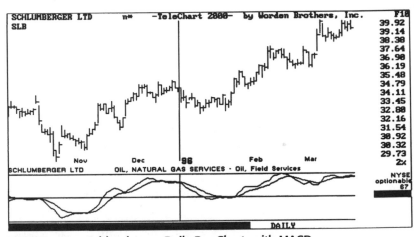

FIGURE 27-8.   Schlumberger Daily Bar Chart, with MACD.

10. **Price Rule.** Yes. Count a Rule 3, with a small gap up on February 9.

11. **Turn at MA/Trendline.** Not applicable.

12. **Key Reversal.** Not applicable.

13. **Double Reversal.** Not applicable.

14. **Chart Pattern.** Yes. Count positive. SLB is clearly trying to break out higher on the daily chart.

15. **Gaps.** Yes. There is a small gap up on February 9, the entry day.

ENTRY CHECKLIST, SCHLUMBERGER: BUY

Stock SLB	Price $35.82	Date 2/9/96	
Confirming Indicators	**Monthly**	**Weekly**	**Daily**
1. W/Zigzag Line	✔	✔	✔
2. 25 Bar MA	✔	✔	✔
3. 40 Bar MA	✔	✔	✔
4. OBV 1	✔	✔	✔
5. OBV 10	✔	✔	✔
6. Fast MACD	✔	✔	✔
7. Slow MACD	✔	✔	✔
8. %K Turn	✔	✔	✔
9. %K Level (under 20)			
10. Price Rule	✔	✔	✔
11. Turn at MA/Trendline	✔	✔	
12. Key Reversal			
13. Double Reversal	✔		
14. Chart Pattern	✔	✔	✔
15. Gap			✔
16. Island			✔
17. Market Conditions	✔	✔	✔
18. Value	✔	✔	✔
TOTAL	**14**	**13**	**14**
Negating Indicators			
1. Adverse W/Zigzag Line			
2. Adv. 25 MA			
3. Adv. 40 MA			
4. OBV 1			
5. OBV 10			
6. Fast MACD			
7. Slow MACD			
8. %K Level (above 80)	✔	✔	
9. Resistance			
10. Channel Line			
11. Adv. T-Line Cross			
12. Value			
TOTAL	**1**	**1**	**0**

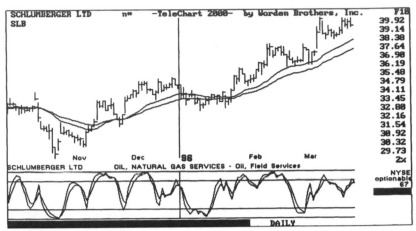

FIGURE 27-9.   Schlumberger Daily Bar Chart, with Stochastics.

16. **Islands.** Yes. There was a small gap down on February 5, now offset with the gap up on February 9, suggesting that the downside correction may have been utterly exhausted and that the price may proceed steadily upward from here.

17. **Market Conditions.** Covered on the monthly list.

18. **Value.** Covered on the monthly list.

Daily Negating Indicators

1. **Adverse W/Zigzag Line.** Not applicable.

2. **Adverse 25 MA Direction.** Not applicable.

3. **Adverse 40 MA Direction.** Not applicable.

4. **OBV 1.** Not applicable.

5. **OBV 10.** Not applicable.

6. **Fast MACD.** Not applicable.

7. **Slow MACD.** Not applicable.

8. **%K Level.** Not applicable.

9. **Resistance.** None.

10. **Channel Line.** Not applicable.

11. **Adverse Trendline Crossover.** Not applicable.

12. **Value.** Not applicable.

It would be very difficult to find a better looking breakout than SLB is making. The potential for a big move is enormous.

Setting Stops

The price tested hard down during January, making a low for the month at $32.69. Given the buy at $35.82 and the strength of the chart pattern, especially OBV, it is unlikely that the stock will retrace much. If it does, it is probably a buy, not an exit. Therefore, a stop at $29.50 looks appropriate, under the round $30. That allows a generous 18 percent, but it should not be out of line with the stock's upside potential.

Case Study: Buy Into a Rapidly Moving Market

Don't Think It's Too Late!

Many people find it extremely difficult to buy a stock moving rapidly. It is all too common to hear the echo: What goes up must come down! At the time, the risk seems inordinate. You must, however, relate the risk to the potential reward. After the event, you can often see in hindsight where you might have bought a stock that multiplied by several times the price at which it looked too risky.

Many stocks that multiply by several times over a few years, or in some cases just a few months, do so for good reasons. They are by no means always penny mines promoted by hot air and manipulation. Some of them, like Microsoft in its early days, have truly found the proverbial gold mine. They go on to justify not only their current price, which seems so high, but a price that is immensely higher.

The answer, when considering a stock moving rapidly, is not to pass up the opportunity to buy it. It is to buy only what you can afford to lose in the event of the stock going down far enough to hit your stop-loss. Rapidly moving markets require a focus on probability theory even more than investment in less exciting stocks. One of the great things about stocks is the potential for some of them to multiply by so many times that the gains eclipse losses from the ones that fail. Table 28-1 assumes that you invest $1000 in each of five stocks. One goes up

TABLE 28-1   Invest 5 × $1000

1 × 10,000	$10,000
1 × 5,000	$ 5,000
1 × 1,000	$ 1,000
1 × 0.5	$ 500
1 × 0	$ 0
Total	$16,500
Initial Investment	$ 5,000
Net Gain	$11,500

by ten times, one by five times, one stays at the same price, one halves, and one goes to zero.

You do not have to buy a penny stock in order to find one capable of going up fast. There are many smaller emerging companies with enough substance to be worth looking at on the basis of both fundamentals and market action. There are probably more established and rapidly growing companies in the United States than in all the rest of the world put together. Looking for those companies in one's own backyard is likely to be better than trading penny stocks or looking all over the world for stocks that you cannot follow day by day.

The monthly chart for Cognos shows a stock taking off like a rocket (Figure 28-1). It would be understandable to get a feeling of vertigo and to fear that this stock could be a candidate for a fall as rapid as its advance. There are, nevertheless, reasons to assume that this is not a penny mine or a fly-by-night company. It happens to be a software company based in Ottawa, Canada (essentially operating within the U.S. computer environment). The stock has traded on NASDAQ for many years and is certainly not a start-up company without a track record. On the contrary, it is a company that labored away on product development which, to judge by the action of the stock, was likely starting to bear fruit.

Using the Entry Checklist on page 276, we review a decision to buy Cognos on February 2, 1996, at $13.86. That is long after the stock has broken out and started running.

The Entry Checklist for Cognos

Monthly Confirming Indicators

1. **W Formation/Zigzag Line.** Yes. After the small dip in the monthly price line in January 1996, the monthly price line has turned right up again. It is reasonable to assume that this blip was enough of a retracement to shake stock out of weak hands so that it could make another leg up.

2. **25-Month Moving Average.** Yes. The price has moved a long way from the 25-month moving average. This is clearly a sign of strength, although it also suggests vulnerability to a retracement at any time. At some point, the stock and the moving averages are likely to converge, but it is reasonable to assume that this rapidly moving stock can continue to move higher. Ask yourself: Why should the stock suddenly stop now?

3. **40-Month Moving Average.** Yes. Even more than the 25-month moving average, the 40-month shows a stock that is may be hugely overbought; for certain, it is moving powerfully.

4. **OBV 1.** Yes. The bulge in OBV suggests the possibility of climactic buying. Nevertheless, the OBV line turned right up again along with price, and there is no sign of it faltering.

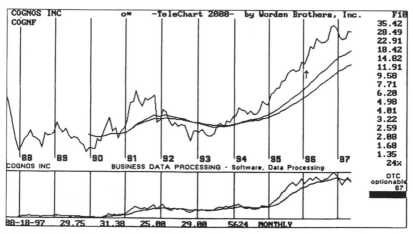

FIGURE 28–1. Cognos Monthly Line Chart, with 25- and 40-Month Moving Averages and On Balance Volume.

In November 1994 there was a clear breakout by OBV above all highs for the preceding four years. This action strongly suggested that money was flowing into the stock. It should continue to do so.

A final confirmation occurred when OBV completed a W and confirmed its upward zigzag with the upturn in price in January 1995.

5. **OBV 10.** Yes. The hesitation in OBV 1 has done no damage to OBV 10. OBV 1 may have to converge toward its moving average, but as long as it remains above, there is no cause for concern about this indicator.

6. **Fast MACD.** Yes. There is no tiring in fast MACD. This looks like a stock to keep if you own it and to buy when there is an opportunity.

7. **Slow MACD.** Yes. Both MACD lines are maintaining a steady upward incline and a steady divergence between each other. This shows that the underlying trend of momentum is solid.

8. **%K Turn.** Yes. %K is jammed at its upper extremity and blips at this overbought level are virtually meaningless in a rapidly moving stock.

9. **%K Level.** No. The fact %K remains jammed at an overbought

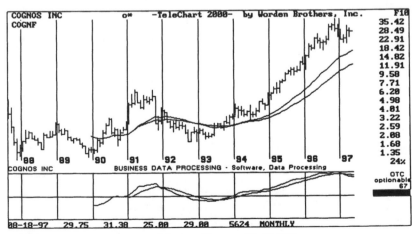

FIGURE 28-2. Cognos Monthly Bar Chart, with MACD.

extremity indicates power more than it suggests the likelihood of an imminent collapse in the stock price.

10. **Price Rule.** Yes. The upside monthly reversal in January is immensely powerful. This alone suggests a buying opportunity.

11. **Turn at MA/Trendline.** Not applicable.

12. **Key Reversal.** Yes. A bull's-eye!

13. **Double Reversal.** Yes. A monthly upside reversal in October and another one in January.

14. **Chart Pattern.** Yes. There is really nothing to say except that this is a stock steadily working higher. There is nothing to suggest that the strong trend in force is likely to falter, let alone to end suddenly.

15. **Gap.** Not applicable.

16. **Island.** Not applicable.

17. **Market Conditions.** Yes. The major stock indexes are clearly bullish, especially the software subindexes. Cognos looks like a prime stock to own within a group where upward momentum is likely to continue.

18. **Value.** Yes. Cognos has been working on various software programs. In all honesty, it is impossible to know much about their chance of success in the marketplace. They have been in busi-

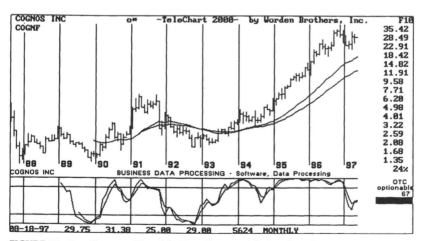

FIGURE 28-3. Cognos Monthly Bar Chart, with Stochastics.

ness for some time, which is a big plus, and chart action suggests that knowledgeable investors are buying.

Monthly Negating Indicators

1. **Adverse W/Zigzag Line.** Not applicable.

2. **Adverse 25 MA Direction.** Not applicable.

3. **Adverse 40 MA Direction.** Not applicable.

4. **OBV 1.** Not applicable.

5. **OBV 10.** Not applicable.

6. **Fast MACD.** Not applicable.

7. **Slow MACD.** Not applicable.

8. **%K Level.** Yes, but unlikely a cause for concern.

9. **Resistance.** None.

10. **Channel Line.** Not applicable.

11. **Adverse Trendline Crossover.** Not applicable.

12. **Value.** Not applicable.

Weekly Confirming Indicators

1. **W Formation/Zigzag Line.** Yes. The weekly price line has just ended a major correction, which probably strengthens the market rather than shows risk of further weakness.

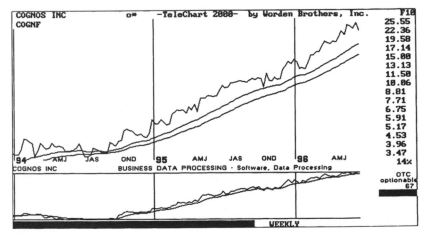

FIGURE 28-4. Cognos Weekly Line Chart, with On Balance Volume.

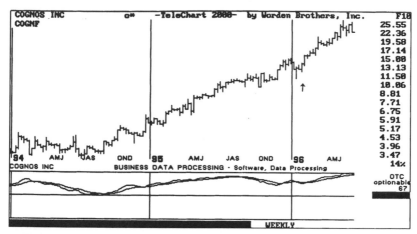

FIGURE 28–5. Cognos Weekly Bar Chart, with MACD.

2. **25-Week Moving Average.** Yes. Confirms with a strong upward incline.

3. **40-Week Moving Average.** Yes. Confirms with the same positive indications as the 25-week.

4. **OBV 1.** Yes. OBV confirms with a strong upward zigzag.

5. **OBV 10.** Yes. Confirms with OBV 1 crossover turning up again near the strongly rising OBV 10.

6. **Fast MACD.** Yes. There was weakness in November and there has been some in January, although fast MACD holds well above

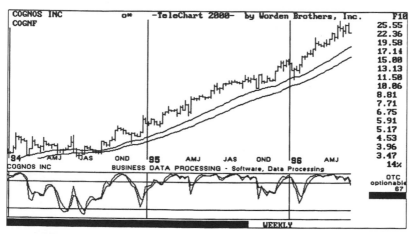

FIGURE 28–6. Cognos Weekly Bar Chart, with Stochastics.

the November low. MACD shows momentum and may weaken without affecting price.

7. **Slow MACD.** Yes. Slow MACD has barely turned up after a decline from September to December. This faltering is unlikely a cause for concern.

8. **%K Turn.** Yes. Count %K positive.

9. **%K Level.** No. Count neutral. %K may have retraced enough to relieve the immensely overbought condition. The fact that it failed to retrace down to the 20 oversold level may be a sign of strength, not weakness.

10. **Price Rule.** Yes. Count a Rule 5 and a Rule 8 on February 2! You could hardly have a more bullish price rule than one where the second bar is a double reversal and also an outside bar.

11. **Turn at MA/Trendline.** Yes, a perfect turn at the weekly moving averages!

12. **Key Reversal.** Yes.

13. **Double Reversal.** Yes.

14. **Chart Pattern.** Yes. Count as a positive indicator. Everything about this stock is bullish.

15. **Gaps.** Not applicable.

16. **Islands.** Not applicable.

17. **Market Conditions.** Covered on the monthly list.

18. **Value.** Covered on the monthly list.

Weekly Negating Indicators

1. **Adverse W/Zigzag Line.** Not applicable.

2. **Adverse 25 MA Direction.** Not applicable.

3. **Adverse 40 MA Direction.** Not applicable.

4. **OBV 1.** Not applicable.

5. **OBV 10.** Not applicable.

6. **Fast MACD.** Not applicable.

7. **Slow MACD.** Not applicable.

8. **%K Level.** Count neutral.

9. **Resistance.** None.

10. **Channel Line.** Not applicable.

11. **Adverse Trendline Crossover.** Not applicable.

12. **Value.** Not applicable.

Daily Confirming Indicators

1. **W Formation/Zigzag Line.** Yes. The daily price line sustained a major correction during January. If you wanted to buy the stock on the basis of the daily chart, you might think that the action was too violent for comfort, even though no damage occurred on the monthly and weekly charts. The stock now seems to be shaking off its lethargy ahead of a potential upward surge. The correction probably occurred as a result of profit-taking by value investors. Thanks for the opportunity to get in!

2. **25-Day Moving Average.** Yes. Confirms with an upturn right here.

3. **40-Day Moving Average.** Yes. Confirms with a gentle upturn.

4. **OBV 1.** Yes. OBV confirms with a textbook upward zigzag developing again.

5. **OBV 10.** Yes. Confirms strongly, with OBV 1 back above again.

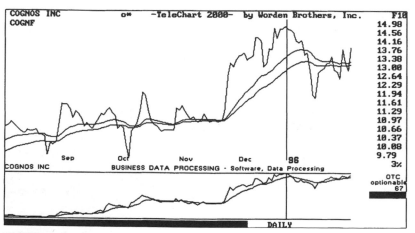

FIGURE 28-7. Cognos Daily Line Chart, with On Balance Volume.

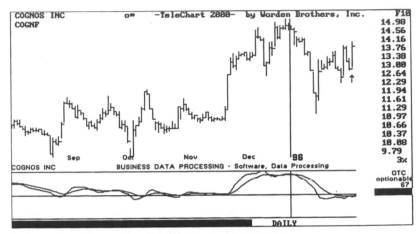

FIGURE 28-8. Cognos Daily Bar Chart, with MACD.

6. **Fast MACD.** Yes. Confirms with a small W and a new upside crossover right here.

7. **Slow MACD.** Yes. Slow MACD appears to be rounding out after declining during January. Count this indicator neutral to positive.

8. **%K Turn.** Yes. Count %K positive, with a good W pattern.

9. **%K Level.** No. Count neutral. The decline to zero maximum oversold levels in January almost certainly completed a selling climax.

10. **Price Rule.** Yes. Count a Rule 5, with the added bonus of two gaps up within the formation.

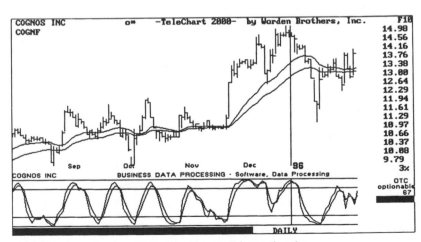

FIGURE 28-9. Cognos Daily Bar Chart, with Stochastics.

11. **Turn at MA/Trendline.** No. The price should not have penetrated so much below the 25- and 40-day moving averages. However, this probably signifies the importance of the correction rather than suggesting the potential for weakness ahead.

12. **Key Reversal.** Not applicable.

13. **Double Reversal.** Not applicable.

14. **Chart Pattern.** Yes. Count as a positive indicator. The single price line appears to be coiling, with a strong upward bias. The amplitude of the correction from $15.19 to $11.12 is $4.07. The initial price projection is $19.26, based on adding the amplitude of the correction to the price at the December high.

15. **Gaps.** Yes. A very bullish gap up on the entry day.

16. **Islands.** Not applicable.

17. **Market Conditions.** Covered on the monthly list.

18. **Value.** Covered on the monthly list.

Daily Negating Indicators

1. **Adverse W/Zigzag Line.** Not applicable.

2. **Adverse 25 MA Direction.** Not applicable.

3. **Adverse 40 MA Direction.** Not applicable.

4. **OBV 1.** Not applicable.

5. **OBV 10.** Not applicable.

6. **Fast MACD.** Not applicable.

7. **Slow MACD.** Not applicable.

8. **%K Level.** Not applicable.

9. **Resistance.** None.

10. **Channel Line.** Not applicable. The resistance at the December high is not likely to cause more than hesitation.

11. **Adverse Trendline Crossover.** Not applicable.

12. **Value.** Not applicable.

It would be very difficult to find a better market in rapid motion than COGNF. The potential for a big move is enormous, possibly a double, a triple, or who knows what.

ENTRY CHECKLIST, COGNOS: BUY

Stock COGNF	Price $13.86	Date 2/2/96	
Confirming Indicators	**Monthly**	**Weekly**	**Daily**
1. W/Zigzag Line	✔	✔	✔
2. 25 Bar MA	✔	✔	✔
3. 40 Bar MA	✔	✔	✔
4. OBV 1	✔	✔	✔
5. OBV 10	✔	✔	✔
6. Fast MACD	✔	✔	✔
7. Slow MACD	✔	✔	✔
8. %K Turn	✔	✔	✔
9. %K Level (under 20)			
10. Price Rule	✔	✔	✔
11. Turn at MA/Trendline		✔	
12. Key Reversal	✔	✔	
13. Double Reversal	✔	✔	
14. Chart Pattern	✔	✔	✔
15. Gap			✔
16. Island			
17. Market Conditions	✔	✔	✔
18. Value	✔	✔	✔
TOTAL	**14**	**15**	**13**
Negating Indicators			
1. Adverse W/Zigzag Line			
2. Adv. 25 MA			
3. Adv. 40 MA			
4. OBV 1			
5. OBV 10			
6. Fast MACD			
7. Slow MACD			
8. %K Level (above 80)	✔		✔
9. Resistance			
10. Channel Line			
11. Adv. T-Line Cross			
12. Value			
TOTAL	**1**	**0**	**1**

Setting Stops

With the entry at $13.86 on February 2, there are several choices of stops. By far the best one for well-financed investors is to put the stop under the January 16 low, which took the price down to $11.12. A stop at, say, $10.75 is extremely unlikely to be hit unless there is something very wrong with the assumptions for buying Cognos. This stop allows for a loss of 23 percent. Some people would find that too rich, despite the prospect of the stock going on to double or triple. Nevertheless, that is the best available chart point for the stop.

A second choice is to put the stop under the January 29 low, at $12.32. Then the stop could be placed at $11.75. That would represent a 16 percent loss in the event of the stop being hit.

There is a conflict. On the one hand, a rapidly moving stock should keep on going if it is truly good. On the other hand, even the greatest stock needs to be allowed room to move. Otherwise, there is the risk of inviting an unnecessary loss. On balance, the looser stop is normally better.

What Happened

Cognos went on to $39.50 by the end of the year, after a three-month pause during June, July, and August. The stock then retraced savagely to a low at $21.50 before resuming its advance. Trailing protective stops should have allowed for at least some stock to be sold well above that retracement low, probably at $26.50. During 1997 and 1998 COGNF went into another long period of consolidation during which there was little or no money to be made. However, the stock continued to be worth watching to see whether the market might decide to appreciate the company's apparently substantial efforts toward reaching for a higher plateau in the marketplace along with, presumably, another surge in the price of the stock.

When to Sell and When to Sell Short

CHAPTER 29

When to Sell

Reasons to Sell

It is much easier to buy than it is to sell. You do not set sail or buy a stock without checking for fair weather. Selling requires interpretation of a wide range of unpredictable variables. What looks initially like a summer shower may be the start of a hurricane. A severe squall that looks like the start of a hurricane may be no more than an unpleasant but isolated interruption that soon passes.

When in doubt, it generally pays to stay in a stock in which you have a good profit, and it generally pays to sell one in which you have a loss. This is the exact opposite of what comes easily to most people. When there is conflicting evidence, it generally pays to live by the principle of running profits and cutting losses. Of course, you do not want to give back all of a big profit, right back to your buying price, by staying in a stock long after the technical indicators have turned negative, as a buy-and-hold strategy might seem to dictate.

There are two primary reasons to sell a stock.

1. You See Something Better to Do with the Money

There is always the risk of constantly seeing something better to do with the money. It is all too easy to turn into a trading junkie. When, however, you see a really good stock that is timely to buy, it makes a lot of sense to weed out one or more weak ones and upgrade the quality of the portfolio. Many investors do the opposite, taking profits in order to buy stocks at an earlier stage of development. This is almost invariably a loser-play. It seldom pays to sell a Microsoft in order to buy a General Motors, however seductive GM looks. You should do the opposite when a Microsoft delivers a strong signal to buy.

The technical analyst has to say that there is a poor technical case for owning Woolworth from about 1991 on (Figure 29-1). The stock was going nowhere. You should always be able to find something better to do with money invested in a stock with that kind of dismal chart pattern. If the stock ever stops going sideways, it is just as likely to go down as up, which we now see actually happened. Here is a stock for which its time in the sun came to an end. You might have tripled your money or more as a very long-term shareholder, but staying in it no longer warrants the risk relative to the prospect of further gains. Failure to face that reality amounts to an exercise in unjustifiable complacency, or even of incompetence, in light of probabilities that have turned unfavorable.

2. The Stock Runs Its Stop

The difficulty with this approach is that it requires both discipline and judgment when setting the stop, which was discussed in Chapters 21 and 22. You can have the best guidelines in the world for setting stops, but it is impossible to make the process entirely objective and mechanical.

You have to get the hang of setting stops. Just as important, you have to get the hang of living with the outcome. Once you do, it is possible to do very well by relying on stops as the only means of getting out

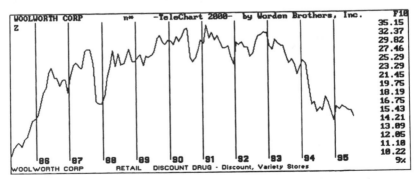

FIGURE 29-1. Woolworth Monthly Line Chart, with On Balance Volume.

of the market. Stops are set at the level where you decide that a stock would be in violation of its major trend and of your expectations. Stops relieve you of the psychological difficulty of making under pressure a decision whether or not to stay in the market. Logically, therefore, you should be satisfied to know that you traded well when a stop is hit. There's nothing wrong with that, although a more proactive approach to analysis of the prospects for a stock may pay better in the long run.

Warning Signs

Here are some of the things to look for when taking a more aggressive or vigilant approach than simply waiting for stops to be activated. When pulling the trigger to sell a stock, it is generally best to do so on activation of a daily price rule signal to sell. That probably shows that the price is indeed heading lower, at least in the near term.

1. The Head-and-Shoulders Top. The head-and-shoulders top is one of the most reliable of all chart formations. It comes in all shapes and sizes on every chart. On the monthly chart, it often serves to warn of a substantial trend reversal. However, it is one of those patterns of which it can be said that when it works, the outcome may be dramatic, but when it does not, the continuation in the previous, upward direction is likely to be powerful.

The idea behind a head-and-shoulders formation is that the stock surges strongly to a new high, making in the process the left shoulder. Then it settles back and surges again to a higher high, making the head, before settling back yet again. Next it surges a third time to make the right shoulder. This time the stock fails to exceed the previous high before turning down again. Only after completion of the right shoulder can you designate a potential head-and-shoulders top. To signify a top with the greatest reliability, the pattern should take a significant time to form on the monthly chart, often a year or more. It should also be as symmetrical as possible and ideally, the right shoulder should be equal to or lower than the left one.

Confirmation of a head-and-shoulders formation occurs when the stock breaks below the so-called neckline. Some people draw a neckline by joining the lows of the retracements. When there is a choice, it is often better to draw a horizontal line across from the lower low, rather than draw a diagonal line.

Sometimes other indicators start confirming a top, or at least the start of sideways action, well before the stock breaks the neckline. However, you need good reasons to sell a stock before the breakdown, such as confirming OBV and MACD. Otherwise, you may find that the stock is doing no more than backing and filling before its next move up. Even the strongest and most wonderful stocks can make a more lasting top. Buyers push the price beyond what value analysts are prepared to pay for it, and the stock goes out of favor with them. Once out of favor, interest may back off and stay backed off for some time.

The chart for Bethlehem Steel shows the stock making a high in mid-1988, forming what develops into the left shoulder (Figure 29-2). A surge in early 1989 forms the head. Finally, there is a feeble right shoulder in mid-1989.

Confirmation of the formation occurs when the stock breaks below the end-1988 and September 1989 lows. It is worth noting that there was a rally back to the breakdown level, as frequently occurs. After breaking down below the neckline, the stock was to fall by almost 50 percent by the time it made its low in 1990.

This chart shows a second head-and-shoulders top, this time with a double-top at the head, between 1993 and 1995. Both these head-and-shoulders patterns showed that Bethlehem might be a stock to sell short, and that it was certainly not a stock to own.

2. The Descending Triangle.   A large descending triangle is equally reliable as the head-and-shoulders top at indicating a probable downward break in a stock.

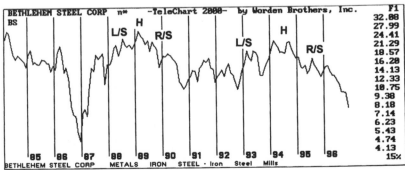

FIGURE 29-2.   Bethlehem Steel Monthly Line Chart, with Head-and-Shoulders Top and On Balance Volume.

Goodyear Tire & Rubber (Figure 29-3) went sideways during 1988–1989. It made a succession of three distinctly lower highs but always more or less stayed above the October 1987 low. Once the stock broke decisively down out of the triangle, there was almost no interruption in the decline from the $22 level to $6.50. Note that the triangle has to be drawn on the monthly line chart. It omits the range of the October 1987 collapse shown on the monthly bar chart (Figure 29-4), which initially provided support.

The chart pattern and the action of other technical indicators showed Goodyear was no longer a stock to own under any circumstances once the bottom of the descending triangle gave way. It was now a prime candidate for a short sale.

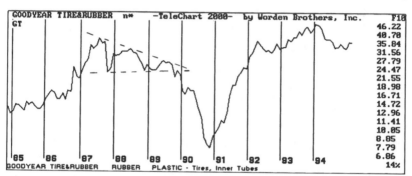

FIGURE 29–3. Goodyear Monthly Line Chart, with Descending Triangle.

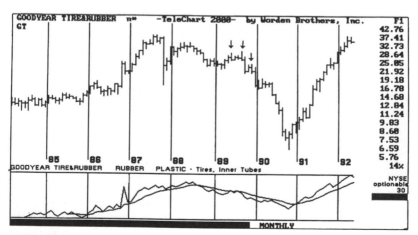

FIGURE 29–4. Goodyear Monthly Bar Chart, with Monthly Downside Reversals and OBV Failure.

3. Monthly Downside Reversals.   Monthly downside reversals often give warning of an impending top or of a potential breakdown. It is easy to misinterpret the occasional monthly downside reversal in a strong market. However, when other indicators agree, and especially when there is more than one downside reversal with a low close, there may be a significant decline soon. This alert is particularly significant when the close of a second or third monthly downside reversal is lower than one or more earlier ones. Weekly downside reversals, particularly outside down weeks, also serve as a warning of potential near-term weakness. Nevertheless, it seldom pays to be too hasty to move to sell unless over-all price action and performance of other indicators is conspicuously weak. All too often, a short period of weakness merely shakes shares out of weak hands before the stock goes higher again.

The monthly bar chart for Goodyear shows two monthly downside reversals toward the end of 1989, as the stock price was breaking down out of its descending triangle (Figure 29-4). There is a third outside down month in June 1990 before the stock really fell apart, going from $15.57 to an eventual low of $6.44.

4. OBV Failure.   OBV generally shows the likely direction of the breakout from a consolidation, including a head-and-shoulders formation and a descending triangle. From the second half of 1988 OBV was giving no encouragement to owners of Goodyear (Figure 29-4). Any idea that the rally in the first half of 1989 might have the makings of a new upward zigzag should have been dispelled by the weak performance of OBV. By mid-1989 it supported the case for short sales when OBV 1 was trending steadily below the declining OBV 10.

5. MACD Failure.   When MACD on the monthly chart starts topping out, there is a high probability that the stock price will begin to consolidate, if not necessarily to change direction. So a weakening MACD serves as an alert, not a call for action. The stronger a stock has been previously, the more it is entitled to a rest, and therefore a weakening MACD. In that case, MACD may turn severely negative without forecasting a trend reversal.

Figure 29-5 shows MACD with a double top at the same level in January 1992 as in mid-1991, although price went a lot higher. The relentless decline in MACD in conjunction with price breaking below the mid-1992 lows was an ominous sign. The downturn in fast MACD at the end of 1992 from a much lower high, together with slow MACD trending down, suggested bad news for this stock.

6. *200-Day Moving Average Breakdown.*   It seldom pays to continue owning a stock trading below its declining 200-day moving average.

The 200-day moving average is an industry standard for defining whether or not to own a stock. Contact here is often a pivotal level where a stock is either a wonderful buy or a must-sell, depending on price action and other indicators. You may inadvertently throw the towel in on a good stock because of an apparent failure, only to see it turn powerfully up again. In that case, admit being wrong and simply buy back the stock, even if you have to do so at a higher price than where you sold.

In practice, it is generally better to use the close equivalent, the 40-week moving average, because of the better view it gives of the big picture. By looking at other indicators, it is often possible to make a reasonable guess, as to whether this moving average is rolling over and likely to continue down or whether it is just temporarily losing steam. When the moving average is strongly pointing up, the probabilities favor buying at or near the 200-day moving average, not selling.

Figure 29-5 shows Merck initially supporting well at the 40-week moving average in 1992. However, with other bearish signs developing, you could have sold on the 40-week moving average breakdown in

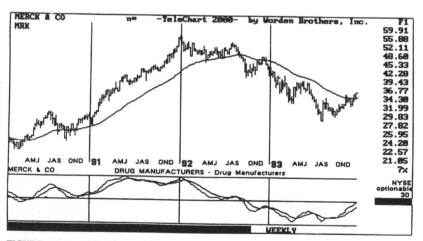

FIGURE 29–5. Merck Weekly Bar Chart, with 40-Week Moving Average Crossover and MACD Failure.

Merck in October 1992 at $47.00. If you failed to act then, there was another even more compelling time to sell when the rally in December failed at the declining 40-week moving average, allowing you to get out at $44.63. This action shows how support and resistance work both ways. Initially, the 40-week moving average supported Merck. After the breakdown, it served as resistance. The single weekly close above the declining 40-week moving average proved to be a trap, not an indication that the stock was resuming its long-term bull market.

Often there is no second chance as good as the one to sell Merck in December 1992. Although in due course MRK resumed its advance and far surpassed its previous highs, there was no knowing how low the stock could go once it topped out. In fact, the low for the move turned out to be at $28.13 in April 1994. That was almost a 50-percent decline from its high at $56.63 in January 1992.

Remember that selling, even more than buying, is an art as much as it is a science. It is guaranteed that there will be many frustrations when selling. You keep a stock only to see its price fall apart. You sell a stock only to see its price turn around and continue higher. As a rule, it is better to keep a great stock and give it room to move. On the other hand, it is best to act as soon as possible on strong signals to sell. Of course, these two rules often seem totally contradictory in practice. You cannot avoid that altogether. Nevertheless, these approaches to selling are likely in the long run to work a lot better than mindlessly holding stocks forever or constantly getting in and out of the market.

Of course, a stock well bought is likely to cause less difficulty when making the decision to sell. It is always easier to make decisions when you are making money.

Selling Stocks Short

Sell First, Then Buy

The standard investment approach is to buy a stock, expecting it to go up. However, there are times when an individual stock or the general market is going down, not up. Owning stocks then is an invitation to lose money. The obvious remedy for avoiding losses, or the disappearance of profits, in a stock going down is to sell it.

After identifying a stock that is going down or is likely to go down, it is both logical and possible to sell a stock you don't own, and then buy it back at a profit when the price is lower. This is what selling short is. Few people sell short, mainly because so few people know how to do it. Learning how to do it successfully is by no means as difficult as you might believe.

Many people think selling short is unethical. Not so. Selling short is, in effect, something many businesses do as a matter of course. A business often delivers goods or services, such as an airline ticket or a tailor-made suit, after the customer has placed the order and paid for it. A short sale in the stock market does essentially the same thing.

No doubt, you will have noticed that losses seem to come fast while profits from stocks you own tend to come more slowly, if they come at all. There is a reason for this. It takes new money coming into the market to make a stock go up. All it takes for a stock to go down is for the inflow of new money to fade. As a result, a stock often goes down between two and three times as fast as it goes up.

Selling short with a manageable risk is not difficult. But it is not suitable for everyone. It is generally advisable only when the major trend for all stocks, or for an industry sector such as gold or steels, is down. Then you can win three ways. You keep your profits from the bull market. You make money on the way down. You have more money than you would have otherwise to buy stocks low at the start of the next bull market.

A chart often shows at once that you do not want to own a stock. We have seen, for example, Digital Equipment and IBM when they were clearly going down. At times, they were in such clearly entrenched downtrends that it was obvious you could make money by selling them short.

Short-Sellers Perform a Service

As for the morality of selling short, many short-sellers perform a useful service. When a stock is skyrocketing, short-sellers who think the stock has gone too far allow demanding buyers to buy their stock at some price, even if not necessarily at one that seems favorable. Much of this short-selling is done by the short-term excess traders who intentionally sell into market bulges in the expectation that the price will settle back once the initial flurry ends. The same thing happens in reverse when there is panic selling and the excess traders buy into the decline. The excess traders tend to stop prices getting so far out of line that it is impossible to do business at any price at all.

Every short sale creates latent buying power. At some point, most short-sellers want to bank their profit, if there is one. When they buy back their shorts, they support the market in a stock that has gone down. Alternatively, their buying power adds fuel to an upward move if they get it wrong and have to cover their short sales at a loss. On balance, short-sellers tend to make money, particularly the professionals and those who have learned the skill of doing it profitably over time. However, selling short is not a one-way street to profits. When a short-seller gets it right, big profits come fast. When a short-seller gets it wrong, particularly when attempting to sell a high-flyer that has caught the popular imagination, the losses may be huge.

Risk and Reward

There is a common belief that selling short is very dangerous or, in any case, that it is not worth the risk. If you sell a stock short, the most you can make is the total amount you sold it for. Since a stock sold short can go up by several times instead of going down, the potential for loss is unlimited. It is natural, therefore, to think that the odds are heavily stacked in favor of buying and heavily stacked against selling short. That is true as far as it goes, but it is an extreme oversimplification. The risk depends on market conditions and how you set about selling short. In a general bear market, you should generally do nothing but sell short, if you are in the market at all.

Consider the difference it makes whether you buy a stock or sell short one that goes down. Say you bought Digital Equipment at $100. You ride the stock down to $30. Finally, you throw in the towel and bank a loss of $70 per share. You lose 70 percent of your investment. Your money has gone down the drain forever. But if you sell the stock short instead of buying it, then you have a profit of $70 per share, not a loss. To make the same money by buying the stock at $100, it has to go up to $170.

Responsible, planned short-selling of a declining stock in a bear market can deliver profits comparable with what you can make by buying a good stock in a bull market. As we shall see, under the right circumstances the risk of selling suitable stocks short when the time is right need be no greater than when buying strong stocks in a bull market.

During every major stock market decline, you can be certain that almost all stocks go down. That is what a bear market is. An entrenched bear market is generally obvious, although it may be confused with a short-lived panic sell-off. In a normal bear market, about 90 percent of all stocks go down. That compares with the 70 percent of all stocks that are normally rising at any given time in a strong bull market. Even if you sell a stock short that holds up in a bear market, it is very unlikely to go up much.

In a truly entrenched bear market, the statistical risk of picking a loser when selling short is smaller than the risk of picking a loser when buying in a bull market. In addition, the probabilities favor making more money more quickly because of the greater rapidity of decline and the greater reliability of a bear market. Of course, the key question is whether, in fact, you have a truly entrenched bear market. Even when that designation is ambiguous, make sure to sell a stock that is carving its own proprietary bear market or looks ready to begin one.

Selling short is the logical extension of going to cash to avoid a bear market. It is the means to profit from the stock market rather than just sitting on the sidelines waiting for the time to buy stocks again.

Stocks Not to Sell Short

Selling short is a byword for risk and loss because of the way many people set about it. Many people think selling short means selling stocks that are absurdly high on the assumption that they are worth only a fraction of their current price. A stock captures the public imagination and seems to go to the moon for no good reason. You find a company with a million dollars a year in sales and a market capitalization of a billion. The stock has assets behind it of 50 cents, but it sells for $50. How can it not be a short sale? Sure as you try to sell that stock short, the chances are that it will go on to $75 or $150. There is no price so high that a stock cannot go higher still, especially when a lot of people sell it short. Then buying back by those that sold it short drives the price higher still.

Sell a high-flyer short only when the run-up has had its back well and truly broken. The $50 stock that has gone up on helium and hype may be a short at $20 or at $15 when it has been truly busted and is heading back to earth and possibly to nothing.

Short Sale Candidates

Opportunities for short sales fall into five categories:

1. *A general bear market.* Sell short a stock that is in a clear bear market and when, in addition, stocks generally are in a bear market.

    When both of these conditions are met, there is little risk in selling short. The biggest challenge, however, is not to succumb to believing that there is a general bear market when there is no more than a correction in a continuing bull market. Real bear markets tend to decline relentlessly day after day. Corrections in a bull market may be extremely severe but of short duration.

2. *A stock-specific or sector bear market.* Sell a stock short that is carving out its own proprietary bear market, or a stock in a sector that is in a bear market, even as stocks generally are rising or going sideways.

   Depending on the intensity of the stock's bear market, the chances of a dramatic reversal are probably small. Normally, there are conspicuous business problems behind stocks carving out their own proprietary bear markets. Ideally, the company represented by the stock should be losing money, and there should be little prospect of that changing soon. Ideally, too, the company should be in an industry plagued with chronic overcapacity and low profit margins, and the entire subindex for the group should be in an entrenched bear market. Most gold mining stocks met these conditions during 1997. The stock should not be attractive as a takeover target.

3. *An emerging bear market.* Sell a stock short that is completing a long, drawn out distributional top. At major tops there is often a distributional phase that is the counterpart of the long-term base-building or the reverse head-and-shoulders from which come many of the most substantial bull markets.

   There are various topping patterns, but the best of all is generally the head-and-shoulders. For some reason it tends to work even better than any random double, triple, or even quadruple top. Sometimes you see rounding, like an upside-down saucer, that is the counterpart of the rounding bottom when a stock is starting to turn up and gather speed as it takes flight.

4. *The vacuum crash.* This involves selling short a stock at an absurdly high level that appears to be riding for a major fall, if not a total collapse. Once buyers stop pushing the stock, there is a vacuum underneath the market, a complete absence of interest in buying into a crash.

   This is the most hazardous assumption when considering a short sale. For the most part, candidates for a vacuum crash short sale fit the category of stocks where short sales should be avoided. Break the rule only very sparingly and when there is pronounced topping action such as two or more monthly downside reversals or what may be interpreted as exhaustion gapping up and down. It is best to assume the potential for a vacuum crash only when selling the stock of a major company with a considerable number of shares outstanding.

5. *Sell short to spread.* The case for spreading comes in two flavors.

   a. Sell short a weak stock while simultaneously owning a strong stock.

   There are two main reasons for considering the short sale of one stock while continuing to hold another one, putting on what the professionals call a spread.

   The first is that you expect to lessen the risk in holding what you own and, ideally, to make money on both the long, the one you own, and the short. You might see Wal-Mart winning and K Mart losing in the battle for retail sales. Alternatively, you might think Wal-Mart vulnerable to a setback for any number of reasons, ranging from its apparent high price to the possibility of a general weakening in retail sales. In the event of Wal-Mart setting back, you hope that K Mart falls by at least as much as Wal-Mart.

   This approach seldom has much to recommend it unless the case for both the long and the short can be justified on their own merits. It may simply offer two opportunities to lose money.

   b. Sell short another stock as a deliberate strategy for protecting profits in a stock you own. Then you may be able to delay payment of the capital gains taxes that would result from selling a stock that has made a lot of money.

   When a stock has gone up by several times and there is a sell signal, but you expect only temporary weakness, you may want to make an offsetting short sale to lock in the profit. If both stocks go down by roughly the same amount, you may be able to bank a profit on the short that is roughly equal to what you lost on the stock that you still own. Keep the drug stock Merck, for example, while selling the nearest equivalent you can find, which might be Pfizer.

   As a general rule, it pays better in the long run and it is psychologically more liberating to clear the decks by banking a profit and to accept that you have to pay some taxes. Otherwise, you may find yourself married to investment in a market sector where the sun is no longer shining. The main thing when banking profits is to make sure that you also take losses to offset the gains. If you have to pay taxes, so be it. It shows that you have done well.

The Short Interest Ratio

When everyone wants to sell short, in all likelihood the market will be at or near an important bottom, and it is more likely to go up than down. When any investment concept becomes too popular, firepower may run out at any time, causing a sharp reversal. Logically, most shortselling should happen at market tops, not at bottoms, but the opposite almost always happens. Logic generally rules only the professional market-makers and more astute investors. Emotions rule the general public at major tops and bottoms.

Some technicians use the Short Interest numbers as a contrary indicator with which to measure investment sentiment. Although not a timing indicator as such, it often works in the big picture. The list of Short Interest published monthly in *Barron's* represents a useful but by no means infallible guide to the advisability of selling short any individual stock. This list shows net changes since the previous report as well as the ratio of the number of stocks short to the average daily volume for the stock. Thus, if there is a short interest of 200,000 shares and average daily volume is 100,000 shares, the ratio is 2. The most desirable stocks to sell short generally have a short interest of between two and four days' average daily volume. When the ratio is too low, it means that few people want to sell the stock short, and it is probably unwise to do what few other people want to. When the short interest ratio is too high, it may mean that selling that particular stock short may be excessively popular. There may therefore be a short squeeze. Any rally may start a scramble in the stock that leads to a big upward surge in price.

Short Sale Procedures

There are some minor procedural differences between selling a stock that you own and selling a stock short.

Ordinarily, when you own a stock and want to sell it, you deliver the stock to the buyer. When you sell a stock short, you have to tell the broker you are selling short. Since you have no stock to give to the buyer, the broker has to borrow stock to deliver for you. Most likely, the stock comes from the margin account of another client. It may come from stock owned by the firm, or it may even be borrowed from another firm. The important thing is that except by special agreement, you cannot keep the buyer waiting for delivery.

Occasionally, the person from whom you borrowed the stock may want it back. Your broker may then be unable to borrow stock anywhere else to cover your short sale. This situation generally occurs only in a thinly traded stock. However, it can happen that aggressive buyers wanting to push the price higher refuse to lend stock to be sold against them. When there is an extreme imbalance of demand over supply, holders of short positions unable to borrow stock may be forced to buy in the stock that they are short. One way or another, they must either borrow the stock or pay it back. The result is the technical condition called a *short squeeze*. Regardless of how much the short-seller has to pay, there is no choice but to pay up to buy the stock back. For all practical purposes, a short squeeze never occurs in a stock that a prudent investor would ever normally want to sell short. But you have to know what it is.

After selling a stock short, you are responsible for making good the value of all dividends and any other benefits of ownership issued to stockholders by the company. If the stock pays only a small dividend or none, this obligation counts for little. If the stock pays a large dividend, the obligation may be heavy.

There is a technical requirement for execution of a short sale on the exchange. Regulations require that a short sale occur only by an uptick. It is allowed only after someone is prepared to pay more than the price of the last trade in the stock. It can occasionally happen in a rapidly falling market that you cannot execute a short sale. Every trade is at the same price or lower, so your order is never filled. If you do get a fill, it may be only at a price far lower than you expect, especially when the market is falling apart all around you. To avoid getting an appalling fill, give the broker a limit below which you do not want to sell.

There is no time limit for covering a short sale (by buying back the stock). You can stay short for as long as you like unless the person from whom you borrowed the stock wants it back and the broker cannot find a replacement borrowing. Occasionally, you may want to hold a short position for years. If the company issuing the stock you sold short goes bankrupt, you never have to cover the short position.

Short Sale Margins

Margins work differently when selling short than when buying on margin. When buying a stock on margin, the broker requires the account to have cash equal to half what you pay for it. The other half is advanced as a debit balance on which you pay interest. Even if the stock goes up by several times, you still owe the same amount of money to the broker. When a stock bought on margin goes up enough, you can, of course, use the excess to buy more stock.

If you sell short $10,000 worth of stock, you must put up cash of $5000, or 50 percent. When you sell, $10,000 in proceeds from the sale is deposited in your account, so you have on hand $15,000 in cash. Instead of owing 50 cents for each dollar of stock that you buy on margin, you own $1.50 in cash for each dollar of stock that you are short. Some brokers will pay interest on that $10,000. It is hard to find one that will, but it is worth working on it when interest rates are high. Normally, brokers keep the interest earned on that credit balance in exchange for the favor of finding the stock for you to borrow. That is why some brokers execute short sales without charging any commissions at all.

If the stock you sell short goes down by 50 percent, it takes only $5000 to buy back what you sold for $10,000. To be fully margined at 150 percent, the broker now requires only $7500 in the account, half the $15,000 originally required. You can stay in your short position and draw off your entire profit of $5000 as well as half what you put up as margin in the first place.

Calculate the Stop-Loss

As when buying a stock, you have to budget for a short sale not to work. The broker allows a rise in price against you until your margin falls from 50 percent down to 40 percent. This is roughly equivalent to a 10 percent rise in price against you. It means that you lose $1000 of the $5000 that you started with. You will not have a margin call if you have other money or stocks in the account. In that case, you have to do your own homework to monitor your short sale.

Instead of a sell stop below the market, as when you buy a stock, when selling short, you place a buy stop above the market. Depending on the chart pattern for the stock, you might place a stop 20 percent above your selling price.

Before selling a stock short, work out where the stop has to be, as you would before buying. Then consider how much of a loss you can withstand, both financially and psychologically, in the event of the stop being hit.

You have to work out your own tolerance for losses using the total value of your portfolio as the starting point. Say that you have a portfolio worth $100,000. A short sale of $10,000 worth of stock represents a 10-percent commitment of your total funds to the market, as it would when buying an equivalent amount of stock. If the stop dictates getting out when the stock goes up by 20 percent, you lose $2000, or 2 percent of the total value of your portfolio. That should be acceptable for most people.

As when you own a stock, you must give a short sale room to move. In addition, you must allow for contingencies. Every venture into the stock market, whether you buy or sell, involves the risk of a market accident. When you own a stock, there can be an announcement of some devastating piece of corporate news that sends the stock plummeting. When you are short a stock, there can be an announcement about the launch of some wonderful new product or a bid for the stock from another company. Most surprise announcements have an impact on the stock price that falls within about a 30-percent range up or down for the stock. You should budget to absorb a sudden 30-percent loss on a single short sale that backfires.

Start Short Sales Slowly

When starting to sell short, sell only half of what you think you can handle. Remember that Gerald Loeb seldom put at risk more than one-third of his total capital at any one time, or more than 10 percent in a single stock. That is a reasonable maximum exposure for most accounts selling any stock short. Some people plunge into selling short, learning the hard way. Even if you are successful, at some point the probabilities are likely to turn against you if you overtrade or take a bigger position than you can afford should things go wrong. As well as learning the mechanics of how to do it, almost everyone needs to get the psychological hang of short-selling. As with all investment, it is worth remembering how much money you can make when you are right. So there is no point in risking a squeeze that endangers the overall value of your investments.

It pays to set about short sales with the mind-set that the general direction of stocks over the long term is up, not down. If you buy a stock at a bad price, things may turn out all right just by holding on until it comes back. You cannot make that assumption about a short sale. A short sale that runs your stop could, instead, be a stock to buy. You may have sold toward the end of a move down, and the next significant move could be higher, possibly very much higher.

It is essential to look at the big picture for the overall market. Selling any stock short in a general bull market is an invitation to lose money unless the case for doing so is overwhelming. In a bull market, it is generally much better to stay with the major uptrend, looking for stocks that are timely to buy rather than seeking out short sales.

You can make very big money selling short when the conditions are right, but you have to select stocks with patience and care and most important, manage your capital conservatively. Joseph Kennedy, father of the U.S. President, is said to have made much of his fortune by selling short between 1929 and 1932, but he was not selling short until the bear market began.

On balance, professional traders who sell short tend to be better versed in market timing than the majority of investors. They tend also to be better traders, whether buying or selling, because they use the techniques of market timing. They understand the meaning of the truism that the stock market fluctuates and that there are bear markets as well as bull markets. Logically, it makes equal sense—no more and no less—to make money when the market goes down as when it goes up.

Pyramiding Margin

A curiosity of the way that margins work on short sales is how much money you can make if you add to the short position when you use your profits as new margin. When you make a short sale, you are always at 150 percent of margin, so new short sales do not add to a debt, although, of course, they add to the potential for loss.

Table 30-1 shows what you could theoretically have done with $6000 after starting with an initial short sale of IBM at $114.13. You sell more stock short when the stock goes down by enough to support the new short sale and, in addition, there is a new sell signal.

In real-time trading you would never use your available margin so fully if that were all you had. Nevertheless, here is how you might have turned $6000 into $18,000, tripling your money, while the stock went from the initial entry price of $114.13 until the position was covered at $49.75.

The table shows the current position in the account before and after each new transaction.

In this example, a decline in the price of 55 percent multiplies the initial margin by more than three times, before allowing for a small

TABLE 30-1   Use of Margin When Selling IBM Short

Date	Buy/Sell	Qty	Current Price	Market Value	Cash On Hand	Account Value
3/19/91	Opening Deposit				$ 6,000	$6,000
3/20/91	Sell	100	$114.13	$11,413	$17,413	6,000
11/15/91		100	96.25	9,625	17,413	7,788
11/16/91	Sell	50	96.25	4,812	22,225	7,788
8/17/92		150	88.63	13,294	22,225	8,931
8/17/92	Sell	40	88.63	3,542	25,767	8,931
9/18/92		190	78.50	14,915	25,767	10,852
9/18/92	Sell	50	78.50	3,925	29,692	10,852
10/15/92		240	72.88	17,491	29,692	12,201
10/15/92	Sell	50	72.88	3,644	33,336	15,845
11/4/93		290	49.75	14,427	33,336	18,909
11/4/93	Cover Short	290	49.75	14,427	17,752	18,909

Account starting value: $6,000; account ending value $18,909 deduction for commissions and slippage. At the time of each new short sale, the account was always fully margined, with at least 50 percent more money in the account than was required to cover the short position. There was never an addition to the short position greater than the previous total number of shares already held short.

At the bottom of the market in IBM in August 1994 the stock sold down to $40.63. At that price the short position in 290 shares could have been covered at a profit of $21,554. However, as we have seen, it is almost impossible to buy at bottoms and sell at tops.

Even without adding to the position at all, you could still have more than doubled your money. In a full-fledged bear market, there may be many stocks that go from a very high price to almost nothing, and declines of 80 or 90 percent are quite commonplace. Then there are even greater opportunities for adding profitably to short positions. You have to remember that you will get a margin call when the market price of a stock you sell short goes up by more than about 20 percent from the price where you sold it, unless you have other money and securities in your account.

It pays to keep watch on the margin requirements for your short positions and not to shelter from reality simply because you have other money in the account. It seldom pays to depart from the saying: Never meet a margin call! Even if there is not a margin call as such, because you have other investments, you should almost certainly close out a short position that has gone more than about 20 percent against you.

CHAPTER 31

Entry Checklist: Sell Short

Differences Compared with Buying

The checklist for selling stocks short is almost identical to the one for buying stocks except that the overbought and oversold indicators are reversed (Table 31-1).

Short sales having the highest probability of success are normally in an established bear market. There should ideally be a downward zigzag that has established a minimum of a triple top, or a *double* M. Larger Ms developed over a longer time are more significant than smaller ones.

It is not mandatory to have the monthly 25- and 40-month moving averages already pointing downward, with price trading below them, but these confirmations reinforce the likelihood of success and lessen the risk of failure.

If a downtrend in the monthly moving averages is not yet established, there should be strong evidence of an extended distributional top forming. OBV and MACD should show clear evidence of the potential for a decline in price. One of the best indications of an impending top is a long, drawn out head-and-shoulders formation. It can be lethal to own a stock that completes a big head-and-shoulders top. The other side of the coin is a corresponding prospect of a big gain from a short sale. This pattern can be a very rewarding place to start looking for potential short sales.

As when buying, there is always a trade-off between entering a short sale early or late. Enter early and you have a manageable stop. Enter later and the evidence of a breakdown is much stronger. However, the distance from a reasonable stop requires a bigger budget in case the short sale aborts. When a decline is underway, it is generally better to sell into rallies rather than into breakdowns unless the breakdown is both decisive and the decline is at an early stage of development.

As when buying, it is not necessary for every indicator to confirm, although the more indicators confirm, the better the probability of success—but only up to a point. If you wait until every possible indicator confirms, there is a high probability of an imminent retracement, if not necessarily a trend reversal. You can have too much of a good thing.

Confirming Indicators

1. **M Formation/Zigzag Line.** There is no more powerful indicator of a bear market than the downward zigzag on the monthly line chart, preferably with markedly lower highs and lower lows. You can identify an emerging bear market when there is an M on the monthly line chart. The bigger it is and the longer it takes to form, the more likely it is to signify an important top. An M occurring in conjunction with a head-and-shoulders formation is particularly powerful.

2. **25-Bar MA.** The 25-*month* moving average should show a downward direction, and ideally, it should be below the 40-month moving average.

3. **The 40-Bar MA.** The 40-month moving average takes longer to turn down than the 25-month. Tops often form too fast for confirmation by the 40-month moving average. However, a declining 40-month moving average shows a solidly entrenched bear market.

4. **OBV 1.** The direction of the simple unsmoothed line for on balance volume shows the immediate weight of buying or selling pressure in a stock. This line is particularly encouraging for downward continuation in the price of a stock when it comprises its own downward zigzag pattern.

ENTRY CHECKLIST: SELL SHORT

Stock	Price		Date
Confirming Indicators	**Monthly**	**Weekly**	**Daily**
1. M/Zigzag Line			
2. 25 Bar MA			
3. 40 Bar MA			
4. OBV 1			
5. OBV 10			
6. Fast MACD			
7. Slow MACD			
8. %K Turn			
9. %K Level (above 80)			
10. Price Rule			
11. Turn at MA/Trendline			
12. Key Reversal			
13. Double Reversal			
14. Chart Pattern			
15. Gap			
16. Island			
17. Market Conditions			
18. Value			
TOTAL			
Negating Indicators			
1. Adverse M/Zigzag Line			
2. Adv. 25 MA			
3. Adv. 40 MA			
4. OBV 1			
5. OBV 10			
6. Fast MACD			
7. Slow MACD			
8. %K Level (under 20)			
9. Support			
10. Channel Line			
11. Adv. T-Line Cross			
12. Value			
TOTAL			

There are two conditions in the action for OBV that you have to be careful with. When OBV 1 has moved a long way from OBV 10, it may indicate a selling climax rather than the kind of persistence that keeps a stock moving steadily lower. You also have to beware when price moves to a new low but OBV makes a higher low.

Although not included on the checklist, this indicator delivers a sell signal in its own right when it crosses below its 10-bar moving average. It is most significant when the crossover occurs after a period of rounding by the two OBV lines.

5. **OBV 10.** The smoothed OBV line takes the wrinkles out of the ebb and flow of supply and demand. It shows persistence more reliably than does OBV 1. You want it to confirm direction.

6. **Fast MACD.** Fast MACD should be pointing down.

    This is often a lagging indicator when buying, but it seldom pays to go against its direction when selling. The best short sales have MACD solidly zigzagging down.

7. **Slow MACD.** This indicator should be pointing down.

    Some of the biggest and best declines start when fast MACD crosses below the slow and they both begin to move hard down.

8. **%K Turn.** The %K fast stochastic should point down to confirm, regardless of whether it is at a high or low level.

    Sloppy action in %K at a high level, when the price of the stock also seems high, may indicate that the stock needs to consolidate and that the stock may sell off. However, this is not a good indicator for selling short unless there is a pronounced pattern of lower highs and lower lows over an extended period of time.

9. **%K Level.** This indicator confirms when %K is above 80 in a clearly defined bear market.

10. **Price Rule Signal.** You need a new price rule on the daily chart to pull the trigger to sell. Ideally, there should be a clear price rule signal on the monthly chart and on the weekly chart in force when selling a stock short. In practice, it is often enough to get a general impression that bars on the weekly and monthly charts are generally bearish, with closes mostly in the lower end of their respective bars.

11. **Turn at MA.** Count this indicator positive when the price stops and turns at a level at or near the 25 and 40 moving averages, after completing a retracement. Then there is very high probability that the moving averages will contain the retracement, and there is a much higher probability of success than when a price rule occurs randomly.

    The 25 and 40 calibration may seem arbitrary. Nevertheless, the probabilities tend to be more favorable on retracements to these levels for two reasons. First, they show that the stock is not exceptionally overextended and vulnerable to a retracement. On the contrary, it has returned to an equilibrium level within the major trend. Second, many traders watch the 25 and 40 moving averages so that their effectiveness in containing retracements tends to be self-reinforcing.

12. **Key Reversal.** A key reversal with a strong close increases the probability of a stock continuing in the direction of the close. A downside key reversal provides the visible means of showing that buyers have failed to turn the market up. Also, timid shorts have probably been flushed out of the market.

    Downside key reversals on the monthly and weekly charts tend to show a weak stock, especially when there have recently been one or more additional downside reversals.

    A key reversal occurring in conjunction with a sell signal on the daily chart generally provides a much-enhanced probability of a stock moving sharply lower right away.

13. **Double Reversal.** A double reversal in the direction of an established trend is as powerful as a key reversal, if not more so. They both indicate cleansing of the market of weak holders and preparation for a strong continuation of the move.

14. **Chart Pattern.** Count a favorable indicator when the overall chart pattern is clearly bearish. Also count a favorable chart pattern when a stock is breaking out of a trading range or is completing a head-and-shoulders pattern.

15. **Gaps.** Count a favorable indicator when there are downward gaps on the weekly or daily charts. Gaps on the weekly chart tend to have more significance than you might expect because so many people make investment decisions over the weekend.

16. **Islands.** Count a favorable indicator when the price has gapped up and then gapped down. Best of all is when there are several days of market consolidation above the market prior to a sharp downside resolution of the standoff between buyers and sellers. This can be one of the most favorable formations for selling at the end of a retracement in a bear market.

   On the other hand, an island below the current price that results from downward-upward gapping may show the stock has exhausted its downside potential.

17. **Market Conditions.** It is essential to look at the bigger picture for the market generally, for interest rates, and for the group index for the stock that you are considering.

   When the stock market in general is either going sideways or is at a very low level, be careful. That means that you should sell lightly, not that you should pass when there is a strong signal.

   In a general bull market, be wary of selling any stock short.

18. **Value.** The best stocks to sell short generally have an external reason to sell them. It should be obvious that the company is badly run, is not making money, and has little prospect of doing so. Ideally, the stock should represent a company in an industry that has substantial overcapacity. On the other hand, beware of selling a stock so beaten down that it could be a takeover target.

Negating Indicators

1. **Adverse M/Zigzag Line.** It practically never pays even to think about selling short a stock without a clearly defined downward zigzag on the *monthly* chart, or at least the beginning of one. Lack of this confirming indicator virtually amounts to a total embargo. However, a very overbought condition in a bear market can establish an adverse zigzag on the weekly chart or even more frequently, on the daily chart.

   The weekly and daily charts may not have a downward zigzag pattern after a severe retracement.

The main thing is to have a strong monthly chart pattern confirming a major downtrend.

2. **Adverse 40 MA Direction.** An upward incline in the 40-month moving average counts as a negating indicator.

   Many stocks sell off before the 40-month moving average turns down, so this indicator may take some time to come on side. Count it negative, if adverse.

3. **Adverse 25 MA Direction.** An upward incline in the 25-month moving average counts as a negating indicator.

   Given that tops often occur more rapidly than bottoms, the most important thing is to have the weekly and daily moving averages, both the 25 and the 40, pointing down.

4. **OBV 1.** When OBV 1 points up, count this indicator negative.

5. **OBV 10.** Count this indicator negative when pointing up.

6. **Fast MACD.** Count a negating indicator when fast MACD is pointing up.

7. **Slow MACD.** Count a negative indicator when slow MACD is pointing up.

8. **%K Level.** Count a negative indicator when the fast stochastic %K is at 20 or lower.

   This condition often occurs when a stock is oversold and vulnerable to a retracement. It also occurs, however, in the fastest moving markets and when a stock first breaks out of a consolidation. Therefore, a low %K level may be a sign of a stock capable of collapsing. So you have to interpret %K in the context of specific market action at the time.

9. **Support.** Support counts as a negative indicator when a stock is approaching a historic low where it has previously turned up.

10. **Channel Line.** Count this a negative indicator when a stock is pressing against a lower channel line. Then, there is a high probability of retracement back to the downtrend line.

11. **Adverse Trendline Crossover.** Count a negative indicator when price is above a clearly identifiable downtrend line. That means that the stock has lost its immediate downward momentum. A

strongly downtrending stock should not require ever shallower trendlines.

12. **Value.** Count a negative indicator if the stock represents a company that is asset-rich and merely going through a bad patch that may only be temporary.

Stops

Don't sell a stock short without knowing where to place the stop. You must also, of course, enter the order with the broker. You cannot live without disaster insurance!

CHAPTER 32

Case Study: Sell Short into an Approaching Waterfall

IBM Takes a Slide

Sometimes you see a chart for a stock that looks like a river gathering speed as it approaches a waterfall. Trading into a waterfall can be extremely rewarding when you know what to look for. Inevitably, some of these short sales backfire. Nevertheless, those that succeed repay many times over the losses incurred by the ones that fail.

This case study illustrates the homework for selling IBM short on August 5, 1992 at $91.63. The monthly chart shows the stock accelerating downward at the end of 1991 (Figure 32-1). Instead of a regular pattern of lower highs and lower lows that permits drawing a straight trendline, the highs are significantly lower than the previous ones, allowing for a curved trendline. Lows are also significantly lower than previous ones. There is little or no horizontal support as a result of previous rebounds from the current level, so there is a high probability that selling will intensify, taking the stock down far and fast.

The Entry Checklist

Monthly Confirming Indicators

1. **M Formation/Zigzag Line.** Yes. The monthly price line for IBM shows an erratically declining zigzag gathering downward mo-

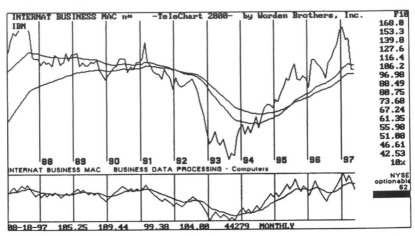

FIGURE 32-1. IBM Monthly Line Chart, with 25- and 40-Month Moving Averages and On Balance Volume.

mentum from its 1987 high. The early 1991 high turned out to be no more than a bull trap, confirmed once the next low exceeded the previous one. The 1992 rally achieved no more than a retracement to the breakdown level represented by the end-1990 low and the mid-1991 low. A downturn here strongly suggests the possibility that owners of the stock may throw in the towel in a panic sell-off.

2. **25-Month Moving Average.** Yes. This average has been pointing hard down from mid-1991. After crossing under the 40-month average, it gathered speed from early 1991.

3. **40-Month Moving Average.** Yes. The aberrational upside crossover by price in 1991 did nothing to slow the general downward slope. Since price closed back under the 40-month moving average, both price and the moving averages have picked up downward momentum.

4. **OBV 1.** No. The upward slope requires counting this indicator negative. OBV remained surprisingly neutral from 1988 to early 1991. Some big money managers must have been prepared to step up to the plate to buy. After the failed rally that crested in January 1991, selling picked up in earnest. The sharp rally in OBV in June 1992 conspicuously failed to establish an upward zigzag and did little to break the overall downtrend in this indicator.

5. **OBV 10.** Yes. From early 1991 OBV 10 assumed the same pattern as the moving averages for price. The adverse crossover in June turned out to be no more than a trap, a false move counter to the major trend.

6. **Fast MACD.** Yes. The downturn in fast MACD in November 1991 reinforced the bear market designation, which was barely disturbed by the June rally.

7. **Slow MACD.** Yes. The relentless downward trend in fast MACD below the slow confirms the big picture for a continuing bear market.

8. **%K Turn.** No. This indicator has not yet turned. It may not be necessary to wait for a turn, given the overall bearish cast of other indicators.

9. **%K Level.** No. %K rallied significantly as price rallied to the June high, but nowhere near an overbought reading of 80. It has rallied enough to relieve the extreme oversold readings at the end of 1991 and 1992.

10. **Price Rule.** Yes. The single monthly downside reversal in July completes a Rule 6 sell signal, assuming the confirmed and unmistakable downtrend in the market.

11. **Turn at MA/Trendline.** Yes. The June 1992 rally stopped just short of the declining 25-month moving average. This action

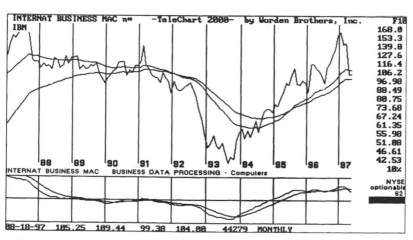

FIGURE 32-2. IBM Monthly Bar Chart, with MACD.

suggests that the retracement could be all that the rally can do and that there may be a prime entry to sell IBM short.

12. **Key Reversal.** Not applicable.

13. **Double Reversal.** Not applicable.

14. **Chart Pattern.** Yes. The January 1991 high looks like the head of a head-and-shoulders formation within the continuing down-trend—an exceptionally bearish pattern. Normally, head-and-shoulders patterns appear at tops. Appearing during the course of the bear market, this pattern also indicates here the exhaustion of buying power.

15. **Gap.** Not applicable.

16. **Island.** Not applicable.

17. **Market Conditions.** Yes. Neutral to bearish. The overall condition of the Dow Industrials and interest rates is not particularly bearish, although stocks look a bit tired. There is a case for selling IBM short while continuing to own strong stocks.

18. **Value.** Yes. IBM appears to be in serious trouble. It has been completely overtaken by newcomers like Microsoft, Intel, and Compaq. The company, once so powerful, has become so ossified that it is hard to see how it can be turned around any time soon. If business conditions generally become difficult, IBM could be in great difficulty. On the other hand, the company is

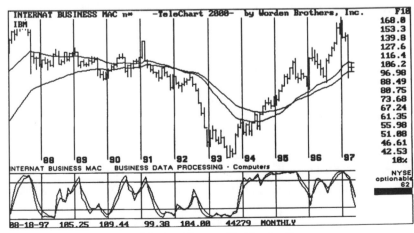

FIGURE 32-3. IBM Monthly Bar Chart, with Stochastics.

asset-rich and could turn around after major restructuring, if it happens.

Monthly Negating Indicators

1. **Adverse M/Zigzag Line.** Not applicable.
2. **Adverse 25 MA Direction.** Not applicable.
3. **Adverse 40 MA Direction.** Not applicable.
4. **OBV 1.** Not applicable.
5. **OBV 10.** Not applicable.
6. **Fast MACD.** Not applicable.
7. **Slow MACD.** Not applicable.
8. **%K Level.** Not applicable.
9. **Support.** Not applicable. Penetration of the end-1989 and end-1990 lows suggests that IBM may be heading much lower. There are often false breakdowns (bear traps), and you never know until after the event whether there will be a capitulation and an ensuing waterfall. In the overall picture, support at the April 1992 low looks weak and unlikely to hold. However, we have to be prepared for the possibility that the April low will prove to be the bottom of the market.
10. **Channel Line.** Not applicable.
11. **Adverse Trendline Crossover.** Not applicable.
12. **Value.** Not applicable. Covered on the monthly list.

The case for selling IBM on the basis of the monthly chart looks good. There is an overwhelming preponderance of confirming indicators and almost a complete absence of negating indicators.

Weekly Confirming Indicators

1. **M Formation/Zigzag Line.** Yes. A new M.
2. **25-Week Moving Average.** Yes. This average is pointing down.
3. **40-Week Moving Average.** Yes. This average is pointing down.
4. **OBV 1.** Yes.
5. **OBV 10.** Yes.

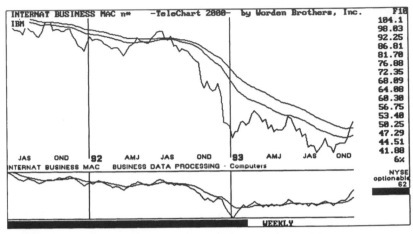

FIGURE 32-4. IBM Weekly Line Chart, with On Balance Volume.

6. **Fast MACD.** No, but this indicator often turns late.

7. **Slow MACD.** Yes. This indicator is flat but count it as confirming.

8. **%K Turn.** Yes. The downturn from maximum overbought levels should confirm the crest of a bear market rally.

9. **%K Level.** Yes. This is where %K really comes into its own. It shows that we are right to be assuming the possibility of a crest of the rally. The downturn in %K here could signal a prime place to sell IBM short. Thank you, %K, for resolving the ambiguities in the weekly price line, OBV and MACD!

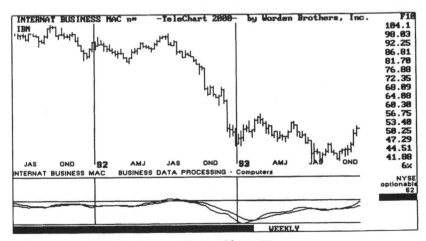

FIGURE 32-5. IBM Weekly Bar Chart, with MACD.

10. **Price Rule.** Yes. The outside down week ending on July 17 looks like the final exhaustion of a bear market rally. This extremely powerful week makes it look as if the weekly chart is signaling a prime entry to sell short.

11. **Turn at MA/Trendline.** No. The price rallied too far. The crossover above the 25- and 40-week moving averages may serve either as a warning or as a manifestation of an extremely overbought condition in a bear market rally. %K strongly suggests the latter.

12. **Key Reversal.** Yes, completed on July 17.

13. **Double Reversal.** Yes, if the week closes on the low.

14. **Chart Pattern.** Ideally, the price should not have exceeded the January high. However, apparent failure just above it could well signify resumption of the downtrend. Count this indicator positive for selling short.

15. **Gap.** Not applicable.

16. **Island.** Not applicable.

17. **Market Conditions.** Covered on the monthly list.

18. **Value.** Covered on the monthly list.

Weekly Negating Indicators

1. **Adverse M/Zigzag Line.** Not applicable.

2. **Adverse 25 MA Direction.** Not applicable.

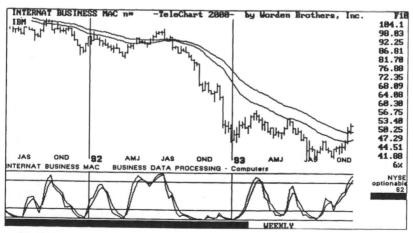

FIGURE 32–6.   IBM Weekly Bar Chart, with Stochastics.

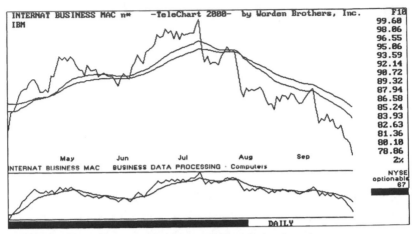

FIGURE 32-7. IBM Daily Line Chart, with On Balance Volume.

3. **Adverse 40 MA Direction.** Not applicable.

4. **OBV 1.** Yes, but the monthly chart takes precedence.

5. **OBV 10.** Yes, but the monthly chart takes precedence.

6. **Fast MACD.** Yes, but feeble.

7. **Slow MACD.** Yes, but very feeble.

8. **%K Level.** Not applicable at all but, on the contrary, inviting a sale at the crest of a bear market rally.

9. **Support.** There is support at the April 1992 low but it does not warrant counting.

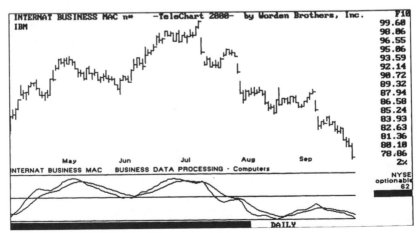

FIGURE 32-8. IBM Daily Bar Chart, with MACD.

10. **Channel Line.** Not applicable.

11. **Adverse Trendline Crossover.** Not applicable.

12. **Value.** Not applicable. Covered on the monthly list.

Daily Confirming Indicators

1. **M Formation/Zigzag Line.** Yes, a perfect new M.

2. **25-Day Moving Average.** Yes. It has just rolled over again.

3. **40-Day Moving Average.** No. It has not yet rolled over, although it is encouraging that price has just closed below it.

4. **OBV 1.** Yes.

5. **OBV 10.** Yes.

6. **Fast MACD.** Yes.

7. **Slow MACD.** Yes.

8. **%K Turn.** Yes. The downturn on July 17 comes from a level sufficiently overbought for a market top, particularly given the extreme negative divergence.

9. **%K Level.** Yes. %K has been high enough for long enough to suggest that the price on the daily chart is likely to decline.

10. **Price Rule.** A great price rule on August 5, with a gap down! This looks like an exhaustion top *par excellence.*

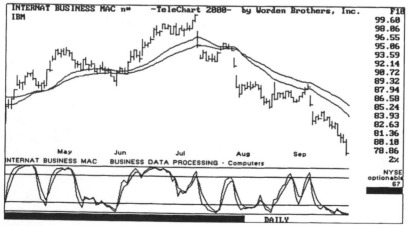

FIGURE 32-9. IBM Daily Bar Chart, with Stochastics.

11. **Turn at MA/Trendline.** Yes. After the initial sell-off, price rallied back to the declining 25-day moving average and then failed.

12. **Key Reversal.** Not applicable.

13. **Double Reversal.** Yes, with two very small ones on July 31 and August 4.

14. **Chart Pattern.** Yes. The 13-day island top is extremely significant.

15. **Gap.** Yes, a real break!

16. **Island.** Yes, a beautiful five-day island!

17. **Market Conditions.** Covered on the monthly list.

18. **Value.** Covered on the monthly list.

Daily Negating Indicators

1. **Adverse M/Zigzag Line.** Not applicable.

2. **Adverse 25 MA Direction.** Not applicable.

3. **Adverse 40 MA Direction.** Yes, but it may be losing upward momentum and follow the 25.

4. **OBV 1.** Not applicable.

5. **OBV 10.** Neutral. It does not count against the trade.

6. **Fast MACD.** Not applicable.

7. **Slow MACD.** Not applicable.

8. **%K Level.** Not applicable.

9. **Support.** Yes. There is support at the April 1992 low.

10. **Channel Line.** Not applicable.

11. **Adverse Trendline Crossover.** Not applicable.

12. **Value.** Not applicable. Covered on the monthly list.

The great thing about selling IBM short is the combination of a confirmed bear market on the monthly chart in parallel with an immensely overbought condition on the weekly and daily charts. On their own, the shorter-term charts might have seemed to suggest a trend reversal. However, stochastics really came into their own here to show that the probabilities favored interpreting the crest of a major bear market rally and in consequence, a superb opportunity to sell short.

ENTRY CHECKLIST, IBM: SELL SHORT

Stock IBM	Price $91.63	Date 8/5/92	
Confirming Indicators	Monthly	Weekly	Daily
1. M/Zigzag Line	✔	✔	✔
2. 25 Bar MA	✔	✔	✔
3. 40 Bar MA	✔	✔	
4. OBV 1		✔	✔
5. OBV 10	✔	✔	✔
6. Fast MACD	✔		✔
7. Slow MACD	✔	✔	✔
8. %K Turn		✔	✔
9. %K Level (above 80)		✔	✔
10. Price Rule	✔	✔	✔
11. Turn at MA/Trendline	✔		✔
12. Key Reversal		✔	
13. Double Reversal		✔	✔
14. Chart Pattern	✔	✔	✔
15. Gap			✔
16. Island			✔
17. Market Conditions	✔	✔	✔
18. Value	✔	✔	✔
TOTAL	11	14	16
Negating Indicators			
1. Adverse M/Zigzag Line			
2. Adv. 25 MA			
3. Adv. 40 MA			✔
4. OBV 1		✔	
5. OBV 10		✔	
6. Fast MACD		✔	
7. Slow MACD		✔	
8. %K Level (under 20)			
9. Support			✔
10. Channel Line			
11. Adv. T-Line Cross			
12. Value			
TOTAL	0	4	2

Stops

Given the immensely bearish big picture for IBM, the stock could be allowed to retrace to the top of the weekly downside reversal. With its high at $100.38, there is also significance attributable to the $100 round number. A daily close above $100.38 should be the signal to run for cover.

IBM is a great short sale on August 5, 1992, at $91.63. As the stock started collapsing and breaking under support with downward gapping, there were additional entry points. The stock was also a great short sale on September 15 at $85.50 and on September 29 at $81.00. After that, it was enough to sit back and watch the barrel go over the waterfall.

The collapse in IBM occurred when overall market conditions were not particularly bearish. When overall market conditions are bearish, there are likely to be many stocks as bearish as IBM was in 1992. The more that conditions generally are bearish, the more the probabilities favor selling stocks short. Then, there may actually be less risk in selling short than when buying in a bull market.

CHAPTER 33

Case Study: Sell into an Emerging Bear Market

K Mart Makes a Top

This chapter shows the case for selling K Mart short on December 1, 1993, using the checklist on page 334. The monthly chart for K Mart shows a stock that has been laboring in an erratic sideways pattern from 1986 to 1993 (Figure 33-1). The monthly chart at the end of 1993 clearly shows the possibility that the stock may be carving out a huge head-and-shoulders formation, one of the most deadly chart patterns for owning a stock and one of the most promising for entering a short sale at an early stage of development.

The Entry Checklist

Monthly Confirming Indicators

1. **M Formation/Zigzag Line.** Yes, except for a small wrinkle formed by the May high. The big picture without this wrinkle looks quite bearish. The monthly price line already established a bear market designation with a succession of two consecutively lower highs off the top and three consecutively lower lows. However, this pattern alone scarcely justifies jumping the gun on a short sale—just a warning to beware of continuing to own the stock.

The downturn in November 1993 from a high close equal to the one in April, with its corresponding double top, strongly suggests that the bear market designation is correct. Potentially, this downturn sets up a "double right shoulders" that has its approximate counterpart with the double left shoulders at the highs in 1991 and early 1992.

The downturn in November 1993 might be early but a short sale here can be entered with a tight stop.

2. **The 25-Month Moving Average.** No. The 25-month moving average went flat in April and has stayed more or less flat, showing that by this criterion there was no upward momentum in the stock. At this point, we cannot count a declining 15-month moving average.

Price fluctuating either side of the average did not in itself suggest that there would be a worthwhile move down any time soon, but it suggested a loss of upward momentum.

3. **The 40-Month Moving Average.** No. The 40-month moving average showed K Mart in an uptrend from 1991, with price holding above the average until the cross underneath in June, by which time the average had gone flat. One adverse crossover does not necessarily end a bull market. A second one is much more likely to do so.

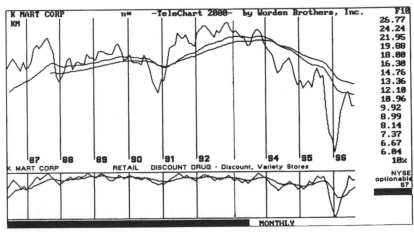

FIGURE 33-1. K-Mart Monthly Line Chart, with 25- and 40-Month Moving Averages and On Balance Volume.

4. **OBV 1.** Yes. Here, too, we have a double top with a lower second high after a big bulge and a downturn in OBV. It made its high in mid-1991, after which the price of the stock went to two successively higher highs without OBV confirming. However, OBV did not establish a downtrend either, except for a brief period of weakness in 1993 when the monthly price line was setting up its bear market designation.

   After the event we can see that the high at the end of 1993 was no more than an aberrational bulge, although at the time it might have been interpreted as a sign of returning strength in the stock. Once the price and OBV turned down, it was likely that both OBV and price were ending a failed rally.

5. **OBV 10.** No. There is a slight upward incline in OBV 10, which might signify a return of buying pressure, but the overall trend appears to be downward. The apparently bullish pattern requires an upward zigzag in OBV 1, which is definitely not apparent. In the meantime, the bearish pattern developing in early 1993 has turned ambiguous.

6. **Fast MACD.** Yes. Fast MACD turned down from the April 1992 peak in price and stayed hard down even as the price of the stock made a new high and later attempted to rally.

   This action in MACD strongly reinforces the likelihood that the stock is making a long-drawn-out distributional top.

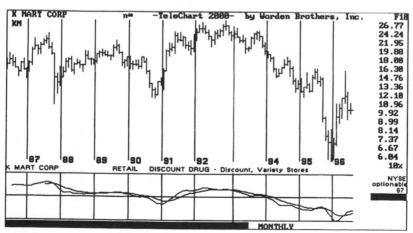

FIGURE 33–2. K-Mart Monthly Bar Chart, with MACD.

7. **Slow MACD.** Yes. The MACD crossover in July 1992 confirmed this indicator's indications that the stock was unlikely to rally and, on the contrary, could well begin a more significant decline.

8. **%K Turn.** Yes. The downturn in %K in December 1992 strongly suggested that K Mart might be making no more than a major bear market rally from which a substantial decline could begin.

   Note the triple tops in %K in 1991, early 1992, and late 1992 versus the action in the price of the stock. This is a textbook example of stochastics showing negative or bearish divergence and that the upward momentum has gone out of the stock. The downturn in November 1993 makes a fourth high, with each of the last three at a lower level than the one before. This is extremely impressive bearish divergence.

9. **%K Level.** Yes. The rally in October 1993 took %K well above 80. Obviously, with such an overall bearish-looking top, the probabilities were weighted overwhelmingly toward an interpretation of this as a rally that should be sold, not as strength capable of driving the stock out to new highs.

10. **Price Rule.** No. There is no monthly price rule yet. However, market action in October and November 1993 suggests the possibility of a top.

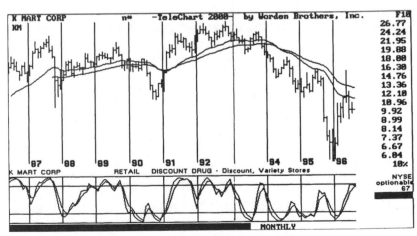

FIGURE 33-3. K-Mart Monthly Bar Chart, with Stochastics.

11. **Turn at MA/Trendline.** Not applicable. The 25-month moving average has not yet turned down decisively, and price closed above it for two consecutive months in September and October.

    The 40-month moving average still suggests a feeble bull market, although not so strongly as to prevent short sales.

12. **Key Reversal.** Not applicable.

13. **Double Reversal.** Not applicable.

14. **Chart Pattern.** Yes. As already discussed, the head-and-shoulders pattern is the first tip-off that K Mart warrants serious examination for a potential short sale.

15. **Gap.** Not applicable.

16. **Island.** Not applicable.

17. **Market Conditions.** Yes. The pattern for interest rates and the major indexes suggests the possibility of a more significant market top. In that case, K Mart is unlikely to go up, and the stock might decline significantly in the event of the general market decline.

18. **Value.** Yes. K Mart's business could well be laboring as a result of fierce competition from the likes of Wal-Mart. It is clear that this company is by no means the market leader in retailing that it once was. Therefore, profits and the stock price could both come under pressure, and possibly severe pressure.

Monthly Negating Indicators

1. **Adverse M/Zigzag Line.** Not applicable.

2. **Adverse 25 MA Direction.** The 25 moving average is still pointing up, though barely, and with an interesting potential double top. It could form an M if it turns down here.

3. **Adverse 40 MA Direction.** The 40-month moving average is still pointing strongly upward, as often happens when attempting a top-pick.

4. **OBV 1.** A big bulge and bullish crossover at the last high. Count this indicator negative, and if you trade, make sure the other indicators are really good for a short sale.

5. **OBV 10.** The adverse direction counts negative, along with the adverse crossover.

6. **Fast MACD.** Not applicable. The strongly downtrending MACD may well override negating OBV given the overall bearish chart pattern.

7. **Slow MACD.** Not applicable. (The declining slow MACD looks really solid.)

8. **%K Level.** Not applicable. The reach above 80 is extremely positive for a short sale, suggesting the potential crest of a rally.

9. **Support.** There is support at the July low at $19.50, although the overall bearish chart pattern suggests that it is unlikely to hold for long. One low does not show that buyers are prepared to come in strongly at that level.

10. **Channel Line.** Not applicable.

11. **Adverse Trendline Crossover.** Not applicable.

12. **Value.** Not applicable. Covered on the monthly list.

Apart from OBV, there is almost a complete absence of significant negating indicators, and there is an overwhelming preponderance of confirming indicators.

Weekly Confirming Indicators

1. **M Formation/Zigzag Line.** Yes. The weekly price line shows an M completed in September 1992 that fits into a very bearish overall chart pattern.

2. **The 25-Week Moving Average.** Yes. This average steadied when price rallied above it in July and August, although it never crossed above the 40. A downturn here is very bearish.

3. **The 40-Week Moving Average.** Much the same as the 25-week.

4. **OBV 1.** No. It looks as if it should turn down right away at a level far below its last high, but it has not yet done so. OBV 1 developed an upward zigzag during the summer rally. However, the overall trend appears to be sideways to down after completion of an M with a lower low. There appears to be a small and very bearish head-and-shoulders forming in this indicator.

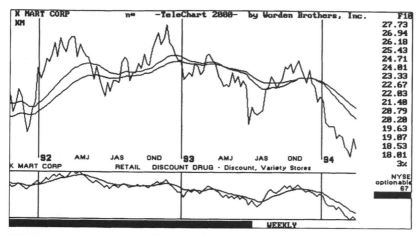

FIGURE 33–4. K-Mart Weekly Line Chart, with On Balance Volume.

5. **OBV 10.** No. However, this indicator appears to be making a rounding top prior to turning down.

6. **Fast MACD.** Yes. Fast MACD appears to be making a rounding top and is just turning down.

7. **Slow MACD.** No. The rally from mid-summer could signify the start of a new move up, but that is unlikely. Much more likely is that slow MACD will complete a bear market rally well below the high in early 1992 and the one at the end of 1992.

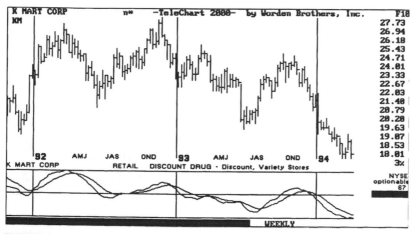

FIGURE 33–5. K-Mart Weekly Bar Chart, with MACD.

8. **%K Turn.** Yes. The downturn from maximum overbought levels after multiple topping should confirm the crest of a bear market rally.

9. **%K Level.** Yes. The highs in %K near the 100-percent level make it look as if this could be a prime place to sell short.

10. **Price Rule.** Yes. A Rule 1 sell signal was completed on November 19. There now appears to be a weekly Lindahl sell signal developing, which is extremely bearish.

11. **Turn at MA/Trendline.** No. The price crossed above the 25- and 40-week moving averages, which may serve either as a warning or as a manifestation of an extremely overbought condition in a bear market rally. %K strongly suggests the latter.

12. **Key Reversal.** Not applicable.

13. **Double Reversal.** Not applicable.

14. **Chart Pattern.** Yes. There appears to be a huge and very bearish head-and-shoulders formation. The right-hand shoulder is much below the left, confirming extreme weakness in the stock.

15. **Gap.** Not applicable.

16. **Island.** Not applicable.

17. **Market Conditions.** Covered on the monthly list.

18. **Value.** Covered on the monthly list.

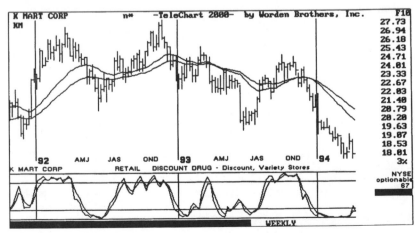

FIGURE 33-6. K-Mart Weekly Bar Chart, with Stochastics.

Weekly Negating Indicators

1. **Adverse M/Zigzag Line.** Not applicable.

2. **Adverse 25 MA Direction.** Not applicable.

3. **Adverse 40 MA Direction.** Not applicable.

4. **OBV 1.** Yes, a negating indicator.

5. **OBV 10.** Not applicable.

6. **Fast MACD.** Not applicable.

7. **Slow MACD.** Yes, a negating indicator. It looks as if slow MACD should crest about here, but it has not yet turned down.

8. **%K Level.** Not applicable.

9. **Support.** Not applicable.

10. **Channel Line.** Not applicable.

11. **Adverse Trendline Crossover.** Not applicable.

12. **Value.** Not applicable. Covered on the monthly list.

Daily Confirming Indicators

1. **M Formation/Zigzag Line.** Yes. The daily price line shows a classic bear market with the downturn at the beginning of December.

2. **The 25-Day Moving Average.** Yes. This average appears to be trending hard down despite the small flattening and upturn at the end of November.

3. **The 40-Day Moving Average.** Yes. Much the same as the 25-day.

4. **OBV 1.** Yes. OBV 1 shows an established downtrend.

5. **OBV 10.** Yes. The overall trend is hard down.

6. **Fast MACD.** Yes. There is a steady succession of lower lows and lower highs.

7. **Slow MACD.** Yes. Much the same as for the MACD slow line.

8. **%K Turn.** Yes. The downturn at the end of November makes a triple top in this indicator along with a triple top in price, confirming a very bearish picture.

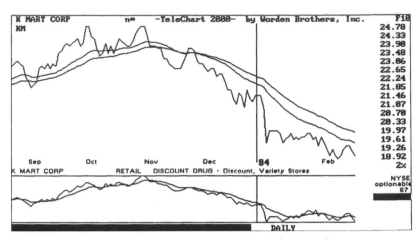

FIGURE 33–7.   K-Mart Daily Line Chart, with On Balance Volume.

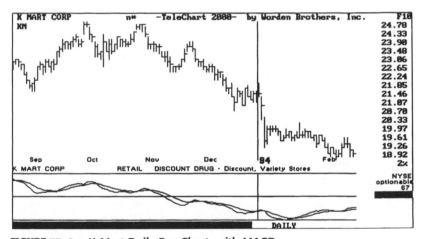

FIGURE 33–8.   K-Mart Daily Bar Chart, with MACD.

9. **%K Level.** Yes. %K above 80 sets off an alert to look for a place to sell short.

10. **Price Rule.** Yes. A powerful Rule 1 sell signal on December 1 appears also to be setting up a weekly Lindahl sell signal.

11. **Turn at MA/Trendline.** The brief upside crossover of the moving averages looks strictly aberrational, allowing us to count this indicator positive when price closes back under the moving averages on December 1.

12. **Key Reversal.** Not applicable.

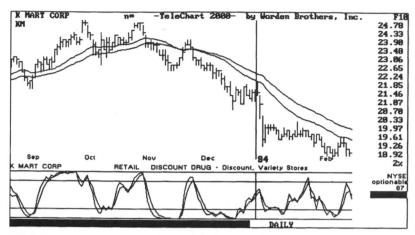

FIGURE 33-9. K-Mart Daily Bar Chart, with Stochastics.

13. **Double Reversal.** Not applicable.

14. **Chart Pattern.** Yes. A great head-and-shoulders formation on the daily chart. The daily chart shows two tops with islands, one in October and one in November. This is extremely bearish, suggesting that not one but two buying climaxes have exhausted themselves.

15. **Gap.** Yes. Price gapped down on the open and closed low.

16. **Island.** Yes. The gap down today has its counterpart with the gap up on November 26.

17. **Market Conditions.** Covered on the monthly list.

18. **Value.** Covered on the monthly list.

Daily Negating Indicators

1. **Adverse M/Zigzag Line.** Not applicable.

2. **Adverse 25 MA Direction.** Not applicable.

3. **Adverse 40 MA Direction.** Not applicable.

4. **OBV 1.** Not applicable.

5. **OBV 10.** Not applicable.

6. **Fast MACD.** Not applicable.

7. **Slow MACD.** Not applicable.

ENTRY CHECKLIST, K-MART: SELL SHORT

Stock KM	Price $23.13	Date 12/1/93	
Confirming Indicators	**Monthly**	**Weekly**	**Daily**
1. M/Zigzag Line	✔	✔	✔
2. 25 Bar MA		✔	✔
3. 40 Bar MA		✔	✔
4. OBV 1	✔		✔
5. OBV 10		✔	✔
6. Fast MACD	✔		✔
7. Slow MACD	✔		✔
8. %K Turn	✔	✔	✔
9. %K Level (above 80)	✔	✔	✔
10. Price Rule		✔	✔
11. Turn at MA/Trendline			
12. Key Reversal			
13. Double Reversal			
14. Chart Pattern	✔	✔	✔
15. Gap			✔
16. Island			✔
17. Market Conditions	✔	✔	✔
18. Value	✔	✔	✔
TOTAL	**9**	**10**	**15**
Negating Indicators			
1. Adverse M/Zigzag Line	✔		
2. Adv. 25 MA	✔		
3. Adv. 40 MA			
4. OBV 1		✔	
5. OBV 10	✔	✔	
6. Fast MACD			
7. Slow MACD		✔	
8. %K Level (under 20)			
9. Support			
10. Channel Line			
11. Adv. T-Line Cross			
12. Value			
TOTAL	**3**	**3**	**0**

8. **%K Level.** Not applicable.

9. **Support.** Not applicable.

10. **Channel Line.** Not applicable.

11. **Adverse Treadline Crossover.** Not applicable.

12. **Value.** Not applicable. Covered on the monthly list.

Conditions on the monthly, weekly, and daily charts are all very favorable for a short sale on December 1, 1993, at $23.12. If that entry is missed, there is another prime opportunity on December 6 as a result of the downside key reversal day, with its close at $22.75.

This case study shows particularly well how to achieve a really good entry that occurs within a relatively small window of opportunity.

Stops

The high for the formation on the monthly chart is at $25.

Add a small allowance beyond the high and we enter a stop at $25.50. Assuming an entry at $22.75, we budget for a loss of $2.75 per share, or about 12 percent.

Subsequently, the stop would have been lowered to about $19.50 and $15.50 as a result of repositioning the TPS. In all likelihood, you would therefore have been stopped out of the short position by the blip up in July 1995. However, the short position could have been reinstated after the next month's downside reversal, going in again at $14.75. Then you were positioned for the big one! The drop to an intramonth low at $5.75 shows two things. First, it shows how much money you can make by selling short. Second, it shows how you must be prepared to reenter in the event that you are inadvertently stopped out. You must not quit in the mistaken belief that there is only one opportunity to trade per stock or per market move.

CHAPTER 34

Case Study: Short into a Vacuum Crash

What Happened in October 1987

Sometimes what goes up does come crashing down. A stock, generally a small and speculative one, takes flight far beyond all reason, and then plummets. It practically never pays to try to sell short a small, speculative stock high, but occasionally the opportunity to do so occurs in a big stock or for the stock market generally when it is spectacularly high and riding for a fall.

An absurd rise in price often occurs when a concept catches the popular imagination. Once a parabolic climb starts, it attracts new buyers and the Greater Fool Theory supplants reason. The theory holds that you can make money by climbing on a bandwagon as long as there is always another buyer prepared to pay a higher price.

Everything goes well for a time, sometimes spectacularly. Nevertheless, you have to know when to get off the bandwagon. Generally, the chart for a parabolic climb goes far beyond what anyone expects, so the exit is a challenge; still more the short sale. After a while, there are people who see how little value there is in the current price. So a trickle of selling starts from people taking profits. A few people begin to sell short in the expectation of a crash. However, continuation of the parabolic ascent continues, squeezing short sellers with losses beyond their endurance. So they join the bandwagon of buyers, pushing the price ever higher.

At some point the bubble bursts, much as a balloon bursts. Suddenly, there are all sellers and no buyers. The price crashes. It is as if there is a vacuum under the market, as there is when an airplane flies into an immense downdraft. Sometimes the topping process lasts long enough to deliver signals reliable enough to justify entering short sales.

There is often no choice but to assume a massively overbought market on the basis of the monthly chart and then to trade off the weekly and daily charts rather than the monthly. If you wait for the monthly chart to come on side, it may be all over. These situations offer opportunities to sell short with the prospect of an exceptional gain, although sometimes too with greater risk than most people can assume.

In the nineteenth century there were frequent stock market crashes of 10 percent or more. In the twentieth century, there have been far fewer crashes, although some of them have been huge. A huge crash occurred in the general level of stock prices in October 1987, as shown by the monthly chart for the Dow Jones Industrial Average (Figure 34-1). Here it serves as a proxy for almost all major stocks and stock index futures, exemplifying the adage that in a real bear market 90 percent of all stocks go down.

It should have been clear to every market timer that the stock market in September and October 1987 was screaming an invitation to look for an entry to sell short. The technical indicators strongly suggested the possibility of an important market top. In addition, interest

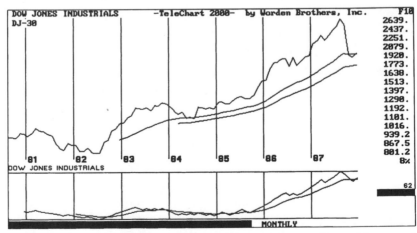

FIGURE 34–1. Dow Jones Industrial Average Monthly Line Chart, with 25- and 40-Month Moving Averages and On Balance Volume.

rates had been rising steeply all year, so this was clearly a time for extreme caution for anyone owning stocks. That should also have been obvious to everyone who ever heard the saying: "Don't fight the Fed!" You did not have to be short, of course, but at least you should have gotten out of the way in good time by selling all the stocks you owned.

Here is how the checklist, printed on page 349, looks for a short sale for the Dow Jones Industrial Average on October 15, 1987, at 2355.

The Entry Checklist

Monthly Confirming Indicators

1. **M Formation/Zigzag Line.** No. There is a parabolic acceleration in the monthly price line. The market has been rising without a significant pause for three years and has doubled in price.

2. **25-Month Moving Average.** No. The 25-month moving average is rising strongly and is far above the 40-month. The price level is so far beyond both of them that it is highly vulnerable.

3. **40-Month Moving Average.** No. The 40-month moving average is also rising strongly and without interruption.

4. **OBV 1.** OBV is in a strong uptrend, possibly too strong for its own good.

5. **OBV 10.** OBV 1 looks as if it is drawing unsustainably far away from its 10-month moving average.

6. **Fast MACD.** Fast MACD shows no sign of tiring. (Remember that this is a slow-acting indicator.)

7. **Slow MACD.** Slow MACD is the same as the fast.

8. **%K Turn.** %K turned down in September 1987 from maximum overbought. That in itself means very little.

9. **%K Level.** There has been a maximum overbought reading for almost three years with only minor interruptions. That shows how powerfully the market has been moving up. It may show vulnerability, but it does not show impending weakness.

10. **Price Rule.** Not applicable.

11. **Turn at MA/Trendline.** Not applicable.

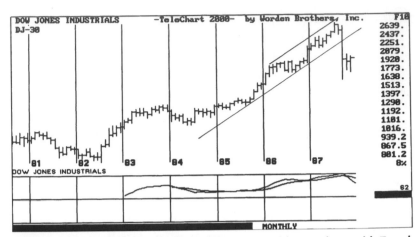

FIGURE 34-2.   Dow Jones Industrial Average Monthly Bar Chart, with Trend-line, Channel Line, and MACD.

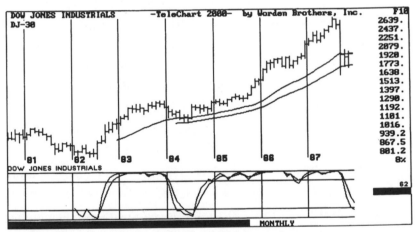

FIGURE 34-3.   Dow Jones Industrial Average Monthly Bar Chart, with 25- and 40-Month Moving Averages and Stochastics.

12. **Key Reversal.** Not applicable.

13. **Double Reversal.** Not applicable.

14. **Chart Pattern.** Yes. Count this indicator positive, given the prox-imity to the upper channel line. Otherwise, the bull market looks solid.

15. **Gap.** Not applicable.

16. **Island.** Not applicable.

17. **Market Conditions.** Interest rates could hardly be more hostile to the market. It is true that a bull market does not need declining interest rates and can live a long time with rising interest rates. But this is getting ridiculous (Figure 34-4). The bond market declined by 22 percent from its peak, from 105 to 81, even as the stock market was soaring.

18. **Value.** The stock market is more overvalued than at any time since 1929 by all conventional criteria, such as yield, ratio of price to earnings, and price to book. Can this really be a "new era?"

Below are some comparisons between the yield on stocks, Treasury bonds, and Treasury bills:

	Yield at Year-End 1986	Yield in September 1987
30-year Bond	8.2%	10.2%
3-month T-Bill	5.7	8.7
Dow stocks	3.6	2.6

Until about 1960 stocks generally yielded significantly more than bonds. The premium in bond yields over stock yields in October 1987 was 7.6 percent, near a record. The yield on the Dow stocks was also a near-record low. And people said stocks represented value?

FIGURE 34–4. U.S. 30-Year Bond Monthly Chart.

Monthly Negating Indicators

1. **Adverse M/Zigzag Line.** Yes.

2. **Adverse 25 MA Direction.** Yes, but price is way above and by this criterion overbought and vulnerable.

3. **Adverse 40 MA Direction.** Yes, as for the 25.

4. **OBV 1 Direction.** Yes.

5. **OBV 10.** Yes, but there could be a climactic bulge.

6. **Fast MACD.** Yes.

7. **Slow MACD.** Yes.

8. **%K Level.** Not applicable.

9. **Support.** No. It is difficult to identify support on the monthly chart other than the uptrend line from the 1985 low. That is absolutely critical. Violation of it means that there is almost no case for continuing to own most stocks.

   The May monthly low at 2180, from which the last upturn in the monthly price line occurred, is significant. A 5-percent allowance from there gives a level of 2071. A break below that level could lead to a trend reversal and a big decline.

   The very long-term support is at the 40-month moving average, now just under 1700! The September close for the Dow Industrials was at 2570, so this support is 34 percent below the current market. At some point, the index and the 40-month moving average are certain to meet again, either by the index falling or the average rising.

10. **Channel Line.** Not applicable.

11. **Adverse Trendline Crossover.** Not applicable.

12. **Value.** Covered on Confirming Indicators. Very dangerous conditions for owning stock, with the potential for a major letdown.

The monthly chart is immensely overbought. There could be a substantial decline without necessarily ending the bull market altogether.

Weekly Confirming Indicators

1. **M Formation/Zigzag Line.** Yes. The weekly price line shows an M completing on October 9, with a lower low and a lower high. This downturn makes the lower high.

2. **25-Week Moving Average.** No. This average remains strongly bullish.

3. **40-Week Moving Average.** No. Much the same as the 25-week.

4. **OBV 1.** Yes. OBV 1 has made almost no upward progress since August, but it has not gone down either. There is a beautiful double top, indicating major bearish divergence.

5. **OBV 10.** Yes, but barely.

6. **Fast MACD.** Yes. Fast MACD made its high all the way back in April. There was a conspicuously lower top in August. This indicator shows substantial bearish divergence.

7. **Slow MACD.** Yes, but it has really just turned flat. A bearish crossover after a prominent second high is very bearish.

8. **%K Turn.** Yes. A downturn from maximum overbought levels might confirm the crest with a break below 80.

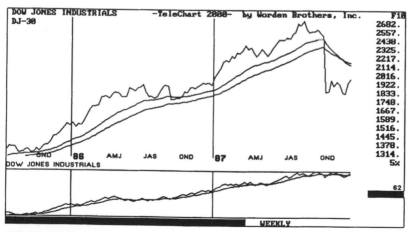

FIGURE 34–5. Dow Jones Industrial Average Weekly Line Chart, with 25- and 40-Week Moving Averages and On Balance Volume.

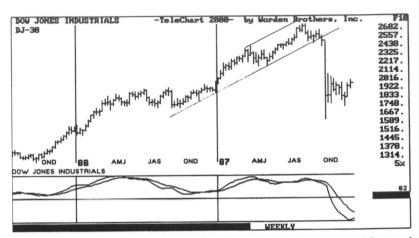

FIGURE 34-6. Dow Jones Industrial Average Weekly Bar Chart, with Trend-line, Channel Line, and MACD.

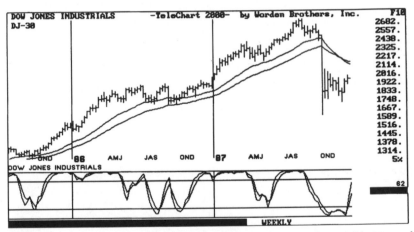

FIGURE 34-7. Dow Jones Industrial Average Weekly Bar Chart, with 25- and 40-Week Moving Averages and Stochastics.

9. **%K Level.** Yes. %K has been high enough for long enough to suggest that it could turn decisively down.

10. **Price Rule.** Yes. A weekly Lindahl sell signal occurring on the close of Friday, October 9, is exceptionally bearish. The overall pattern for the formation is very bearish.

11. **Turn at MA/Trendline.** Not applicable.

12. **Key Reversal.** Not applicable, but almost, for the week ending October 9!

13. **Double Reversal.** Yes, and very bearish.

14. **Chart Pattern.** Yes. The weekly chart pattern, when considered in conjunction with the weekly Lindahl sell signal and other factors, suggests a probable top. Of course, you never know until after the event how far a snowball, once in motion, will actually go.

15. **Gaps.** Not applicable.

16. **Island.** Not applicable.

17. **Market Conditions.** Covered on the monthly list.

18. **Value.** Covered on the monthly list.

Weekly Negating Indicators

1. **Adverse M/Zigzag Line.** No.

2. **Adverse 25 MA Direction.** Yes.

3. **Adverse 40 MA Direction.** Yes.

4. **OBV 1.** No.

5. **OBV 10.** No.

6. **Fast MACD.** No.

7. **Slow MACD.** No.

8. **%K Level.** No.

9. **Support.** No. There is some support around the 2200 to 2300 level, although it is unlikely to mean anything if the market starts sliding.

10. **Channel Line.** Not applicable.

11. **Adverse Trendline Crossover.** Not applicable.

12. **Value.** Covered on the monthly list.

Daily Confirming Indicators

1. **M Formation/Zigzag Line.** Yes. The daily price line shows an extremely bearish pattern. It looks like a river heading for a waterfall.

2. **25-Day Moving Average.** Yes. This average has been flat to down since early September and looks very bearish.

3. **40-Day Moving Average.** Yes. Much the same as the 25-day.

4. **OBV 1.** Yes.

5. **OBV 10.** Yes.

6. **Fast MACD.** Yes.

7. **Slow MACD.** Yes.

8. **%K Turn.** Yes. Extremely bearish.

9. **%K Level.** Yes. %K is coming off a maximum overbought reading. Extremely bearish.

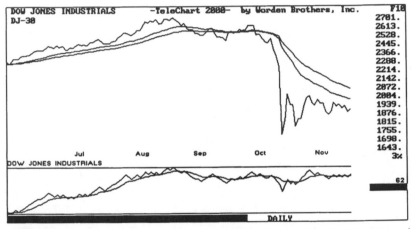

FIGURE 34-8. Dow Jones Industrial Average Daily Line Chart, with 15- and 40-Day Moving Averages and On Balance Volume.

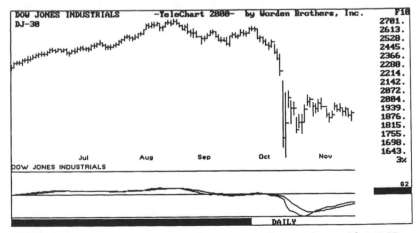

FIGURE 34-9. Dow Jones Industrial Average Daily Bar Chart, with MACD.

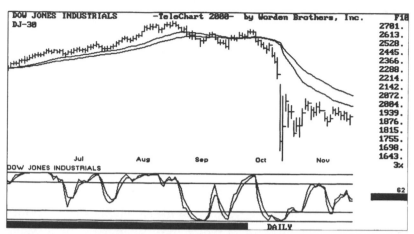

FIGURE 34–10.   Dow Jones Industrial Average Daily Bar Chart, with 25- and 40-Day Moving Averages and Stochastics.

10. **Price Rule.** Completed on October 6 with a Rule 1 sell signal at 2548. It is repeated on October 14 at 2412, on October 15 at 2355, and on October 16 at 2246—extremely bearish action.

11. **Turn at MA/Trendline.** Not applicable.

12. **Key Reversal.** Not applicable.

13. **Double Reversal.** Not applicable.

14. **Chart Pattern.** Extremely bearish.

15. **Gaps.** The gap down on October 14 is very bearish. Considered in conjunction with the low close on October 15, the market appears to have its back broken.

16. **Island.** Not applicable.

17. **Market Conditions.** Covered on the monthly list.

18. **Value.** Covered on the monthly list.

Daily Negating Indicators

1. **Adverse M/Zigzag Line.** Not applicable.

2. **Adverse 25 MA Direction.** Not applicable.

3. **Adverse 40 MA Direction.** Not applicable.

4. **OBV 1.** Not applicable.

5. **OBV 10.** Not applicable.

6. **Fast MACD.** Not applicable.

7. **Slow MACD.** Not applicable.

8. **%K Level.** Not applicable.

9. **Support.** Not applicable.

10. **Channel Line.** Not applicable.

11. **Adverse Trendline Crossover**. Not applicable.

12. **Value.** Not applicable. Covered on the monthly list.

The conditions are never perfect for a short sale when picking an entry for a potential vacuum crash. By their nature, vacuum crashes develop fast and dramatically, so it is impossible for all of the pieces to fall into place to confirm a new bear market. It is generally clear, as here, that there is a compelling conjunction of bearish weekly and daily chart indicators as well as massive overvaluation in historical terms.

The situation is particularly intriguing, given the staggering divergence between interest rates and the stock market. This stock market has been fighting the U.S. Federal Reserve and winning—until now. Market action, as it appears on the weekly and daily charts, suggests that there is no case for continuing to own stocks. There is a strong, although obviously more speculative case for selling short. This could not at that time be accomplished with the Dow Jones Industrial Index as such. However, it could be done with many individual stocks or with other stock index futures such as the S&P or the New York Composite Index (NYFE).

If the market falls apart, the reward could be very substantial. There is a fair risk of a rebound, possibly above 2600, which would be hard to take. However, a short sale can be justified on the basis of probabilities. When this kind of short sale succeeds, the rewards pay for many attempts that fail.

Setting Stops

Assume a short sale on the basis of the weekly chart signal on October 9 at 2482. A daily close above 2600 looks to be enough to allow. That may be a bit tight, but it would be better to book a small loss than to try to fight renewed strength.

ENTRY CHECKLIST, DOW INDUSTRIALS: SELL SHORT

Stock Dow-30	Price 2355	Date 10/15/87	
Confirming Indicators	**Monthly**	**Weekly**	**Daily**
1. M/Zigzag Line		✔	✔
2. 25 Bar MA			✔
3. 40 Bar MA		✔	✔
4. OBV 1		✔	✔
5. OBV 10		✔	✔
6. Fast MACD		✔	✔
7. Slow MACD		✔	✔
8. %K Turn	✔	✔	✔
9. %K Level (above 80)	✔	✔	✔
10. Price Rule		✔	✔
11. Turn at MA/Trendline			
12. Key Reversal		✔	
13. Double Reversal		✔	
14. Chart Pattern	✔		✔
15. Gap			✔
16. Island			
17. Market Conditions	✔	✔	✔
18. Value	✔	✔	✔
TOTAL	**5**	**12**	**14**
Negating Indicators			
1. Adverse M/Zigzag Line	✔		
2. Adv. 25 MA	✔		
3. Adv. 40 MA	✔	✔	
4. OBV 1	✔		
5. OBV 10	✔		
6. Fast MACD	✔		
7. Slow MACD	✔		
8. %K Level (under 20)			
9. Support			✔
10. Channel Line			
11. Adv. T-Line Cross			
12. Value			
TOTAL	**7**	**1**	**1**

Prepare for the Next Bull Market

As a postscript to the 1987 crash, it is worth noting that in the overall scheme of things, very little net selling occurred. Yes, there was heavy liquidation when the market sold off. However, there was no general shift by institutions such as mutual funds and pension funds from stocks into cash. It all happened too quickly. OBV for many stocks sustained relatively little damage, and most stocks, including the major indexes, remained above their rising 40-month moving averages. The crash occurred, much like ones in the nineteenth century, more because of an absence of buyers than as a result of heavy or persistent selling. At the bottom, there was a buying opportunity once the dust settled, not the beginning of the end for stocks.

When it was all over, there was plenty of time over the next couple of years to select stocks for the next bull market. There was no need to rush since even the best stocks needed time to build a new base, and some never did. At the time, it was necessary to consider whether a longer-lasting bear market might be starting, as many said it was. However, the 40-month moving average did its job of holding major long-term support. The rest is history.

Different Perspectives

CHAPTER 35

How to Use Options

Trade with the Professionals

Options have their place for serious long-term investors, but that place is not what most people think it is. Most people try to buy options in the hope of scoring home runs, thinking they are limiting risk to the cost of the option. While you can make huge profits in options when you buy one that multiplies in price by many times, the probabilities in favor of making money over the long term are stacked against you. They are the long shot that misses the mark too much of the time. The probabilities are weighted in favor of the option seller, not the option buyer. The bias is weighted against the option buyer as decisively as it is against the casino gambler.

For those unfamiliar with options, here first is how they work. Then we proceed to suggestions for using them to make money, putting yourself in the position of the house rather than that of the gambler playing long shots.

A *call option* allows you to buy a stock at a fixed price some time in the future. Every optionable stock has a series of strike prices and expiry dates. Assume that it is January 1 and you expect U.S. Widgets (USW), now trading at $95, to go to $130 by May. For $10 you can buy an option to buy USW at $100 any time up to the third Friday in May. If you are right in your assumption that USW will go to $130 in five months, you make three times your money. However, the stock has to go to $110 and change just to get your money back, plus two commissions.

A *put option* allows you to sell a stock at the designated strike price. So the option buyer makes money if the stock goes down.

Many speculators regard options as a means of making a lot of money quickly. A call option on USW makes a huge profit if the stock skyrockets from $95 to $130 or more. You make an immense profit if USW not only goes to $130 but keeps on going to $200. Then you make ten times your money. You also make a huge profit by buying a put option if the stock plummets.

To repeat the point, as at the casino, in options trading the house is the seller of options, not the buyer. Therefore, let's see what the house does.

Professionals Sell (Write) Options

Professionals sell (or write) options. A mostly unwary and amateurish public buys them. It pays to be a professional, not an amateur. (The exception is when someone in the know buys call options ahead of a takeover or buys a put option ahead of bad corporate news. That is not supposed to be legal, but it happens. It is impossible to keep news of all corporate developments secret. Sometimes people can simply make an educated guess and be right about what might happen. When a lot of people think they smell something happening in a stock, their buying or selling may start to show up in market action. However, this action is seldom on a scale big enough to attract much attention.)

The buyer of an option assumes a risk in the hope of making a superior gain. The seller receives money for a smaller but more certain immediate one, but forgoes the prospect of a huge windfall gain. Many informed investors sell options on stocks that they own. The procedure is called *covered writing*. Sometimes the stock is *called away,* or sold at the strike price, because the stock has gone up. Often the option writer simply keeps the option premium as a kind of extra dividend.

It is January 1 and you own 100 shares of USW, now trading at $95. You can sell an option that gives the buyer the right to buy the stock from you at $100 any time up to the third Friday in May. You receive $10 per share and put the money in the bank. If the stock goes above

$100, the option buyer will come and ask for the stock. Then you receive the agreed $100 per share. Since you have already received the $10 option premium, the effective result is that you sell the stock for $110. A 16-percent gain over five months is a good return on your money by any standard. If the stock goes much higher, you miss out on that big gain. Nevertheless, it is hard to complain about the reward received versus the risk. You receive in five months a return that in normal times would be very good for a year of owning the stock.

If USW goes down instead of up, you are covered by the sale of the option for a decline down to $85. In that case you are in the same position as if you sold the stock at $95. Relative to your position on January 1, you lose money only if the stock goes under $85.

There is an obvious reason why it is so hard for the option buyer to make money in the long run. The price of the option reflects the likelihood of the stock moving strongly higher. A strong stock has an expensive call option, and only a weak stock has a low-priced one. The option seller does not willingly give away more than necessary, charging what the freight will bear.

Another obvious problem with buying a call option on USW is that the stock has to go up by May. You may be right on the stock but wrong on the timing. Options start losing value the moment you buy them, since the clock starts running against the expiry date. For the option buyer, being wrong on the timing is just as bad as being wrong on the stock. Either way, you lose money. The option seller merely has to sit back and hope the stock does not fall in the meantime below the $85 level for which selling the option gives protection.

When you own a stock, you can keep on selling call options time and again against that stock unless it is called away by an option buyer. In that case you may or may not simply decide to buy the stock back. When one option expires, you repeat the process. Every so often, you sell an option and have the stock called away. Sometimes, too, you forgo a huge profit. That hardly matters. Over time, the option writer can achieve excellent returns with limited risk.

The downside is that writing options is a waste of time compared with owning stocks like Microsoft and Intel when those stocks are really running. Nevertheless, even those stocks take a rest in a bull market and sometimes provide opportunities for covered writing.

Professionals Also Sell Put Options

Many speculators try to make huge profits by buying put options in the expectation of a crash in a particular stock or in the market generally.

You might wonder who the sellers are. Some money managers generally have a steady inflow of money to invest. They also have a list of stocks that they want to buy, and often want to buy cheaper than the current market price. One may want to buy USW if it goes to $85 but not at the current price of $95. Selling a $90 strike-price put option for $5 brings the stock half the way to the desired buying price. If the stock stays above $90, the option writer simply keeps the $5. If the option writer has to buy the stock at any price between $85 and $90, he pays the option buyer $90. The effective cost is $85, the intended purchase price in the first place, represented by $90 minus the $5 proceeds from the sale of the put option. The option writer loses money by writing the option, compared with doing nothing, only if the stock goes below $85.

Of course, buying low intentionally may not be such a good thing to do if the stock goes down significantly. However, if the stock merely retraces, it still may be better to buy it at an effective cost of $85, compared with just going out and buying it at $95.

Sell Naked Options against the Trend

There is another approach that gives the speculator a chance of beating the odds: Sell options without owning the stock, a procedure called *selling naked options*. As when writing covered options, the returns are smaller than the home runs you can make by buying options that make big gains. However, the likelihood of making money consistently is more important than hitting home runs.

Sell naked *call options* on stocks that you expect to go sideways or *down*. When you expect a stock to go sideways or *higher*, sell naked *put options*.

Make sure that you get this concept the right way around. Do not sell naked call options on a stock in a strong uptrend. That is a bet on shooting yourself in the foot. Similarly, do not sell a put option on a stock in a strong downtrend.

To illustrate, you do not own any USW, now trading at $95. You expect the stock to continue going higher. Instead of buying a call option, you sell a put. You sell the $95 strike-price put option for $7 and put the money in your account. When the put option buyer exercises his right, you have to buy the stock if its price is at or below $95. However, you already have $7 protection from the money you sold the option for. You lose money only if the stock goes below $88. If the stock stays above $95 by the option expiry date, the $7 stays in your account and there is no more exposure to risk either.

When USW is going sideways or down and trading at $95, sell a call option at the May $100 strike price. Since, when the stock is going down, the likelihood of the stock going up is relatively small, you may receive only $7. Here you lose money only if the stock goes above $107. If the stock does not exceed $100, you keep the entire $7.

You can protect yourself from ruinous losses when selling naked options. Sell a call option on USW and you lose your shirt if the stock soars. You can protect yourself against disaster by selling a call option at a lower strike price, say at $100, and simultaneously buying one at a higher strike price. The $120 call option might cost you only $2.00. Sometimes you get caught in between $110 and $130 and lose money, but the high strike-price call option saves you from a disaster in the event of the stock going to $200.

Advantageous Strategies

In practice, there are two different approaches that work when selling naked options. The first is to define the major trend and then to sell options on the other side of the market, selling put options in a bull market and call options in a bear market. If you have confidence in the trend, you can sell options that are close to the strike price and have a longer time to run. This approach ties in with our timing techniques for buying stocks or selling them short. Then you can sell the naked options at very good prices, maximizing the amount of premiums coming into your account.

An alternative approach is to sell naked options that have a strike price far out of the money and also having a short time to expiry. For example, it is May 1 and USW is selling at $95. With three weeks to run, you might sell the $110 call option for $2. The chance of the stock going past $110 is almost infinitesimal. The reward may seem small but the probabilities are very favorable for simply keeping the option premium. It takes a major corporate development to move the stock so far within that short time.

Responsible capital management is essential when writing naked options. It generally pays to budget for potential losses of about two to three times what you receive in premium. It also pays over the long term to accept smaller but more reliable returns than to risk more in the hope of making superior gains.

Because of the risk of a market accident, diversification is more important when writing options than it is when buying stocks. As with any investment approach, there are certain to be losses as well as gains. Occasionally, a stock may lunge against you on some completely unforeseeable corporate development. The option writer is in a position somewhat similar to an insurance company. You pocket premiums but occasionally have to pay out big claims. Options writing, like writing insurance, can be a very good business in its own right.

CHAPTER 36

Market Myths I

The Savings Myth

There is a myth spread with urgency by those in the investment business who make money when you save. It is that you must save and save, and start saving early. Only then can you expect to reap the benefits of compound interest and build a fortune. Only by saving regularly can you make your dreams come true.

Saving is good, of course, and financial planning is essential. However, saving should not dominate your lifestyle, particularly when the first priority should be to provide for a young family. It is true that you need some money to invest. It is not true that you need a large amount. Far more important than how much you save is what you do with what you have.

You can see in hindsight that an investment of just $5000 in Microsoft in 1988 would have grown to half a million dollars by 1998. While that return was exceptional, you can also see that there were many, many stocks that advanced during the decade by ten times or more. There are almost always superior opportunities somewhere if you are patient and know what to look for. If you used new savings to buy natural resource stocks instead of buying Microsoft and other great stocks, you might as well have spent the money. If you bought Microsoft, that stock did your saving for you. On the other hand, a dollar saved and invested badly can easily become a dollar lost.

The urgency of the savings myth is contradicted by the sales pitch aimed at retired people by the Templeton group of mutual funds. Invest $100,000 in an equity fund and they will then pay you each year a blend of capital and interest equal to 10 percent of your investment. Over the long term, Templeton succeeded in making these disbursements as well as multiplying by several times the money originally invested. They have been able to do so by consistently achieving investment returns in excess of the 10-percent annual payout rate. The only problem, and it is a real one, is whether Templeton would be able to continue this performance during a severe bear market and afterwards if you invested a lot of money near the top of the market.

Templeton proves the point that it is more important to use investment techniques that work than it is to have or to save an immense amount of capital. The corollary is that money is meant to be spent, not merely to be saved for its own sake. That is true whatever your time of life.

The Myth of Corporate Profits

Contrary to popular belief, in the 1990s the real underlying rate of increase in corporate earnings was almost certainly not what it seemed.

Much of the increase in corporate profits during the 1980s and 1990s occurred as a result of nonrecurring shifts. These included declining interest rates and lower corporate taxes. Corporations starting the 1980s with high-interest bank loans outstanding gained considerably from declining interest rates, with the benefit flowing immediately to profits. Savings from the extensive introduction of a new generation of cost-saving computer technology are not likely to continue their rapid enhancement of corporate profits in such industries as banking and telecommunications. There were substantial but nonrecurring savings from laying off personnel and rehiring on contract, often at a lower rate of pay and without the staggering cost of employment benefits.

The improvement in productivity and in corporate profits in the United States was immense relative to companies abroad. In Germany, for example, business long remained shackled with many onerous and hard-to-change restrictions on lowering costs and improving productivity. Nevertheless, even Germany took on its labor costs and other impediments to improving productivity. If everyone becomes more efficient, then everyone is more competitive. The ability to make easy profit gains does not recur.

A study in *Grant's Interest Rate Observer* (August 15, 1997) set out assumed true results for the thirty Dow stocks and several other major stocks, as opposed to their reported earnings. *Grant's* used operating income before taxes less any net interest expense and backed out non-recurring gains and losses. To neutralize the effect of share repurchases, the study used total dollars, not per-share results. On this basis, Kellogg delivered a 4.3 percent decline in sales and a 4.6 percent decline in earnings, not, as reported, a huge increase in sales and earnings. The mighty Coca-Cola, popularly thought to have an annual growth rate above 15 percent, had true sales growth of 0.4 percent and a decline of 3.7 percent in net earnings. The story was repeated almost across the board.

The average reported growth rate for corporate profits during the 1990s was 16 percent. This reported and to a significant extent, mythical rate of gain in profits occurred in conjunction with a growth rate in sales of only 4 percent. It is mathematically impossible to sustain this divergence between the rate of gain in profits and that for sales. Profits can never reach 100 percent of sales.

Most real and substantial growth during the 1980s and 1990s was attributable to a very small percentage of the total corporate universe, and it was mostly concentrated in such areas as computer technology and pharmaceuticals. Even within apparent growth sectors, there were many companies that were stagnant or losing money.

The Myth of Pension Profits

Most corporations provide pensions funded by money charged against corporate profits. Pensions are generally paid at a rate that relates to employment earnings during the years leading up to retirement, and they are generally paid at a predetermined rate. There is seldom provision for major increases in benefits in the event that the pension fund achieves conspicuously good returns on the fund's investments. Nor are pensions normally reduced after a period of conspicuously bad returns. The company reaps the benefit if the fund is actuarially over-funded. It has the obligation to make up the difference if the pension plan is underfunded.

During the great bull market many pension funds were invested successfully enough to achieve big surpluses. Since its plan was fully funded, General Electric, for example, was able to stop making contributions to its corporate plan after 1987. At the end of 1997 GE's pension fund had a market value of $38.7 billion, after achieving a return on its investments that year of almost 20 percent. The result was that GE could book $743 million as income that might otherwise have had to be paid into the pension fund and charged against profits accordingly. This gain boosted GE's profits by 6.7 percent. For the first half of 1998 Northrop Grumman reported net pension credits equal to 29 percent of operating income. With numbers like that, investors have to be concerned about the true source of profits and whether they come from operations or from pension fund investments.

While pension fund profits are real income at the time, these unrealized gains should not be taken for granted. Most companies project pension fund returns of between 8 and 10 percent, or about the long-term historic norm for the return on stocks. When portfolios were increasing at 15 or 20 percent each year during the great bull market, those projections looked conservative. However, one must be aware that portfolio returns can turn severely negative in a full-fledged bear market.

The great bull market fed on rising profits fed in part by pension fund credits fed in turn by the great bull market. The loop was a virtuous circle. It could reverse. When bonds yield 5 percent and there is a severe bear market, there is nowhere to hide from returns well below the projected 8 or 10 percent expected from stock market investments. Retention of any stocks at all in a pension fund portfolio during a severe bear market could result in severely negative returns, with a correspondingly adverse impact on profits. Under these circumstances stock prices are likely to keep trending down in response to lower profit expectations. That is how a virtuous circle turns vicious.

The Myth of Professional Integrity

Many people believe in the myth that you can rely blindly on professional integrity. Even under optimum circumstances, professionals can make mistakes. Some are incompetent or misleading even if they sincerely strive to be honest.

Let's come back to Cendant, discussed in Chapter 2. This company provides an example of how many professionals blunder by accepting corporate financial statements at face value. It was necessary to look more closely at what Cendant was really doing. On the basis of published results, the company appeared to have an annual growth rate of around 30 percent. However, much of that growth came from buying great companies at a good price. The rate of growth depended on continuing to make successful acquisitions. The more companies Cendant bought, the greater the risk of eventually buying a bad one, which is what happened when it bought CUC International. That company was the source of the accounting irregularities which, when discovered, caused Cendant's stock to tumble. If you read the fine print in Cendant's financial statements and took out the growth attributable to acquisitions, it turned out that Cendant's internal rate of growth was around 11 percent. That still left it a good company but not good enough to justify a $40 stock price.

The Myth of EBDITA

EBDITA, or earnings before interest depreciation taxes and amortization, is an accounting exercise used to create an illusion of profit and value.

This exercise shows the amount of cash that a company generates. The problem is that taxes and depreciation are both very real expenses, and they must be charged against profits. You can no longer buy machinery to make newsprint, for example, and expect it to last for 50 or 75 years. In many businesses, the useful life of a capital investment may be five years or less. Then it is worth nothing. Failing to charge depreciation as a real expense means that you end up with an entire business worth nothing. Some businesses truly generate surplus cash after all real expenses, and some consume more cash than they generate. EBDITA is not a useful means of distinguishing which is which, or of telling which stocks to buy.

When relying on what other people tell you and when processing information from any source, however prestigious, remember this rule about professionals in any field: Never rely blindly on the advice of someone who stands to profit from it.

The Myth of Corporate Buybacks

There is a myth that a corporate stock buyback is always good for shareholders. In a bull market, the initial reaction to the announcement of a stock buyback is almost always positive. But what does a buyback really mean? A stock buyback is the equivalent of a dividend paid by other means.

In the short run a buyback means that fewer stockholders own the same company, so there is more value in the stock. Or is there? A buyback means that fewer stockholders own a *smaller* company. The value of corporate assets is reduced by an amount exactly equal to what is spent on buying back stock.

The rise in price on the announcement of a stock buyback may be damaging to shareholders. When IBM announced a buyback of $850 million of its own stock, the share price went from the $120 level to the $160 level, increasing the market value of the company by—*yes, that's right!*—$850 million. The announcement of the intended buyback had the effect of raising the price in a bidding war against itself.

If a buyback program pushes the price of the stock higher only temporarily and then it falls back, stockholders are clearly worse off. It is the same as if you yourself bought the stock high and then saw the price fall. You as a shareholder and the company that you own as shareholder have an exactly interchangeable interest in the price paid for stock.

There is a case for a company to buy stock back if that is an inherently profitable thing to do. If it buys stock at a price below the replacement value of the underlying assets, that should be good for stockholders. It should also be a good deal if the company can buy back its stock so as to earn 15 percent or more on corporate equity. In most cases, companies buying back stock at an earnings multiple greater than about eight are playing with smoke and mirrors. Dividends alone provide the proof that a company is really earning its keep over the long term. A sustained and, ideally, rising rate of dividend payout provides a wonderful, if only partial support for the stock price in a general bear market.

Corporate stock buybacks occur when business conditions are good and stock prices are high. But what happens if there is a recession, profits decline instead of rising, and the stock price falls? Many a company buys back stock only to find that it needs the money after all. The case of IBM in the early 1980s is typical. Having parted with its cash to buy back stock, it had to sell bonds at an exorbitant rate of interest when it needed money. For a time there was no return at all on the money invested in the stock bought back.

A stock buyback weakens a company unless the return on the investment is both immediate and high. If these conditions are not met by a company whose stock you own, review whether you want to continue owning stock in a weaker company. Any rise in the stock price spurred by the buyback program could well provide a prime opportunity to sell stock. On the other hand, a buyback at four or five times earnings should in due course strengthen the company and lead to a higher stock price. It's almost certain to be a good buy when, in addition, price action is favorable.

The Myth of Stock Options

Reported corporate profits may be mythical to the extent that employees are paid with stock options instead of money.

The cost of paying employees with stock options comes at a cost to shareholders that is insufficiently recognized and in some cases is huge. At first sight, there is no cost to existing shareholders when employees are granted stock options. There is no charge against profits for the options' value as there is with a paycheck. The cost to shareholders, however, is real. It comes directly at their expense by diluting their interest in the company by an amount exactly equal to the value of the option granted. From the shareholder's viewpoint, the granting of a stock option amounts to the equivalent of a stock trading ex-dividend, except that the shareholder is not the beneficiary of the option. The stock market generally pays no heed to the grant of a stock option because the granting of individual options is generally imperceptible. Collectively, however, they can amount to real money over time. The shareholder has a smaller investment in the company as surely as when a dividend is paid out of the corporate treasury.

Depending on how the option is structured, the real cost to shareholders may be the entire difference between exercise price and current market price times the number of options outstanding. In early 1998 Microsoft had options outstanding on that basis for 500 million shares at an average exercise price of $17.50. The pretax liability amounted to $30 billion, or more than four times the general estimate for what the company was expected to report as "earnings" for 1998. Many companies in the computer industry became accustomed to paying employees with stock options instead of money. Microsoft was merely one of the more conspicuous ones to do so.

For 1997 it was estimated that reported profits for the stocks in the Standard & Poor's 500 index should really be adjusted downward by 10 percent to provide for employees receiving stocks and options instead of money. An apparent 16-percent increase in profits was really no more than 6 percent.

CHAPTER 37

Market Myths II

The Myth of New Eras

Toward the top of a bull market there is always a myth that busts belong in another age. Then the current wisdom says there is a "new era." There has been a "paradigm shift."

Every really big and long-lasting boom breeds the myth that "this time is different." President Calvin Coolidge delivered the all-time classic new-era story in his last message to the new Congress on December 4, 1928. "No Congress of the United States ever assembled," he said, "on surveying the state of the Union, has met with a more pleasing prospect. . . . The great wealth created by our enterprise and industry, and saved by our economy, has had the widest distribution among our people, and has gone out in a steady stream to serve the charity and business of the world. . . . The country can regard the present with satisfaction, and anticipate the future with optimism. . . ."

It took ten months more to arrive at the stock market crash in October 1929. With the economy enjoying an apparently never-ending prosperity, stock prices were high relative to all reasonable expectations for earnings and dividends. At last, in June 1929 an economic slowdown began. Production was outrunning consumption, so manufacturers began to rein in production. As production faded, profits not only failed to maintain their rate of increase but declined.

Declining profits led to lower expectations from the stock market. So investors and speculators sold. Some sold to take profits, some to meet margin calls, some to enter short sales. The declining stock market made people feel less comfortable with their finances, so they spent less. The so-called wealth effect went into reverse, so profits declined further, so stock prices declined further. The depression fed on itself in a downward spiral that was the opposite of the preceding boom.

The bad news, however long it might take to come, is this: Slump follows boom as night follows day! When there is talk of new eras and paradigm shifts, it is not necessarily time to head for the exit, for bull markets die hard. However, when everything seems too good to be true, it is time to be wary.

The good news in the depths of a depression is this: Boom follows slump as day follows night!

The Myth of Defensive Stocks

Contrary to popular belief, for all practical purposes there are no stocks to own when the general direction of the market is down. There may be isolated areas of prosperity and rising stock prices, but the odds are against finding them. In a serious depression you have to own government debt, not corporate bonds, and certainly not stocks.

Even apparently rock-solid utilities decline in a full-fledged bear market. Conservative and knowledgeable professional money owns utilities. It is generally the first to leave the stock market when stock prices are too high for comfort. It is generally the first to buy back in when things look most black.

It is true that utilities and some other stocks are defensive compared with the rest of the market. Nevertheless, defensiveness does not stop them going down. It just means that they are likely to go down less than the darlings of the preceding bull market. In hard times people have difficulty paying even their utility bills, and growth in the use of electricity, gas, and telephone service can turn negative. When investors have to sell stocks, they sell what they can because some stocks become unsalable at any price.

The Inflation Myth

Most people think inflation relates to the price of bacon and beans, of holidays and haircuts. They measure inflation by the Consumer Price Index (CPI).

That dangerous oversimplification does not accommodate the two standard definitions of inflation. The first definition is undue expansion of the money supply. The second is a substantial rise in prices caused by undue expansion of the money supply.

In a perfect, noninflationary world a central bank should increase the supply of money at a rate approximately equal to the growth of the economy. Variations in inflation will then be small and will depend on changes in the rate of growth in the economy and the velocity of money (the rate at which people spend it).

During 1998 the U.S. economy was growing at an annual rate of about 4 percent, while the rate of growth in the M3 measure of money supply was almost 12 percent. The excess of about 8 percentage points in the increase in the supply of money was not going into physical commodities or the Consumer Price Index. It was going into stocks and in some places, into real estate. Money supply numbers are printed each week in the Market Laboratory, Economic Indicators section of *Barron's*.

The 1920s and the 1990s provide textbook examples of less immediately visible inflation. Both periods saw a substantial increase in the money supply in conjunction with an asset inflation. With consumer prices steady or lower, the Fed saw no need to rein in the money supply and credit excesses.

Expansion of the money supply was justified in 1982 to bail out of Mexico's bankruptcy. There was another major and undue expansion of the money supply when Citicorp was essentially bankrupt in 1991, and yet another after the Asian financial meltdown in 1997. On each occasion, expansion of the money supply had little impact on the CPI, and Mexico and Citicorp were successfully floated off the rocks.

In addition to expansion of the money supply, there was an immense expansion of credit, which was only partly captured in official records. During the five years from 1993, mortgage lenders Fannie Mae and Freddie Mac extended new mortgage loans at compound rates of 17 percent and 31 percent respectively. It was possible to obtain home equity loans for 125 percent of appraised value. From mid-1997 to mid-1998 U.S. bank loans for the purchase of securities expanded at a 50-percent rate over the previous year. In the meantime, total household debt stood at a record 95 percent of household income, up from 68 percent a decade earlier. However, auto leasing, accounting for 30 percent of new car financing, was not included in the Federal Reserve's accounting for consumer debt.

Fed chairman Alan Greenspan was reported as saying that the level of household debt in the United States was not at worrisome levels relative to the prosperity of the times. Bank of Canada chairman, Gordon Thiessen, correctly observed in his 1997 annual report: "The worse the inflation, the worse the subsequent recession." Neither he nor Mr. Greenspan took the next step: to acknowledge what inflation is.

The Myth of the Fed's Credibility

There is a myth that governments are there to protect the public. History shows that in times when the need has been greatest, government has as often as not been the problem, not the solution. The U.S. Federal Reserve is at the heart of problem-creation in the U.S. economy.

In his essay *Gold and Economic Freedom,* published in July 1996, long before becoming U.S. Federal Reserve Chairman, Alan Greenspan stated the historic challenge facing central banks as follows:

> When business in the United States underwent a mild contraction in 1927, the Federal Reserve created more paper reserves in the hope of forestalling any possible bank reserve shortage. More disastrous, however, was the Federal Reserve's attempt to assist Great Britain, who had been losing gold to us because the Bank of England refused to allow interest rates to rise when market forces dictated it (it was politically unpalatable). The reasoning of the authorities involved was as follows: If the Federal Reserve pumped excessive paper reserves into American banks, interest rates in the United States would fall to a level comparable with those in Great Britain; this would act to stop Britain's gold loss and avoid the political embarrassment of having to raise interest rates.

The "Fed" succeeded: It stopped the gold loss, but it nearly destroyed the economies of the world in the process. The excess credit which the Fed pumped into the economy spilled over into the stock market—triggering a fantastic speculative boom. Belatedly, Federal Reserve officials attempted to sop up the excess reserves and finally succeeded in breaking the boom. But it was too late: By 1929 the speculative imbalances had become so overwhelming that the attempt precipitated a sharp retrenching and a demoralizing of business confidence. As a result, the American economy collapsed.

In *The Communist Manifesto* Karl Marx advocated state-controlled banking because he thought this was the way to avert the periodic cathartic slumps that he saw occurring in the United States and elsewhere. During the worst bust of all in the United States, which began in 1838, the last year of Andrew Jackson's Presidency, there was total debt liquidation estimated at $450 million, more than ten times the total annual budget for the federal government at that time. Once the decks were cleared, the economy recovered of its own accord.

Since 1914 the Fed's record has been disastrous. It fueled one of the greatest stock market bubbles of all time during the 1920s. It presided over the Great Depression and in 1933, more bank failures than at any time before. It presided over the greatest peacetime inflation of all time between 1960 and 1980. During the 1990s it presided over perhaps the absolute greatest stock market bubble of all time.

The Myth of Confidence

A rising stock market does not necessarily forecast perpetual prosperity, and a declining one does not necessarily forecast the end of the world. It is axiomatic that market tops occur when people are most confident and market bottoms when people are most pessimistic.

The record high reading for consumer confidence of 142.3 was registered in October 1968 when the Dow Industrials stood near their record to that point of around 1000. At that time, the stock market had been rising steadily from 550 in 1962 for a gain of 82 percent. The October peak in consumer confidence was also the exact peak in the stock market. During the next 18 months the Dow declined by 36 percent.

The March 1998 reading for the consumer confidence index, 138.3, was the highest since October 1968, almost exactly thirty years earlier. The broad-based Russell 2000 stock index made an important high the next month.

The reason why people feel confident is not because they intend to buy stocks. It is because they have already bought stocks. Market tops occur when they run out of money and credit with which to buy more.

The Myth of Baby Booms and Baby Busts

In May 1996 Dean Witter Reynolds issued a research report which said:

> Low dividend yields reflect a "paradigm shift," as investor preferences tilt toward higher rates of internal investment. Record low dividend yields do not necessarily portend impending disaster. A paradigm shift is what has driven yields down to the 2.2% level on the S&P 500 [and subsequently to 1.5%]—not speculative frenzy.

The report noted that cash flow from rising corporate earning was likely to fuel future dividend increases. They said that the bull market was "not dead yet," and that the effect of the baby boomers on the bull market "cannot be overstated." "More aggressive younger investors and the late-to-the-party baby boomers trying to catch up are directing funds to continue the bull market."

Here is the chronology of how baby boomers fitted into the economy with their demographic impact:

Born	1955 to 1970
School building	1960 to 1975
University expansion	1960 to 1985
Rising house prices, consumption, and inflation	1970 to 1989
Rising investment values	1982 to ?

Dean Witter Reynolds continued to be right for a long time after publication of their research report. However, history does not support the view that a pendulum goes only one way.

The Market Fuel Myth

There is a popular myth that savings drive the market. Curiously, that appears to be wrong. It is more accurate to say that stocks go up because stocks go up. Rising stock markets do people's saving for them. The imbalance that tips toward the buy side mostly occurs as a result of buying fueled by credit, not by new saving; and credit comes, of course, from the Fed. Insofar as accurate numbers exist (which is a problem), in 1997 the U.S. savings rate was 3.85 percent of disposable income, the lowest in 58 years. In boom times people do not save; they spend. That spending makes the boom that makes the pony go.

The big worry about a huge spending boom in parallel with a huge assets inflation is what happens in recession and depression. Then people save. The harder the times, the more they save. They believe they have to, and generally they are right.

The Devalued Currency Myth

There is a myth that a declining currency is good for business and good for stocks. Not so, despite what politicians and central bankers might have you believe. A falling currency reflects economic weakness. A depreciating currency is said to help exporters. Logically, if a small depreciation is good, a bigger one is better. That is nonsense, because imports have to be paid for with exports. At a lower price, you have to sell more volume of goods to buy what you could previously buy with less volume.

A rising currency lowers input costs, suppresses inflation, lowers interest rates, and forces productivity improvement. During the 1980s Japan was the prime example of the beneficiary of a rising currency. A falling currency has the practical effect of subsidizing inefficiency. The competitive pressure to improve productivity is lifted by a declining currency.

When considering a foreign investment, it is essential to know what is happening to the currency. There is no point in seeing stock market gains lost, if they occur at all, to currency depreciation. Consider, for example, the comparative advantage of investing in the United States versus Canada. During the bull market of the 1980s and the 1990s, the

Dow Jones Industrials went up by ten times and the Toronto Stock Exchange Composite Index by five times. However, the Canadian dollar fell by a third during that time. Consequently, the TSE advanced in terms of U.S. dollars only one-third as much as the Dow, which, in turn, advanced much less than many great stocks.

The story of Canada's decline compares with that of many resource-rich countries. With advantages roughly equivalent to those of the United States, Canada did not finance the Marshall Plan, the Vietnam War, or any significant foreign-aid or peacekeeping capability. Instead, it exported billions of dollars to pay for nationalization of foreign-owned oil companies, buying at the top of the market and paying several times the then-inflated prices on the stock exchange. At the same time, Canada turned down the opportunity to build a pipeline along the Mackenzie Valley to transport natural gas from Alaska to the U.S. Midwest. The combined cost and foregone capital investment of these two initiatives alone amounted to some $25 billion. That cost compounded at 15 percent over the next twenty years was to be some US$400 billion, or an amount approximately equal to total Canadian federal government debt.

Canada long had policies that encouraged people to stay where there was no work and to redistribute wealth rather than create it. Like Argentina, one of the world's richest countries in 1946, Canada, with its interventionist policies, lost the opportunity to have full employment, a strong currency, debt-free government finances, and interprovincial harmony. Instead, it has incurred a tax burden and a debt burden among the highest of any country in the OECD, as well as high unemployment, political discord, and social services under pressure from lack of funding.

The long slide in the Canadian dollar began in 1976, the year nationalization of much of the oil industry began and construction of the Mackenzie Valley pipeline was rejected. The monthly chart for the Canadian dollar illustrates an unattractive environment for owning stocks (Figure 37-1).

The Natural Resources Myth

There is a myth that you can measure a country's strength by its natural resources. If that were so, the richest countries in the world ought

FIGURE 37-1. Monthly Canadian Dollar.

to include Argentina, Brazil, Canada, Mexico, Nigeria, Venezuela, and many other resource-rich economies.

The poorest countries in the world ought to include Hong Kong, Japan, North Korea, Singapore, and Taiwan, but of course they have become rich.

The lesson is clear. People in countries that are rich in natural resources tend get complacent and lazy. The absence of natural resources makes people realize that their comparative advantage must rely on knowledge and enterprise.

CHAPTER 38

The Winning Attitude

The Psychological Challenge of Success

Success is as much a psychological challenge as it is a practical one. For a winning attitude, it is not enough to say you want to be successful. Everyone wants to be successful. The question is whether you are prepared to do the things to be successful. To achieve success, you have to ask yourself some questions:

Am I prepared to learn thoroughly the techniques proven to make money in the stock market?

Am I prepared to follow signals and to respond to them as readily as I respond to traffic lights when driving a car?

Will I manage my capital responsibly and not expose it to undue risk, or will I cheat and overload the wagon when an opportunity appears to offer all the chance of gain and none of loss?

Will I do the homework regularly to keep on top of my investments and the technical action in the market?

Few people can be expected to give a totally unhedged answer to all these questions. Fortunately, perfection is by no means necessary for success. However, success is likely to be, at least to some extent, proportional to the quality of the work done to that end. One way of preparing yourself psychologically for the challenge of successful investing is to guard against the following seven deadly sins of investment.

Sins to Avoid

1. Impatience

Impatience afflicts most people some of the time and some people all of the time. You see what looks like a great stock to buy shaping up and you are tempted to jump the gun on a signal. You hope to get in at a good price, only to see the price get "better" by going lower, or to see the stock going sideways interminably. Many people have bought General Motors or Homestake at a good price over a period of several decades.

It is all too easy to be impatient about banking a good profit and doing so prematurely. Great stocks often go far higher than ever seemed possible at the beginning. However, you have only to look at a chart for Microsoft to see the merits of patience. There have been times when the stock did nothing for many months on end, sometimes even for a couple of years or more. Investing for the long term is the right thing to do when a stock and the underlying company represented by the stock continues to perform well. One partial cure for impatience is to look at the rate at which a long-term moving average or a long-term trendline is going up. Then you can make a tentative extrapolation of how patience—and holding a stock—will pay off in the long term.

It is human nature to want to bank a profit "while it is there." Many, many investors are neurotic when making money. They feel constantly challenged by the need to make a decision whether to take their profit in case what went up comes back down. For a pastime, brokers like to call their clients and invite them to bank profits, or at least to bank half. Unfortunately, this is often the worst thing to do. Time and again the profitable stock that you sell is the one that goes on to make huge profits. Then you have to start all over again looking for the next stock in which to invest the proceeds. Not only should you be wary of selling, but the best place for new money may be the stock you already own.

2. Fear

Many investors are afraid to buy the strongest stocks and to act on strong signals. It is hard to believe at the time that the stock that moves most strongly out of a consolidation is the one least likely to look back. However, what goes up does not necessarily come back down. The likelihood of it coming back down is actually in inverse proportion to the strength of the launch.

The remedy for the fear of taking a strong signal is not to miss buying the stock. It is to buy only as much of the stock as you can sensibly afford to buy if you get stopped out at the initial protective stop.

One way to make of fear a desirable sense of caution is to heed the futures trader's saying: Never trade scared money! That does not mean that you should refrain from taking calculated risks, but that you should truly make the calculations in relation to your emotional and financial capital. For many people it really is psychologically difficult to set aside emotions and to be objective. You should be able to treat real money like Monopoly money. If you let the importance of money trouble you, it becomes very difficult to make good decisions. Inevitably, the psychological pressure to succeed leads to poor decisions. The remedy for psychological challenges is to sell down to your sleeping level. If either a bad loss or a big profit affects your emotions, you probably have too much money in the market.

There is a saying about fear that may be helpful. Let's say you find yourself deciding whether to buy a stock that has just delivered a conspicuously powerful signal. You previously sold out the stock at a much lower price. You now fear that the new signal may be an exhaustion move rather than the start of a major new leg up. Remember the saying: Fear can be effectively overcome by the repetition of acts of courage!

3. Greed

Many investors buy more stock than they can afford, either with their financial or their emotional capital. They set aside fear and reasonable caution and go in deeper than they should. The surefire stock often turns out to be no such thing. Joe Granville has a saying worth remembering: "If it's obvious, it's obviously wrong." What that often means is that if an opportunity is obvious, then everyone wanting to exploit the apparent opportunity may already have done so.

Greed leads many people to buy more stocks on margin than they can carry through routine market fluctuations. It is all too easy to buy at highs using all the available margin. On a retracement you get a margin call that necessitates selling some or all of the stock bought high. However, that is likely where you should be buying more, not selling out. Greedy use of margin can double losses instead of doubling profits.

Greed also leads many people to stay with a stock that has run its course. You look at what you might once have sold a stock for, one like Micron Technology at $95. You say to yourself, "I can't sell it at only $60. I'll wait for it to go back to $95 again. Then I'll sell it." The problem is that instead of going back to $95, it goes down to $25.

Ideally, a great stock should be forever. But forever just does not happen. You must have the discipline to accept that every move in a stock has a beginning, a middle, and an end. All you can expect is to take a piece out of the middle. When you score a bull's-eye like Microsoft, it is all middle, and the beginning and the end are barely perceptible.

One of the surest ways of being successful in the stock market, and in any business, is to keep aside capital for a rainy day or for new opportunities. That is the opposite of buying all the stocks you can on margin. The main thing is to remember how much money you can make when you are right.

4. Hope

Investors fall back on hope when the technical case turns against a stock. Hope is an abdication of control, and it seldom works. It is easier to wait for tomorrow than to make a decision today. However, the delay can cost you money. The longer you wait with a market going against you, the more likely it is that hope will prove ruinously costly. When a stock goes up, a trend in force is likely to remain in force. The same applies when a stock turns down.

You sometimes hear it said of a stock that it's too late to sell, too early to buy, but not too late to pray. If you find yourself even thinking of praying about a stock, the chances are that you should not own it.

Reliance on hope is like reliance on luck. There will always be unforeseeable events that can be attributed to good or bad luck. In the long run, however, good luck comes to people already doing the right things.

5. Pride

Pride assails investors who believe that their intelligence and personality are superior to the market or to a systematic approach to buying and selling stocks.

Many otherwise successful people bring to the stock market the attitude of the conquering hero. Successful experience in wrestling with knotty problems can lead to false conclusions about markets. There is no point in perceiving value if the market disagrees and sellers dominate. There is no point in arguing with the ludicrously high price of a stock if other investors keep on buying it.

The power of the mind over markets is no contest when there is a conflict. Markets always win.

6. Carelessness

After a big success or a big loss, depending on your personality, it is easy to get sloppy about doing your homework. Monitor your actions carefully, after both a big win and a big loss. You may find that what looked easy last time just does not work the next time or the time after. Carelessness may lead to failure to do homework thoroughly or cause you to overlook new variables. You might have simply experienced a piece of good or bad luck. Yes, luck is a factor, but it is no substitute for thoroughness.

Sometimes people seem to have runs when they do very well or very badly. Often these runs are an expression of underlying optimism or negativity. It is much easier to take a strong signal when confidence is up after recently making money. It is much harder to take a strong signal when you just took a bath in a stock that collapsed.

7. Gambling

Some people regard the stock market as a substitute for Las Vegas. These people buy into the myth of the high roller, those hugely successful investors whose names are household words. Almost all famous investors become famous by venturing money when the probabilities are overwhelmingly favorable. They refrain from doing so when they are not. Speculation in the true sense of the word means looking ahead. It does not mean gambling. Gambling means taking chances when the probabilities are not in your favor.

The other side of the challenge of staying with winners is what to do about losers. Staying with losers is generally an exercise in gambling. The probabilities have most likely turned against your stock, and responsibility has passed from you to the whims of the market. To reinforce the psychological imperative of handling losers, it is worth remembering the definition of the difference between speculation and gambling just cited above.

Remarkable as it may seem, some people are comfortable only when losing money, whether in Las Vegas or in the market. Getting ahead feeds on a neurosis, the fear of letting the profit slip. There is a constant nagging requirement to confront the decision of whether or not to sell, to take a profit "while it is there." For many people decision making is a process more painful than losing money. If you are in the market "for the long term," holding a losing stock means that there is no requirement to make a decision.

No doubt, you have met people who deny their losses totally. Their loss is a loss only when they sell. Assume that you bought Digital Equipment at $190 and that it is now trading at $20. You had better believe that you lost money! No doubt, too, you have found that the same people who deny their losses are not similarly slow to bank their profits. They run their losses and cut their profits off at the knees, the opposite of what is required for success.

There is one even more devastating gambler's loser-play than the inability to make the decision to stay with winners and to heave out losers. It is the siren song of the mutual fund salesperson who says that you should "average down." Buy more in a declining market and you lower your average cost. Then you make twice as much money when the market goes back up. The logical outcome of many an addition to losing stocks is that you lose twice as much money if the market continues to fall. If you are ever tempted to average down, remember the futures trader's imperative: Never add to a losing position!

Adding to a losing position gets you two ways. First, it truly increases the probability of adding to a loss. If you bought Digital Equipment at $190 and held it "for the long term," you could have bought more at $100. The loss at that level was bad enough. At $20 the double purchase was a disaster. The second way that adding to a losing position gets you is that it doubles the psychological difficulty of facing up to the loss and of doing something about it by getting out.

Capital Should Be Forever

Make Money and Also Keep It

This book is primarily about making money. It is equally important to keep it. That is far more difficult in the long term than is widely believed. Capital once made should be for generations. Some fortunes have remained intact for centuries, but not many. Sometimes the money has simply been spent or gambled away. Nevertheless, many great fortunes have gone down the drain because of poor investment management and disasters that should have been avoided.

A buy-and-hold strategy is almost certain to fail if you invest in almost any area long enough, except possibly in some real estate. It used to be that you could invest in British government bonds forever. Forever lasted from 1660 to 1946, which is almost three centuries. Then they became almost worthless. There was no more prestigious blue chip in the United States than New Haven Railroad. In due course, it went bankrupt, leaving its shareholders with wallpaper. The number of companies that have been in existence and which have also prospered for more than a century is microscopic. Even some companies that have been around for a long time may not necessarily have stocks worth buying. The Hudson's Bay Company, chartered in 1670, has been a three-hundred-year recovery story that never really worked.

The price of financial freedom, like that of personal liberty, is eternal vigilance.

Gerald Loeb was told by his publishers that they did not like his proposed title, *The Battle for Investment Survival*. They said it was too negative for the book to sell. Loeb insisted that investing in the stock market, let alone making and keeping money over the long term, really is a battle for survival. The public should not be misled into thinking otherwise. Loeb's title was accepted. Published in 1936, his book was written with the wisdom of looking back over the best of times as well as the worst of times. Loeb knew well from recent personal observation and participation that a bull market leads to a bear market. Then a bear market leads to the next bull market, and so on, ad infinitum: Slump follows boom as night follows day, and as the earth goes around the sun, so the cycle rotates. The title of Loeb's book, like the book itself, stands the test of time.

There Are Times to Stand Aside

One of the hardest things for many investors and money managers to accept is the wisdom of the saying: You don't have to be in the market all the time! Money burns a hole in the pockets of most people. The question is automatic: Where should I invest my money? Ask most people this question in the 1990s, especially stockbrokers and fund managers, and the only answer is "Put it into stocks!" or "Buy mutual funds!"

It is worth recalling that this was not the standard answer in the late 1970s and early 1980s. Almost no one then was saying to buy stocks (when the Dow sold at seven or eight times relatively depressed earnings). They did not say to buy bonds (when long-term Treasuries sold on a yield basis of 14 percent). There were of course a few wise stockbrokers and advisors, but it took years for the general public to wade into stocks up to their armpits, and in some cases over their heads.

General Loeb was one of the most successful investors of all time because he recognized that he had to keep cash reserves, however wonderful the opportunities in the market. He knew that there would always be new opportunities and probably better ones. He knew that he could profit from those new opportunities only with cash on hand. When fully invested, let alone when heavily committed on margin with borrowed money, you do not have cash on hand.

The Paradox of Cash

It is a paradox of markets that cash is often worth most when it appears to have the least value compared with other investments. When interest rates are low, who wants to own cash? You are better off to own stocks, bonds, real estate—anything other than cash. The risk is that if the public generally is overweighted in long-term investments and underweighted in cash, then the pendulum is likely to swing back with a vengeance. Cash is king when long-term investments are cheap. So you have to raise cash when financial assets are king. Long-term investments are generally cheap when interest rates are high or when the economy is in deep depression. Everyone wants the maximum short-term gain, and few see the merit in looking farther ahead. That is how fashions in investment, otherwise known at extremes as manias, come and go.

Cash was never more valuable than in the early 1980s, when you could get 20 percent from Treasury bills. That, of course, was the prime time to buy stocks and bonds and to part with cash. The immediate yield was half or less what you could get on 90-day money. However, very high interest rates could not be expected to last, and they did not. Investment in stocks and bonds, although offering a much lower immediate return at the time, delivered long-term gains. Stocks, with the expectation of increasing dividends over time, could be expected to pay more income in due course. The return on money market and Treasury bills or, worse, mortgages and investment certificates, could only go down, and it did, with lower rates paid on each renewal.

When interest rates are low, the risk in speculative investments is high. Never mind! All you need is a parking place. Treasury bills and similar cash equivalents provide a safe haven. That is the only place for conservative money to be when stocks are in a bear market. The only conservative strategy is to sit out the decline until the bear market runs its course. Then cash is available for buying stocks cheap for the next bull market.

The Best Decisions Are Often Difficult

Another paradox of investing is that the hardest thing to do psychologically is often the most necessary thing to do. Even with the best methodology in the world for buying or selling, it is still a psychological challenge to pull the trigger. It is genuinely hard to buy into a runaway market and to stay in for as long as it lasts. It is also hard to keep a cash reserve when all about you are proclaiming the wonders of a "new era" or a "paradigm shift." It is equally hard to believe that stocks have a future when all is gloom and doom. It was hard to sell stocks in August 1987 but all too easy to sell them at the bottom in October.

There is always a trade-off between following a trend and going against collective wisdom. Both are right some of the time. However, you must always be aware of the potential for disaster when no one considers disaster possible. Charles Mackay summed up the challenge succinctly in 1841, in his book *Extraordinary Popular Delusions and the Madness of Crowds*: "Men, it has been well said, think in herds; it will be seen that they go mad in herds, while they only recover their senses slowly, and one by one."

Buy the Strong; Sell the Weak

Always buy the strongest stock in the strongest group, when there are signals to do so, and sell the weakest stock in the weakest group. Buy Microsoft and Intel, not Digital Equipment. Buy Coca-Cola, not Seagram. Sell short K Mart, not Wal-Mart. Although, as we have seen, anything can change, that was what you had to do during the ten years to 1998.

Think of stocks as a car dealer thinks of his inventory. When black cars are selling well and yellow ones are not, the dealer does not buy more yellow ones. Price is irrelevant. If the public does not want yellow cars, there is no point in arguing with the market, even if you can buy yellow cars at a discount. Yellow cars cost money waiting for buyers. It is best to get rid of them as soon as possible and at any price you can. Holding a stock and waiting for other investors to show an interest by buying amounts to the same thing.

There is always a trade-off between giving a stock room to move and getting out quickly to bank a small profit or keep a small loss small. Keeping losses small is important, of course, but you have to give some latitude to a stock with strong confirming signals for the big picture. There is almost never a case for taking a profit prematurely. A trend in force is likely to remain in force. Stock market trends can go on so far beyond what seems remotely imaginable that they should not be abandoned lightly, especially not in the absence of signals. Unavoidably, market timing techniques will sometimes get you out of a stock too early or into a stock too late. That's not the point. The point is that you are working with probabilities. You have only to be successful in finding a few great stocks among the ones you buy. Under the best of circumstances, you can hold a great stock for several years. Then those that make huge gains should make far, far more than the losers lose.

Attempting to buy near absolute bottoms and to sell near absolute tops is one of the worst loser-plays. You can do it successfully so seldom that the effort of trying to do it is certain to be counterproductive. It is enough to take a piece from a middle that starts with an entry signal and ends with an exit signal, or an exit with the stop.

Taking Losses

One of the hardest things of all for many investors is to take a loss when it is timely to do so. In the abstract, it is easy to see the car dealer selling off yellow cars at a discount. However, it can be very difficult for some people, even for most people, to admit a mistake when it comes to selling out a losing stock. There is always the temptation to hang on in the expectation that in due course, it will come back. This is the all-time worst-of-all loser-play. Count on a loss getting worse. Sometimes it goes on getting worse until the last possible moment when you and many others throw in the towel at the extremity of the move. That's how climactic market bottoms are made. However, not all stocks come back. In his book, *The Education of a Speculator,* Victor Niederhoffer recalls how the beneficiary of a legacy in the 1930s handled an inheritance of stocks. All those selling above their cost price were sold. All those selling below their cost price were retained. All of the stocks that were sold subsequently went up, sometimes by many times. None of the ones retained went up, and most of them became worthless.

Heed the saying: Remember how much money you can make when you are right! Put the loss in that perspective and take it when it is manageable. You are unlikely to go broke by taking a loss—when you can afford to take it.

In the final analysis, successful investment comprises the art of being wrong. If you master the art of being wrong, of admitting mistakes and taking remedial action, success is not difficult to achieve.

Use Stops

Stops are an essential tool for implementing the art of being wrong. They are an invaluable defense against unexpected market action and a means of enforcing the discipline required to conserve capital.

There is never any excuse for failing to place a stop somewhere, if only for disaster insurance. Look at the chart for Digital Equipment and see where you could have placed stops. Then consider the alternative of not placing a stop. Stops do not diminish the need for the discipline of reviewing stocks regularly, of selling underperforming stocks, and upgrading the portfolio. Nevertheless, it is better to rely on stops as the only means of getting out than it is to stay in a stock forever, without regard to what it is doing.

Sometimes You Have to Pay Taxes!

One reason for the immensity of the bull market of the 1990s was the reluctance of investors to pay capital gains tax as a result of selling stocks in which they had big profits. This reasoning appears to have contributed to the extremely high price of stocks expected to do well for eternity.

For some people it is, of course, difficult to sell a great stock that has multiplied by many times. It may continue to multiply by many more times. If you sell, you may suffer three times over. You may get left behind as the stock continues rising. A big chunk disappears while the technicals are developing to tell you that it should be sold. In addition, a big chunk of capital disappears into the maw of the tax collector.

These concerns are legitimate. However, their legitimacy is not so complete that they should overrule prudent investment timing. There is a serious risk that the excess on the upside caused by tax considerations may have an equal and opposite effect when the bull market finally unravels.

The best attitude toward taxes is to be pleased to have the good fortune that necessitates paying them. The widespread paranoia about avoiding taxes can be counterproductive when there are secular changes in market psychology.

The Foremost Rule: Preserve Capital!

There is nothing more important than conserving your capital. Money not made is but an opportunity cost, but losses lose real money. As long as you have money, you can always find opportunities. Without money, opportunity is worthless.

The remedy for conserving capital value overall is not to avoid putting money at risk in stocks. On the contrary, failure to put money at risk in stocks when it is timely to do so may be a greater risk than not investing at all. However, it is essential to keep a substantial reserve to allow for things that go wrong and for new opportunities or unforeseen requirements. You should be able to sleep equally soundly whether you have a spectacular success in the market or an unwelcome large loss.

Contrary to most popular wisdom in the investment business, there is little merit in widespread diversification. Some of the biggest and most successful investors trade as few as a half dozen stocks, but what stocks when they do trade!

Take time, be patient, and remember the saying: A fool and his money are soon parted. With any reasonable measure of luck, this book should help to impart some wisdom and to dispel some folly. However, remember also these words of caution: Good luck comes to those already doing the right things!

APPENDIX A

How the System Worked in 1998

se of the timing techniques described in this book led to successful identification of a major opportunity for short sales on July 22,
1998, with the suggested vehicle the small-capitalization Russell
2000 stock index futures. That day, the Dow Jones Industrial Average
closed at 9128, the S&P 500 at 1164, and the Russell 2000 cash index at
451. Subsequent lows in October were 7400 for the Dow, 923 for the
S&P 500, and 304 for the Russell. The Russell made its high in April at
492 and was down by 38 percent at the low, with many stocks declining
much more.

The table below shows a list of individual stocks identified as ones to
buy on October 29, 1998. That day, the major stock indexes delivered a
buy signal, and the NASDAQ 100 stock index cleared significant overhead resistance, thereby suggesting completion of the four-year Presidential cycle low for the stock market. The table also shows the opening
price for stocks on the list for October 30, 1998, and their closing price
on January 31, 1999, together with the gain for each stock. The list was
generated without regard to corporate size or business prospects,
except for a general awareness that certain sectors were attractive. It
was considered sufficient at the time to focus on just one pure Internet
stock, America Online, and to avoid intentionally an overweighting in
that speculative sector. There were several other stocks in the sector—
like Yahoo!—that also generated buy signals, but AOL seemed among
the best of them.

Stock	Price (10/30/98)	Price (1/31/99)	Gain (%)
Advanced Micro Devices	$21.00	$23.06	10
Alltell Corp.	45.63	64.56	41
America Online	64.22	175.63	177
American Power Conversion	42.50	42.00	20
Applied Micro Circuit	23.25	42.00	81
AT&T	64.19	90.75	41
Bank of New York	31.81	35.50	12
EMC Corp.	66.00	107.88	63
Erickson LM Tel ADR	22.30	27.88	25
Flextronics International	24.94	42.38	70
Intel Corp.	90.00	140.94	57
IBM	149.50	183.25	22
MCI Worldcom	54.88	79.75	45
Merck	136.75	146.75	7
Newbridge Networks	21.19	35.94	70
Novell	14.94	20.38	36
Oracle	20.75	55.38	167
PMC Sierra	44.88	74.31	66
Seagate Technology	25.00	40.50	62
Sun Microsystems	59.31	111.75	88
Tel-Com LM A	38.06	53.50	41
Texas Instruments	64.88	99.50	53
Unisys Corp.	26.63	33.00	24
Average Gain			**55%**
Dow Industrials	8498	9358	10%
NASDAQ 100 Index	1396	2126	52%

Advanced Micro Devices should have been sold at $22.50 as soon as the price collapsed on the announcement of poor earnings. Although still making money, too much damage was done to its chart by the decline, especially considering that there were many other stocks inviting new purchases. Merck might have been sold at $151.94 after a huge outside down day, although the decision to do so would have been discretionary rather than mandatory. It was clear at the time that other drug stocks were strengthening and had a better ratio of potential reward relative to risk. Bank of New York was acting poorly, and there was a case for selling it and buying something doing better.

At the bottom of the table are the comparative numbers for the Dow Jones Industrial Average and the NASDAQ 100 stock index.

See market timing in action . . .

Let someone else do the homework for you,
or check your current and intended investments
with Stockscom *(Stockscom-dot-com)!*

To order *Stockscom* **or the** *Five Star*
Futures Advisory, **call, write, or e-mail to:**

Colin Alexander
Stockscom
812 Proctor Avenue
Ogdensburg, NY 13669

Telephone: (613) 745-5593 Fax: (613) 745-1156
E-mail: stocks@stockscom.com

Both services are delivered by e-mail and are
also available on a recorded telephone message.

●

Stockscom: Charter Subscription Rate: $99 p.a.
Five Star Futures Advisory: $229 p.a./$129 for 6 months
Five Star Futures Trades: $55 plus handling

Visa/MasterCard/Amex

Website: http://stockscom.com

Index

About the Author

Colin Alexander is the publisher of *The Five Star Bulletin,* a popular advisory service for futures traders. Since 1996, his service has consistently been rated in the top ten by *Commodity Traders Consumers Report.* In 1998 he launched *Stocktimer,* a successful advisory service for buying stocks and selling stocks short. Mr. Alexander is author of several trading books, including *Capturing Full-Trend Profits in the Commodity Futures Market* and the widely acclaimed *Five Star Futures Trades.*